A Theory of Us
Philosophy, God, and the Meaning of Life

Timothy Rowe

First published in 2013 by OpenLine Publishing

Version 1.1.3

ISBN 978-0-473-24906-9 (paperback)
ISBN 978-0-473-24907-6 (kindle)

For my Mum,
for her illimitable support.

Reason works by trial and error. We invent our myths and our theories and we try them out: we try to see how far they take us. And we improve our theories if we can. The better theory is the one that has the greater explanatory power: that explains more; that explains with greater precision; and that allows us to make better predictions.
—Karl Popper (1902–1994)

Contents

Preface to a Question

In October 2012 a fifteen-year-old girl named Anusha went walking with her parents in a remote village in Kashmir. At some point on their journey, Anusha turned around to look at a boy who had passed by on a motorcycle. It was a critical mistake for her to make. Though she immediately apologized, her remorse counted for nothing. Taken home and restrained, Anusha's parents poured acid onto her face. She died not long afterwards in hospital. When questioned in jail about their actions, her mother coldly explained to reporters that it was her daughter's destiny to die this way.[1]

If reflections on humanity reveal anything, it is that what we believe matters, for our beliefs shape the way we interpret and understand the world. When our beliefs go wrong, catastrophic harms can result. The Aztec belief that the existence of the world was precarious and could only be maintained by acts of ritual human sacrifice is a pristine example. Responsibility for ensuring the world's continuation fell to priests, and they met their obligations in a variety of horrendous ways. The most well-known involved taking an obsidian knife and cutting a large wound into the abdomen of their fully conscious victim. Reaching up into the chest cavity with their bare hands, the priest would tear out their victim's heart and lift it skyward in tribute to the gods. Hundreds of thousands of people are thought to have been killed in this way, and all on the basis of a mistaken set of beliefs about the metaphysics of the world.

Europeans in the Middle Ages also believed themselves threatened by an existentially-serious problem. For them, it was people using magic for dark purposes. Exactly *who* was doing it was always rather difficult to say, however, and in efforts to identify and punish those responsible, many thousands of people were tortured and executed.

Unpleasant though these examples are, they highlight a powerful need to evaluate our beliefs in a critical light, lest we believe wrongly, blindly, and harmfully. Unfortunately, this appears to be anything but the goal in one continuing area of human interest: spirituality.

According to the wisdom of the world's two largest religions—Christianity and Islam—the meaning of life is to believe in god, to

---

[1] See reports by the BBC (2012), CBC (2012), and DailyMail (2012).

worship him, and to be obedient to his revelation. Doing this is said to be very important, for it will determine whether we are eternally rewarded or punished when we die.

While this view of life is central to the understanding of more than half the world's population, it is beset by a range of philosophical problems that leave it highly doubtful. Not only this, I believe it stands in the way of seeing something that is incomparably more beautiful and compelling. The primary goal of this book is to explain what that is.

There are a couple of things that readers should bear in mind before proceeding. First, what follows is intended as a largely non-technical treatment of some of the most significant philosophical issues surrounding belief in god and the spiritual meaningfulness of life. Some of the philosophical and scientific terrain covered does require a level of concentration, however, and there are a handful of philosophical words I couldn't get away from using in the course of writing it. If you find that the meaning of these is lost or unclear at any point, be aware that a short glossary has been included at the back of the book.

Second, no importance should be attached to the fact that god is referred to throughout using masculine pronouns like "he" or "his." In using these words, I am not intending to imply that god is actually male, and readers who wish to are more than welcome to read "she" or "her" (or anything else, for that matter) in their place. The use of the lowercase *g* in "god" does carry significance, however, and has been done to try and reclaim the idea of god as a philosophical rather than religious concept—something that is, I think, very much needed.

Third, when I refer to "religion," for the most part what I am really referring to are the two major world monotheisms of Christianity and Islam. This is clearly a rather narrow way of using the word, and it is potentially problematic for that reason. For one thing, Christianity and Islam do not exhaust all of the world's religions, and for another, there are significant differences between them. The reason why they have been grouped together is that they jointly represent a large amount of what needs our attention, and using the word religion to refer to both is far more convenient than writing "Christianity and Islam" over and over again.

Finally, and perhaps most importantly, a word or two about what this book is not. Above all, it is not a claim to any final, exact, or complete truth. There are natural limits to what any person by themselves can see, and this book is no exception to that. For all the possibility of my error, I can only hope to have looked usefully in a certain direction and to have seen things there that are worthy of attention. As for whether I actually have, this is a question that each person must judge for themselves.

Chapter 1
Life as Understanding

Life is a difficult question; I have decided to spend my life in thinking about it.
—Arthur Schopenhauer (1788–1860)

We are far better persuaded by reasons we discover ourselves, than by those given to us by others.
—Blaise Pascal (1623–1662)

Questions of Life

Why does the universe exist? What *explains* its existence? For many people, the answer lies in the existence of god: the universe exists because god chose to create it. If you want to explain the universe, however, it is not enough to simply point to god as the cause behind it all. What you also need to come up with is an explanation of what it could all be for. What you need, essentially, is a theory of the meaning of life.

There we run into a problem, however, for while billions of us do use god as a way of explaining our lives in the universe, the most popular accounts of life's meaning leave much to be philosophically desired. Consider the following list of candidate explanations:

1) Life is a waiting period that everyone must go through before heavenly union with god.
2) Life is a spiritual and moral test. We are here to freely believe in god, to avoid sin, and to fulfill god's plans. Great rewards and punishments await us in the afterlife depending on whether we meet god's expectations during our time here.
3) Life is conducive to instilling moral virtues like honesty, compassion, integrity, and goodwill. By providing us with opportunities for moral learning, it contributes to our moral and spiritual growth.

4) The purpose of life is to create greater spiritual intimacy with god. Life assists with this by helping us to know him personally.

Your analysis may differ, but none of these explanations strikes me as a satisfying or persuasive solution to the riddle of life's mystery.

Take the idea that our lives are a waiting period ahead of union with god. One immediately wonders where the need for waiting came from, or why the universe was the best way of providing for it. This is especially so given the degree of pain and suffering endured by us in the meantime. I think you'd probably agree that if the waiting room at the doctor's office included an assortment of Bengal tigers, the doctor would have earned some pretty hard questions from patients. The same puzzle must apply to god: why create life as a waiting period when, in the midst of that waiting, we end up experiencing so much that is negative? It is difficult to imagine what a satisfactory answer might look like.

What about life as the equivalent of a moral and spiritual test where the goal is to believe in god, obey his commands, avoid sin, and be eternally rewarded for it when we die? This is probably the most widely accepted understanding that people have. However, I can't see why god would have any interest in regulating, judging, and punishing us. As a perfect or ideal being, it would surely sit far beneath his divinity to impose mandates for how we should live, and to back those expectations up with horrific punishments in the afterlife.

Just imagine waking up one day and discovering that you have become godlike. You are immediately aware of everything there is to know, you can do absolutely anything logically possible that you put your mind to, and so on. Finding yourself like this, would your first thought be to ensure that every living human recognizes and worships you? Would you seek to motivate people towards this by threatening them with eternal torture if they don't? If your answer is yes, I can only say that you think and feel very differently on this question than I do. While it's easy to imagine the more Napoleonic in attitude being thoroughly enamored with these possibilities, I tend to think about god in less egocentric, vain, and despotic terms. If god truly is divine, so should we all.

The idea of life as working to facilitate our moral development has the greatest affinity with what I will propose, but it is also only one piece of the puzzle at best. While the development of a person's moral thinking and feeling certainly does qualify as something that is good, is it *so* encompassing of what spiritual goods conceivably fall out of life that the question of life's meaning can be entirely answered by it? I cannot think so. Most notably, it completely overlooks the importance of our own way of thinking and feeling and the relationship we have with ourselves through our own experiences.

To see what I mean, consider the following question: is holding anger against ourselves a sensible thing to do? Does it tend to enhance our experience of life and lead to successful outcomes more reliably than self-forgiveness and self-kindness do? Going by practice, at least, many of us would seem to think so, and the reason why is not hard to understand. Being angry at ourselves, we think, helps keep us safe by acting as a form of self-punishment.

When we set out to achieve something and we fail, or when we set high standards for our behavior and we fall short, the consequences for how we feel can be profound. This is where anger can seem like the correct response, for by directing it against ourselves, we further focus our attention and increase our commitment to succeed.

Harder to identify, though, are the toxic side-effects of self-anger, including the effect it has on the way we feel, the energy it expends in the process, and the way it arises from and sustains negative judgments about ourselves. As I see it, these all tend to be far more effective at limiting our prospects for success than promoting them.

It's a nuanced topic with many qualifications necessary, admittedly, but I suggest that recognizing and internalizing the self-defeating nature of self-anger and negative self-judgment represents a powerful step forward in the development of the self, and it would be amazing to me if truths of this kind were not an essential part of what projects of spiritual development related to. After all, while our moral thinking and feeling in relation to others cannot be separated off from who we are, how we each are *in relation to ourselves* is no less integral. Seeing the spiritual meaning of life as wholly concerned with moral development unfortunately pays no attention to this fact.

Finally, what about life as something that allows us to get closer to god? It's imaginable, certainly, yet surely there would be better ways of achieving the same end. If personal intimacy with the divine is the spiritual meaning of life, for example, then god's distance to (or complete absence from) the world would appear to be strikingly counterproductive.[1]

---

[1] It could be denied that god is actually absent from the world, of course. Many of those who come from a religious perspective would say that god is very much present, and that he speaks to those who listen and open their hearts to him. Even if this is true, it

It could be that the meaning of life is far beyond our ability to understand it, of course, just as it is beyond the ability of an ant to understand the nature and place of Earth in the cosmos. At the same time, it would be unnecessarily defeatist to simply assume this at the outset.

In attempting to come up with a more convincing spiritual answer, let us assume the truth of three 'spiritual' things:

1) A divine being exists.
2) We and the universe stand in a meaningful relationship to that divine being.
3) Our conscious identities (or 'selfhoods') are not annihilated by physical death, but extend beyond it.

These are all contestable propositions, of course, but the goal of assuming them is just to explore what might then be said about life, should they all be true. In other words, what picture of life's meaning stands to make the best sense of it, vis-à-vis god's existence, the creation of the universe, and the extension of consciousness beyond physical death?[2]

The Experience of Life; the Life of Experience

My proposal is the following: life can be plausibly understood as a mode of experience intended to serve as a catalyst for the synthesis of knowledge and understanding from reason and experience. To put that more simply, life is a way for us to "see," so as to know. It is a path to the truth where the truths in question are ones that stand out in a relation of significance to us as indefinitely ongoing conscious beings. As for the universe itself, it is a platform for reality that serves to reveal those truths

---

must still surely be admitted that there are clearer and less ambiguous ways for god to make himself known than what this answer has in mind.

[2] All that a god-based explanation of the universe minimally requires is a good reason for *god* to have created the universe. This won't necessarily imply that our lives have rich spiritual meaning, however. God could have created the universe as the metaphorical equivalent of a doorstop, for example, but that wouldn't mean that life is worth living. If god is divinely good, though, then presumably our lives really do hold some kind of spiritual meaning *for us*. What I will attempt to do is unify these two perspectives by giving an account where to see the spiritual value of life *to us* is to simultaneously see the reason why god would create the universe.

in an effective way. There is obviously much more to be said about it, but on the shortest and simplest way of rendering things, that is effectively all there is to say: the spiritual meaning of life is *the pursuit of understanding*.

This claim needs to be justified, and perhaps the best place to start is by noting that, at a fundamental level, so much of what our lives come down to just are experiences. With nights of dreamless sleep set aside as exceptions, to live in the world is to be presented with an enormous number and variety experiences, and no two people live lives that are exactly the same in this regard. At the same time, one of the things we know about experience is that it plays a key role in the formation of people's beliefs, values, and attitudes. If the world does have an underlying spiritual purpose or function, then, it seems like a sensible first step to try and locate that in terms of the relationship that experience has with knowledge and understanding.

Still, we know that not every belief we form on the basis of our own experiences is true, and that our thinking is subject to a huge range of biological, psychological, and sociocultural influences. Why should we think that life contributes *more* to our correct understanding of things than it does to detract from them, then? The same question could be posed for values and attitudes. Why should we think that life does more to bring us closer to values and attitudes that contribute to positive states of being than it does to draw us away from them?

Much of the answer comes from seeing life not as a single, one-off event, but as a process that is extended out over many lifetimes. With those lives would come many different perspectives and experiences, and that would allow us to make a convergence to the truth in the way we think. The idea here can be easily grasped with an analogy.

One way we might try and assess the concentration of a chemical in a river system would be to take a sample of water at a random point and test it. From this reading we could then infer the overall concentration of the chemical in the river. This approach isn't ideal, however, for if the chemical's concentration varies at different points along it, extrapolating from a single sample to the river as a whole could be quite misleading. A better method would therefore be to take multiple samples at different points in the river system. The more samples we collect, and the more places we randomly collect them from, the more accurate our overall picture of the chemical's concentration can be expected to be.[3]

Life can be thought of in a roughly similar way—not as a one-off, sampling-of-truth event, but as a process or a series of engagements with the world intended to reflectively bring us into a more complete and accurate view of things, beyond the contingencies of individual lives and any error or incompleteness contained in our metaphysically-held understanding. Moreover, just as how you might take steps to avoid contamination between the different water samples, there is a sense in which each life represents a fresh start in our view to things, for each life starts us over anew. This is significant, for by bringing us to assume the position of many different points of view, and by wiping the old epistemic slate partly clean for us each time, life helps to shake us free from the grip of any errors or deficiencies contained in old patterns of thinking and being.[4]

This might all sound rather strange, but unless it can be seriously entertained that every important spiritual good available from life can be achieved within the space of a single lifetime, and irrespective of the conditions under which those lives are lived, there is little reason to suppose within the framework of this spiritual account that the life we have now is the only one.

What is life, then? It is an opportunity to travel down different pathways of experience, to see in old or new ways within the reality of what is possible, and to choose how we are to be, given all that we want for ourselves and understand to be true. It is a chance to see what works and what doesn't about who we are, and, given the totality of what we know, to try to find ever higher forms for ourselves at the level of our thinking and feeling.

Between Knowledge and Understanding

The spiritual value of life can be further illustrated by noting a distinction between knowledge and understanding. To do that, consider our local cosmic environment.

---

[3] Note that any biases or distortions common to all such measurements will not be overcome by relying on this method (which is something that is true of life itself, too).
[4] The other thing to note is that if our lives are in some way lived with specific points of understanding intended for them, the problem with contingent features outlined earlier becomes less severe. The possibility of this is discussed later on in the chapter.

The solar system is formed with the Sun at the center and eight differently sized planets moving in slightly elliptical orbits around it.[5] Because the planets travel at different velocities and cover different distances in doing so, the time it takes them to finish a single orbit varies. Earth, for example, takes just over 365 Earth-days to complete its orbit around the Sun, while Mars (the next furthest planet out from Earth) takes 687 earth-days. Because moons orbit planets in the same way that planets orbit stars, the planets' moons appear to travel around the Sun in a spiral-like pattern. Moreover, because the planets and moons all spin upon their axes as they orbit, to an observer at a fixed point on one of their surfaces the stars appear to move across the sky.

So would go a fairly brief and abstract sketch of the setup and dynamics of the solar system. It is a celestial picture we know to be true, and it is one that has been accepted for a long time. Any person can come along, memorize the statements just made, and claim them as items of knowledge.

Despite that, it can be a remarkable experience to see those same pieces of information represented visually, such as one might find at a planetarium, or, in the case of Earth's rotation, captured in time-lapse video of the night sky. Because we are such highly visual creatures, that way of representing the same facts can bring them to life before our eyes. Indeed, whereas one may *know* in a rather dry and abstract way that the description of the solar system just given is true, seeing a working model of it or a video of the stars moving relative to Earth's horizon can bring us to a far richer and deeper comprehension of what is going on. I would say that the difference in that case is one between knowledge and understanding.

As I see it, part of life's spiritual function is epistemically analogous to a planetarium, for in being here we add to our *understanding* of the nature of being, not simply our formal or abstract knowledge of it. In this way, to recognize the value of understanding over merely knowing it is to see the value of life from this spiritual point of view even more.

---

[5] An ellipse is like a squashed circle; you might imagine a metal ring that has been pressed down against a hard surface, leaving it slightly thinner in one direction.

A Balance of Conflicted Values

Even if deepening and expanding our understanding of being is the reason why we are here, why should we think that life in the universe is the very best way of achieving it? Couldn't god have simply *made* us understand whatever we may need to know about being? Not only would that have saved us from the rather time-consuming process of life, it would have allowed us to avoid all of the pain and suffering we go through in the course of actually living.

Unfortunately, there is a downside to being divinely zapped into a state of enlightenment, and that is that it fails to respect a range of important goods related to independence, self-determination, and self-authorship. Indeed, for god to do that would seemingly require rearranging and reconstituting our minds from the ground up, which would effectively make him the author of who we are. In so doing, god would be delivering us into one profound good while simultaneously and inextricably denying us of another—the state wherein each of us is the author responsible for who and what we most fundamentally are.

One could question whether goods like independence and self-determination really are all that important in the grand scheme of things, of course. Is there really any strong need for us to be thoroughly involved in the matter of what we are? You might doubt it, but imagine that someone was to use advanced technology to dictate all of your beliefs, values, and attitudes to you. They might do this with only the very best of intentions or only the very worst; it doesn't strictly matter for the purposes of the thought experiment. The question is: in what sense would you be your own person afterwards? However that might be, it is surely greatly diminished over the case in which they did not. After all, what could be closer to us than the nature and contents of our own minds and thinking?[6]

But what if, in being divinely thrust into an enlightened state, we could somehow independently validate our understanding as correct? Think of how words entered into a crossword are both limited by and are limiting to what other words have been and can be entered elsewhere. When the crossword is completed, you might well find that there was only really one way the words could have been written in that would have

---

[6] This does not mean we need to be *absolutely* autonomous or self-authored. Being autonomous or self-authored is not the same thing as being completely self-sufficient or causally isolated, after all. The claim is simply that god's intrusion into our thinking would do a meaningful level of damage to us in relation to those goods.

successfully answered all the questions while avoiding inconsistencies between intersecting lines. This in turn would provide grounds for thinking that the way the crossword was completed was right, for what other set of answers could have done so well?

Perhaps something analogous would happen in the mind of someone teleported into a state of enlightenment, such that to see things from that perspective would be to immediately have access to reasons based in accuracy and coherence for thinking that the elements of belief that make it up are unmistakably correct. This in turn would give us an avenue by which to independently validate that understanding's correctness, and therein reclaim something of our lost independence and self-authorship.

Even so, though, I doubt that what would be gained back would be sufficient to solve the problem. It just doesn't appear to do enough to account for the extent to which god's involvement in us would be necessary to even get us to that point. The objection, then, is that by elevating our thinking on our behalf, god would negatively impact us in respect to the independence of our being within existence, and simply being able to note on our own "that all makes perfect sense to me now" would not reclaim enough of it back.

Naturally enough, those who place relatively little weight on the value of independence or self-authorship may not have much time for what has just been argued, for the argument depends on their significance for its persuasiveness. Someone who sees experiencing pleasure and avoiding pain as the most important elements of what a good life looks like, for example, may find the idea that the universe was spiritually intended as a way of allowing us to develop our understanding while respecting and preserving our independence deeply unsatisfying. So far as they are concerned, if god could save us from the pain and suffering we experience here by directly involving himself in our thinking, then that is exactly what he should do, for what is gained in doing that far outweighs what is lost.

Unfortunately, there may be little that I can say to convince someone who thinks like this otherwise. If our highest achievement really does consist in reaching a state of being most free from pain and suffering and filled with pleasure, I freely admit that the account just given doesn't make a compelling case against the idea of god doing it all for us. However, if our highest achievement consists of something more than this—like existing in a state of being maximized along dimensions of value that include independence—then it is possible to see how the spiritual object of life is not something that can be simply given to us, but must be gained for ourselves.

Our Lives from a Spiritual Point of View

What has been outlined so far is a general theoretical account of life's meaning. It is general in the sense that it is intended to apply broadly to the lives of all people in all places. As you might be wondering, though, what does it come to in practical terms? For example, what is a concrete example of a spiritually significant truth that, when apprehended and internalized, contributes to someone's spiritual development? A handful of stories should help to illuminate.

Andrew was motivated to work in stock markets and trading firms for the money and social status it provided him, and he didn't have to wait long before he achieved success there. As good as he was, though, he found life in that world unsatisfying at any deeper level. Indeed, when he was not doing his best to ignore the problem, the truth was that it left him with a sense of emptiness.

His dissatisfaction was aggravated by a lifelong passion for art as a vehicle for creative self-expression. While naturally talented, pursuing art as a career was not something that he had ever seriously considered. Much like him, both of his brothers were successful and status-driven individuals, and he found the possibility of being seen as "less" than they were extremely uncomfortable. Having a high-status job and income rooted in the world of money helped satisfy his need to be seen as powerful and successful.

It wasn't just in relation to his brothers that his need arose, though. Somewhere within him lurked a doubt that he would be able to attract a woman he would love without being successful and wealthy. Fearing that an artistic path would lead him to a life without satisfaction in love, and caught in the grip of wealth and its many attractions, he saw direct pursuit of money and status as the only real choice.

Unfortunately, the emptiness he felt did not abate over time, and the distractions he used to ignore it never succeeded for long. His unhappiness call out a challenge to him: to live more authentically as himself, and to do so even in the face of what it would cost him in terms of his financial freedom, status-driven self-esteem, and fears surrounding his ambitions in love.

How did things turn out? Perhaps he decided to change careers and pursue his passion for art, or perhaps he chose to remain within the world of money. Whichever way it went, though, there is much that life could have shown him. For example, redirecting his energy towards art would have revealed the stark contrast that exists between being true to oneself and not. He might also have been able to change his thinking about the importance of other people's opinions, perhaps seeing that his need to be seen as socially powerful largely emanated in his own case from doubts that he would be liked for who he was. Connected with that, he might have been able to see that his worries around not being able to attract love into his life without the cosmetic assistance of money and status were misplaced.

Choosing to stay where he was would not have shown him what it is like to live life more authentically, clearly, but either way many important insights could have been realized by him on reflection. For example, he could have realized that staking so much of his self-worth on out-competing others in measures of money and social status, and therein being seen by them as "better," is a road that leads nowhere worth truly going.

Next is Clare, who was raised in a family environment where little she did was good enough in the eyes of her parents. While she strove to win her parent's praise, their expectations for her were set very high, and more often than not she did not meet them. Whenever this happened they would express their disappointment and ask her to try harder. Their pressure did nothing to support her, however, and as time went on they became increasingly frustrated and distant. To them she was a disappointment, and that was how she came to see herself at some level, too.

One of the most important side effects of this was to cultivate a deep sense of anxiety in Clare about meeting the expectations of others—something she imagined existed very widely in people. It was all she had ever known from her parents, after all. To help mitigate this, she unconsciously decided that it was simply better to keep other people at an emotional distance. She feared that if she were to allow them in close, they would inevitably burden her with their high expectations for her, and since she viewed herself as intrinsically disappointing, she dreaded that she would end up falling short and feeling terrible in the process.

Thus it unfolded that, throughout her early adulthood, this intelligent, beautiful, and sensitive young woman never really let anyone else in— neither friends, nor family, nor lovers. She wasn't fully aware of the reason *why* she felt an aversion to emotional intimacy, as the reason was located less consciously in her mind than that. All she knew was that the thought of being close to others made her feel anxious, and anxiety being what it is, she did the thing that she had greatest control over in order to reduce it—she danced breezily through other people's lives, and they danced through hers, never pausing for long with any particular one of them.

In the thirty-fifth year of her life, however, something changed. Tired of the loneliness that sat on a level deeper than her aversion to intimacy, Clare began to reflect on the way her life had gone up until that point. Exhausted and frustrated, she resolved to set her life on a new course.

Since we are at liberty to tell the outcome of this story however we want, let us say that she did magnificently. Perhaps she came to understand that the resistance she felt to intimacy was connected with her relationship with her parents, or perhaps she never connected the dots and, recognizing the destructiveness of it, simply willed herself beyond being controlled by fear. Old ways of thinking tend to die hard, of course, and the anxiety she experienced was formidable. In the end, though, she was able to reframe her conception of herself and accept that she was perfectly fine as she was. Though this positive outlook was initially fragile, with time she was able to get it established as something more resilient and stable within herself. The sense of peace this brought was immense, and it transformed her life. No longer subconsciously ripped by anxiety at the prospect of disappointing people, she was free to experience what being close to well-chosen others is like—a profound source of richness, and one of the very best things in life.

Among many other things, then, Clare's path highlighted the powerful grip that fear can hold over us, and how harmful ways of thinking about ourselves can sit within the background of our minds and influence much in what we experience. She saw what it was to resist deeply-held fears, to overcome them as obstacles to ourselves, and to live in a way that is free from them. She underwent a dramatic change in how she saw herself, too: from someone who is intrinsically disappointing, to someone who is more than good enough to be valued and loved simply on account of who she is. In doing so, she witnessed firsthand some of the deep risks that arise when we allow others to serve as the measure of who we are.

Finally, we have Jasmine, who lived with a continual need to place the happiness of other people before her own. Believing that a kind of nobility can exist in suffering, if it was a question of whether to expend her energy seeking her own happiness or that of friends and family, she nearly always chose the latter. While this focus tended to leave her starved of happiness herself, she was good at hiding the truth of that from others, fearing that if they knew then she would become a concern to them—something she could not accept.

The imbalance evident in Jasmine's priorities originated in part from a belief that her life was a form of punishment—though for what crime or deed she could not say—and she felt powerless to free herself from it. She therefore convinced herself that while her life had very little to offer *her*, she could at least use it to benefit others as much as possible. Then at least some good would come out of it.

Something deeper helped drive her to place the interests of others before her own, though, and that was fear. Having witnessed the destructive effects of her father's selfishness on her family while growing up, she feared that any hint of selfishness on her part would lead to the same disastrous consequences. To her young mind, that's just what selfishness did. So great was the resulting fear that she ended up placing the interests of other people over herself as a sort of safety mechanism. If she always put herself last, it followed that she couldn't hurt anyone out of selfishness, for their interests would always be more important. None of this was consciously known to her; she simply knew that whenever she thought about doing something positive for herself rather than for others, feelings of anxiety and guilt would rise up.

Adding yet another layer of complexity to the situation was the fact that, at some hidden level, she also viewed selflessness as a way of imploring the universe to save her. Feeling powerless to right her situation through her own actions and abilities, she sought to be rescued from it by something else, and being selfless struck her as doing two important things there: it called spiritual attention to her suffering, and it made her life morally worthy of being acted upon benevolently by something greater than she was.

This pattern of thinking ended up trapping her in a vicious circle of misery, for while doing everything she could for others at her own expense was a major part of why she felt so unhappy in the first place, to her spiritually-leaning mind it was also the only thing that stood a chance of making things better. As for the universe itself, it never seemed to notice or care—a point that resonated very deeply with her belief that her life was there to punish her. She therefore experienced life from within a cluster of self-sustaining harmful beliefs, and she suffered greatly because of it.

Most people cannot go on living like this forever. If for nothing else, she found that pretending to be fine when so much unhappiness dwelled within was completely exhausting. Feeling hopeless and alone, something had to change.

Her situation finally began to come right when she was given a self-help book by a friend who knew that something was wrong. Picking apart the pieces, she realized that her unhappiness was not a punishment sent from above, but a natural consequence of the way she had deprioritized herself in relation to others, the false powerlessness she felt over her situation, and her low self-esteem. In building up a story in her mind aimed at making sense of things, she had muddled up the causality of it all.

Making great strides to reframe her views, she convinced herself that it is not *wrong* to pursue one's own good as an essential priority in life. It is, in fact, entirely necessary, for one cannot go through life without getting something of value back from it. She also came to realize that there is nothing spiritually meritorious, honorable, or special about suffering, and that wallowing in one's own suffering in the hope of being externally rescued is to needlessly prolong that suffering even longer. She recognized that responsibility for changing her life rested with her, and that she had deferred that responsibility to something else out of a sense of powerlessness and fear of being a bad person.

Embracing her new responsibility, she gradually began putting herself first—not at the expense of all others, as her father had, but in a way that took into account other people's interests as well. Whenever feelings of anxiety, fear, or guilt would rise up, she reminded herself of the truth of what she had come to apprehend. Casting off the sense of powerlessness that had gripped her, hope returned to the way she saw things. When that happened, Jasmine found that a large portion of the unhappiness she felt was swept out as well. With these developments Jasmine began to direct her life towards new ends—ends that for the first time included her own good as a central legitimate goal of her life.

Varied though they are, my suggestion with these stories is that it is this *sort* of thing that life is abstractly all about—reflecting, discerning, learning, growing, being adaptable and moving towards better ways of being by evolving the way we think and feel. While they are all rather dramatic in what they depict, they are intended only to *illustrate*—not to *typify*—the way in which a person's experiences might hold spiritual significance for them in relation to their understanding. The fact is, I highly doubt that so many of the spiritual truths encountered in life can be written up in a few short paragraphs in a way that will make their significance truly stand out—they need to be lived in order for their meaning to be fully appreciated. Moreover, nobody should think that their own life needs to unfold in just as painful, challenging, or unhappy a way as those described to manifest rich opportunities for spiritual advancement; stories that go that way simply make for better telling.

As for the range of things our lives stand to more clearly illuminate, there is no way for me to give a complete list. Nevertheless, it could be safely taken to include truths to do with anger, authenticity, challenge, commitment, compassion, competition/conflict, cruelty, dependence, desire, doubt, emptiness, endurance, error, failure, faith, fallibility, fear, foolishness, forgiveness, freedom, frustration, giving up and letting go, goodness, guilt, happiness, honesty, hope, inaction, independence, intimacy, justice/injustice, limitation, loneliness, loss, love, loyalty, oppression, ostracism, persecution, power, pride, procrastination, rejection, sacrifice, self-belief, self-control, self-deception, self-judgment, self-representation, self-sabotage, self-worth, shame, success, trust, truth and truth-seeking, victimhood, wisdom, and the power of actions, feelings and ideas. Even this is just a small slice of the fuller reality, and for each of them there might be a range of things to be understood, and a thousand ways in which life might put that understanding in front of us.

The scope of life in relation to spiritual truth is clearly very broad, then, and it may be bewildering to try and work out where best to start with it. If you want my advice, though, it would be to do your best to overcome any negative attitudes, emotions, and false beliefs you might hold. After all, whatever other truths life might place before us, there at least lie a great number of the most important and consequential.

The Suffering of the World and Its Problem for God

For all the reasons that life might be said to be good, it can hardly escape attention that it is possible to experience a tremendous amount of pain and suffering in the course of living it. Reflecting darkly, Arthur Schopenhauer mused that

> ...the shortness of life, so often lamented, may perhaps be the very best thing about it. If, finally, we were to bring to the sight of everyone the terrible sufferings and afflictions to which his life is

constantly exposed, he would be seized with horror. If we were to conduct the most hardened and callous optimist through hospitals, infirmaries, operating theatres, through prisons, torture-chambers, and slave-hovels, over battlefields and to places of execution; if we were to open to him all the dark abodes of misery, where it shuns the cold gaze of curiosity...he too would certainly see in the end what kind of a world is this "best of all possible worlds." For whence did Dante get the material for his hell, if not from this actual world of ours?[7]

Moreover, as evolutionary biologist Richard Dawkins has pointed out, the experience of pain and suffering is not limited to merely human horizons. It appears to be everywhere, in fact.

The total amount of suffering per year in the natural world is beyond all decent contemplation. During the minute that it takes me to compose this sentence, thousands of animals are being eaten alive, many others are running for their lives, whimpering with fear, others are slowly being devoured from within by rasping parasites, thousands of all kinds are dying of starvation, thirst, and disease. It must be so. If there ever is a time of plenty, this very fact will automatically lead to an increase in the population until the natural state of starvation and misery is restored.[8]

It seems that if we open our eyes up for just a moment to all the suffering that occurs in the world around us—to the degree of its severity and the multiplicity of its forms—that the universe calls out a very deep and serious challenge to the idea that a divine being was behind it all. This problem—the "problem of evil," as philosophers call it—is perhaps the single biggest difficulty for the rationality of belief in a divine being, and although it does require some patience and concentration to get through the discussion of it to come, it is still a very important one to have. After all, if you are going to assess the merits of believing in god, you should be well acquainted with what is perhaps the single best reason not to.

Philosophers have traditionally drawn a distinction between two different types of evil. On one side are evils that result from human choices and actions—moral evils, such as rape, genocide, war, theft,

---

[7] Schopenhauer (1969).
[8] Dawkins (1995).

racism, slavery, torture, bullying, sexism, and unjustified discrimination. On the other side are evils that come from nonhuman causes and processes—natural evils, like diseases, earthquakes, droughts, flooding, forest fires, tsunamis, and physical and cognitive disabilities.

While the distinction between natural and moral evils is entrenched, it is doubtful whether every form of evil can be placed neatly into one or the other category. For example, depression, frustration, and the pangs of unfulfilled desire don't seem to me to fit very easily into just one or the other of those two classifications. We needn't get caught up in taxonomic issues here, however. The core of the problem of evil is straightforward: with so much evil both possible and actual in the universe, how can anyone reasonably believe that a divinely capable, knowing, and good being was causally responsible for its existence?

Probably the most frequented philosophical response that people give is to appeal to the value of free will. As the argument goes, god could not eliminate all of the moral evils found in the world without simultaneously eliminating human free will as it relates to moral responsibility. After all, if every morally damaging action that people carried out was foiled by god just before it could come to anything, no one would be truly *free* to do any of those things. The possibility of moral evil, then, is an inextricable by-product of our possession of moral freedom.

While I agree, there are two things that need to be noted. First, if god is infinitely capable (meaning that he is not limited by *any* constraint on thought or conduct whatsoever) then it goes without saying that he could prevent moral evil while still preserving moral freedom. Why? Because infinite capability would mean that god could do even the logically impossible, and it is logically impossible to eliminate all moral evil while simultaneously preserving moral freedom.

As it stands, though, the idea of god being infinitely powerful is logically incoherent, and because of that, philosophers have almost always tended to favor a conception of divine capability that stops short of doing the logically impossible. This requires us to say that there are certain things that even god cannot do, like making square triangles, creating rocks so heavy he cannot lift them, or eliminating all of the moral evils of the world without simultaneously compromising our status as free and morally responsible agents.

The second thing to note is that the value of free will can at best only be a partial answer to the problem of evil, for it only accounts for the existence of moral evils while leaving natural evils aside. Appealing to the value of free will and moral responsibility is not enough, then; something more is needed if we are to make sense of the universe by invoking the existence of a divine being.

My own suggestion for this problem involves pointing backwards to the spiritual reason why there is proposed to be a universe at all. Unfortunately, it does get a little bit tricky, but as I don't know of any better answer, it is the only one I have to offer.

Put most simply, if the universe really was intended as a kind of mirror for truths about conscious existence, and if conscious existence simply does fundamentally include the possibility of negative conscious experiences like pain and suffering, it makes perfect sense that those things (and their associated causal relationships) would be represented in the world. Their very existence in the universe is to be expected, in other words, because truths about them are spiritually important.

Note that the complete absence of pain and suffering from the world would not be any minor transformation, either, for it would radically affect how we subsequently came to think. Just imagine how differently we would think about, say, romantic relationships, if the possibility of pain that is inherent to them did not exist. They would be altogether different things for us, and that would almost certainly be reflected at the level of our beliefs and values.

Looked at in this way, the presence of pain and suffering in the world reflects something much deeper about the realities of consciously being, and as such, is partly explicable by the idea that the universe was intended to provide a window to exactly that.

This answer alone will not do, however, for even if we accept that *some* level of pain and suffering was necessary for the world to represent different truths about conscious existence, it still seems as though god should have been able to devise a way of illuminating those same truths that wasn't as experientially harsh as this one. Why allow *so much* pain and suffering in the universe?

Much of the problem stems from the fact that the universe is a natural system. By that I mean that it is completely self-sufficient from a causal point of view. All that the universe needs to go on in a perfectly fine working order is to be left alone. Unfortunately, the same physical properties that allow the universe to go on without any need for outside direction lead to considerable experiential evils as a by-product.

Consider the second law of thermodynamics, which states that the disorder of closed physical systems tends to increase over time. All of us will have experienced something like this firsthand. While initially tidy bedrooms tend to go from ordered to messy seemingly all by themselves, it almost never happens that a gust of wind blows through an open window and makes them tidier for us. If anything, the gust of wind only ends up rearranging the preexisting mess.

Because all living things exist in a highly ordered physical state, they too are subject to the natural tendency of things to fall into disorder. This makes it necessary for living things to work against that tendency somehow if they are to avoid ending up fatally disordered. This is something that life can certainly do, but work requires an expenditure of free energy (just as it takes energy from you to clean up your room). The problem is, to expend free energy you need to have some to begin with, and energy doesn't just come out of nowhere.

While plants have evolved to meet their energy needs by capturing it from sunlight, carnivorous animals like tigers and bears have evolved to obtain energy via an entirely different process: by consuming the bodies of other animals. Because we have excellent reason to believe that many of the animals that tigers and bears eat are capable of consciously

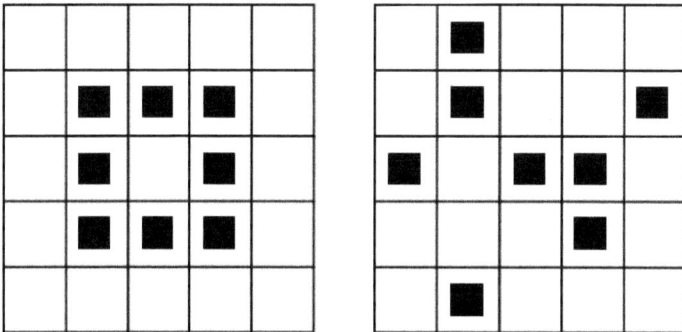

Figure 1.1: The second law of thermodynamics. If we imagine taking a board that has had eight pieces arranged on it in an orderly way and shaking it, the chances are very good that they would end up with a disorderly arrangement afterwards. There are only so many locations on the board that the pieces can occupy, and if they are randomly distributed the odds are good that they won't form up in an orderly pattern. While it would always be *possible* for the pieces to be shaken into an orderly arrangement by chance, the odds of that happening are low, for the number of possible disorderly arrangements greatly outnumbers the possible orderly arrangements.

experiencing pain and fear, the conjunction of the second law of thermodynamics with meat-eating evolutionary solutions to its consequences winds up having the unfortunate side-effect of introducing great volumes of pain and suffering into the world. In a double twist of harm, then, not only do we all naturally veer towards disorder just on account of being highly ordered objects in a thermodynamically decaying universe, some animals have evolved to temporarily get around this issue by consuming the bodies (and, therefore, destroying the lives) of other conscious things. Nothing about this is pretty or fair, but at a fundamental level it is a straightforward consequence of the physics of the universe.

While acquiring energy helps in the battle against disorder, so too does minimizing the need to fix any disruptions to order in the first place. Evolution was wise to this as well, and along with many other animals, the exterior of our bodies come equipped with a vast array of biological sensors aimed at detecting even the slightest hint of damage. The result is unmistakable from the point of view of our experience—stub your toe against a wall or bang your elbow on the doorway and your eyes may water with the excruciating pain of it.

Our brains were constructed under a similar evolutionary mandate for damage avoidance and come packed with cognitive systems geared towards adaptive behavior (like being wary of potential threats in our environment and remembering painful past events). Unfortunately, the qualitative incentives associated with those cognitive mechanisms can be acutely unpleasant to experience, as we can't help but notice with fear, worry, loneliness, sadness, and anxiety. Still, it's not hard to understand why our brains do place such an emphasis upon the negative: it's what worked to keep our ancestors safe and alive, and there was a lot in the world they needed to be kept safe from. In this, we are both the winners and the losers.

Finally, consider evolution itself. As a process evolution requires a number of things to be true: that members of a given population exhibit variation in terms of their traits, that some of those traits are capable of being passed on to the next generation, and that a selective pressure applies to the inheritance of those traits, such that some members of the population do better, the same, or worse by what they inherit. If an inherited trait happens to be an advantage to an organism in its environment, all other things being equal that organism will be more likely to survive and reproduce compared with other individuals in the same population. This will mean that the trait itself will then be more likely to be passed on through those individuals to their offspring, who will in turn be more likely to pass that trait on to *their* offspring, and so on and so on. Because individuals with a beneficial trait do better than those without it, over time this process naturally leads to an increase in the frequency of that trait within the target population.

The selective pressures operating in this process are the various challenges and difficulties that living things face in the battle to survive and reproduce. This includes things like getting enough to eat and drink, battling the elements, avoiding predators, fighting off disease, attracting a mate, and successfully passing on one's genes to the next generation. As noted, those individuals who inherit traits that enable them to meet one or another of these challenges more effectively than others will be more likely to succeed relative to others.

One of the most notable things about all of this is that if by some magical twist life suddenly turned completely utopian tomorrow, such that there was no longer any want for anything, the selective pressure that previously held the numbers of living things back would in effect be turned off. In that case, it would only be a short matter of time before the biomass of what lives entirely filled the volume of the universe. More than that, there could be no thorough-going selection-driven change in such circumstances, for every want and need would be being met regardless of the particular traits of an organism.[9] Not only does evolution require the conditions of life to be at least somewhat difficult for what lives, then, the existence of a universe that isn't filled from horizon to horizon with biomass requires it too.[10]

If these are the kinds of consequences that await us in a dynamic and complex natural universe like ours, why did the universe even have to be like that? What is the spiritual value of having the universe that is a natural system?

One plausible explanation is that, in being causally self-sufficient and complete, the universe achieves a level of authenticity about itself as an independent reflection of being. That is, its naturalness speaks to the truth of itself as a reflection of a divinely-undetermined and independent reality.[11] Its character is not contrived, but is in a sense both *from* and *of* being itself. Or to put that another way again, we are not experiencing

---

[9] Organisms that were faster at reproducing would still reproduce at higher rates than others.

[10] Of course, the fact that life has to be at least a little difficult to avoid these two outcomes does not justify *just any* degree of difficulty, and that is not what I am arguing.

[11] When it is understood as having that broad spiritual intention, at least.

god's version of reality so much as we are experiencing reality directly (as witnessed through the natural character of the universe).

This is significant, for it potentially affects how we frame the truth of any judgments we make on the basis of our experiences. Does the truth of those judgments hold only within the domain of our particular universe? Or does it belong to the nature of being itself? A natural universe—one that can stand happily on its own two legs in its complexity—more easily allows for the latter view.

If that is so, natural evil is partly explicable as a by-product of the need for the universe to be causally self-sufficient and independent, and that is something itself related to the authenticity of the universe as an independent reflection of being and the value of that within spiritual projects aimed at understanding. It's a bit of a mouthful to say, and it is certainly a nuanced idea, but intuitively it has plausibility. If you want the world to reflect truths about being, and if you want those truths to be known independently of god, giving the world a maximally natural character is a sensible thing to do.

There is one more thing to add to this. It is an unmistakable fact that life generally does ask a great deal of us; that it is, for many people, and for much of the time, a very hard and challenging thing. Precisely because of this, though, it seems to me to be very unlikely that life would be thrust upon someone to deal with without their informed consent. Yet if we assume that we have each metaphysically chosen to be here, and have done so knowing well what that might subsequently mean for ourselves in terms of the possibilities for our experiences, the severity of the problem of evil for the existence of a divine being is reduced still further.

Of course, it is all well and good *just to say* that we have each made an informed metaphysical choice to be a part of life, but we have no memory of any such choice being made, and it seems on its surface like a rather convenient way of trying to save the idea of god from the full bite of the problem of evil. I think the existence of such a choice can be plausibly argued for, though, and in just the following way: given the significance of experiential evils and the tendency of the physical universe to realize them for living things, it would be deeply inconsistent with the divine goodness of god to force life upon us without our informed consent. Accordingly, if god really does exist, our participation in the world is almost certainly conditional to our having freely chosen to be a part of it.

So regarded, the experience of natural evil becomes part of an accepted possibility for ourselves as we strive to reach a deeper understanding of being within a physical system that collaterally allows for them as a part of its causal self-sufficiency and independence. Moral evils, on the other hand, are just part of what it is for us to go forward in a universe with others who, like us, have the power to act in either damaging or beneficial ways towards those around them.

So, does *this* provide us with a completely satisfying response to the problem of evil? Alas, not entirely. Even if we accept everything that has been said, we can still reasonably wonder why god couldn't have thought up a design for the universe that risks less collateral natural evil than our universe does, and which still advances all of the same spiritual ends (like our deeper understanding and the preservation of our independence) equally well. For example, couldn't god have designed a less harm-producing alternative to evolution by natural selection for the biological diversification of life? We might not be able to imagine the details of it— certainly, I can't—but god is god, and so surely he could? Moreover, even if no better alternative to this particular universe was possible, we can still wonder whether the experiential evils of life are really balanced out by the spiritual goods outlined as stemming from it. Is spiritual enlightenment really worth that much?

Here opinions may diverge. Even accepting the need for experiential evils to be represented in the world, and for our understanding of being to be independently formed, to the extent that we can plausibly imagine god having come up with a morally more preferable *yet otherwise equally spiritually satisfactory* alternative to the universe, the universe as it is does indeed make it appear less likely that god exists.

How much less likely? That of course is a key question. Because the experience of evil holds foundational moral significance, and because most people expect a lot out of god in terms of his divine capacities, I assume that most people would accept at least *some* incongruity between the way the universe is and how they judge it should have been if divinely created (even accepting all of the various considerations made before). The extent of that judgment will of course vary between individuals. Those who think of god as incredibly far-reaching in his abilities might judge that he probably could have done much better than our universe as it is, and therefore see the universe's moral character as being very disconfirming to his existence. Those who recognize a real dilemma in trying to balance out the conflict between the values identified before as spiritually important may find that the problem of evil is rather less disconfirming to god's existence than that. Either way, I suspect that at least something of the problem would be seen to remain by most people, and it's hard not to agree with them.

In light of this, my response to the problem of evil is only intended as a partial solution, reducing (rather than wholly eliminating) the evidential significance of natural evil for the existence of a divine being. How acceptable it is depends on the plausibility of the spiritual value of understanding facts about being, the importance of our own autonomy and independence in being, the moral significance of evil, and the limitations on god in solving the logical tension that arises between those different values. As a divinely moral being, god would naturally want to try and minimize the level of experiential evil found in the world, yet being limited to what is logically possible, he can't simply transcend the inherent conflict that exists between the aforementioned values to generate a perfectly satisfactory physical alternative.

In framing the problem this way, I have attempted to reduce expectations that the world should be perfectly ideal in respect to suffering, and raise expectations that it should look something closer to the way we actually find it, incorporating experientially good, bad, and neutral aspects of being in a natural and independent way. When life is further qualified as a free and informed choice on our part, the moral pressure that is built up against the existence of god by the incidence of evil is further reduced. Even if the bite of the problem is diminished by this line of reasoning, though, we can still justifiably wonder whether our universe really does represent the very best option god had theoretically available to him.

It's logically possible that god simply doesn't attach the same importance to all of the values outlined before, of course. Suppose god just doesn't care as much as we do about pain and suffering. If so, the universe really could represent the most optimal solution in god's eyes (just not in our own). Another possibility is that there are reasons why the universe needs to take the particular form that it does that we are presently ignorant of. If so, the fact that the universe appears to not to measure up from a moral point of view will be an artifact of our incomplete perspective on things, and something that would disappear if only we could see things from a more enlightened point of view. While both of these are possibilities, we can only go by what we have reason to think is true here and now, and hence noting them doesn't actually do anything to offset the problem.

It is worth emphasizing that the fact that evil constitutes a philosophical problem for god's existence doesn't necessarily mean that god doesn't exist. Just as how juries given the task of weighing the evidence presented before a court may find that there are some things that point towards a defendant's guilt and some things that point away from it, there can be things about the universe that speak in favor of god's existence and others that speak against it. It is only by considering the totality of those reasons that we put ourselves in a position to effectively judge the question.

Still, if belief in god is to be a rational thing, the strength of any reasons for believing in his existence will need to be great enough to overcome the issue brought about by the problem of evil. We shall leave it until chapter four to examine one major reason for believing just that.

The Spiritual Beauty of Our Lives

The philosophical claim we're considering is that life is a mode of experience spiritually intended to help us formulate a deeper understanding of important truths of being. By doing this, life enables us to grow in terms of who we are via the choices that we make for ourselves, given all that we know and want for ourselves. [12] Most fundamentally, then, life can be said to be characterized by three order interchangeable things: *insight, understanding,* and *choice*. [13] How we actually engage in this project will vary between people, however. Simplifying matters somewhat, life can be undertaken in two different spiritually creative modes: passive, and active. [14]

Passive creation is where we move through life largely unreflectively and unselfconsciously, being whatever we're comfortable in being until experiences come along that precipitate making amendments to who and what we are. This could easily describe the situation of someone who

---

[12] Of course, it would be no less true to say that the world is a platform *for* reality, inasmuch as it sits within our ability to take it and shape it in a way directed towards our own interests, both individually and collectively. Since we are all part of the world, the choices we make in respect to ourselves and who we are cannot help but influence the kind of place that the world is for other people, too.

[13] The order is interchangeable in the sense that someone's choice to see things in a different way, or to behave differently, may precede insight and understanding.

[14] This statement isn't intended as a mutually exclusive binary; the modes described can hold in different ways at the same time and vary over time for the same person.

holds deep anger against themselves for a poor decision they once made, and who continues to hold on to it until the consequences of doing so build to a point where they are forced into a position of self-forgiveness and emotional healing. In such a case, the positive changes are largely reactive to the situation they find themselves in, and this indeed is the rule with passive creation—it awaits a need for change before change is engaged in.

Active creation is different and is characterized by a willingness to play a much more reflective role in determining who we are from moment to moment, and to do that in advance of any immediate or pressing need. For example, someone might decide to act against the grain of their fears and strive after what they are passionate about, not because experiences in their life have made the wisdom of that evident, but because they recognize (either abstractly or intuitively) that being constrained by fear can be a pointlessly limiting and happiness-inimical thing. In contrast to passive creation, active creation doesn't wait for experiences to force us into new ways of being, but takes up that challenge in a forward-looking, self-conscious manner. It is harder to do, no doubt, but it has the benefit of not tying us to a pace of spiritual development that is set by feedback from the events of life. Of course, the wisdom of any changes actively undertaken is still *ultimately* evaluated through experience, but because the creative process unfolds at a faster rate, it may represent a more effective path to take in the evolution of the self.

A number of further qualifications and clarifications are needed in order to more fully clarify what is being proposed. First, actually understanding life as having the meaning outlined above is not necessary in order to spiritually benefit from it. One could very easily be an atheist, for example, and live just as reflectively and adaptively as someone who embraces those same values because they see them as playing an important role within life's spiritual function.[15]

Second, the total value of our lives cannot be reduced to their spiritual value, for they have a wider total meaning to us than that. Most people cherish things like friendship, love, and personal success, for example, and see meaning in their lives insofar as they are able to achieve (or stand to achieve) those things for themselves. In claiming that life has a specific spiritual purpose as well, I am not intending to detract from the

---

[15] Moreover, it would surely be possible to reflectively come to all of the same realizations after one's life is through.

meaningfulness that life holds for us in relation to any of those other things. Indeed, the value we place in those things plays a crucial role in its overall spiritual meaning.[16]

A third clarification relates to the causal independence of the universe. I have rested quite a lot on this, having connected it with the value of independently seeing the reality of being for what it is, and in that, of possessing a more comprehensive level of autonomy about ourselves. I should stress that the importance of this value need not be understood as absolute, and hence as something that can never be outweighed by other considerations.

Consider the moral value of not stealing from other people. As a rule of thumb, we regard it as wrong to steal from others, for it does harm to them in a way that is morally illegitimate. There is always going to be some imaginable situation in which it would be morally right to steal, however, such as if it would save the life of a person or prevent a great calamity from happening. There are clearly limits to the value of not stealing, then, and those limits can in principle be superseded by the importance of other values. I hold the same to be true for the causal independence of the universe and the value of that in relation to the preservation of our autonomy.

As such, the claim I wish to make is not that the universe is entirely free from any external spiritual involvement whatsoever, but that that is at least *significantly true of it*, for so much of its spiritual function depends on that being the case.

This leaves open the possibility that our lives are (or can be) influenced and moved in spiritually significant ways. If they are, what would that mean for the kind of freedom we have in life? It is hard to say without knowing the details of it, but perhaps the following analogy is accurate.

Imagine a firefly that has been placed inside a glass jar that is inside a room full of exotic artifacts and items. Inside the jar the firefly clearly has a degree of freedom to move about on its own, and thus by turning itself about within the jar, a certain degree of freedom to choose what it looks at. Suppose, however, that the jar itself is picked up and moved about within the room as well. In what sense is the firefly free to choose what it looks at? Clearly, its freedom is mixed. On one hand, it is free to

---

[16] Though as we'll see in the next chapter, the matter is complicated by the possibility that without a spiritual purpose to life, the value of whatever else is held to be valuable within it may be undermined.

turn about within the confines of its own space, but on the other, it is subject to the movement of the jar within the wider environment.

Perhaps we too are like this—being simultaneously both the mover and the moved. I can't say this actually is the case, but it does illustrate at least one way our freedom in life might conceivably exist once higher spiritual interests are taken into account.

There is one warning to offer concerning the possibility that our lives are subject to spiritual influences, however, and that is of the danger of "promiscuous teleology"—here meaning reading into every little happening of our lives some kind of higher intention. While it is strictly possible that very many things that happen to us in life might have some spiritual purpose or planning underlying their occurrence, the central thesis of this book requires that this cannot be true for everything, and it doesn't appear to be a very sensible thing to believe in any case. It is crucial to recognize that it would be possible to learn something of great importance from a particular experience without that experience having been put into our lives in order to be learned from. Nor can the significance what happens to us be taken as a reliable guide for whether it happened for some higher reason or not. Simply put, big things can happen for no other reason than that that is simply the way the world is. While that doesn't mean those events don't also offer valuable opportunities for understanding and reflection, it does mean that they needn't have happened *in order* to bring those opportunities before us.[17]

Finally, it is worth taking a moment to see that, if this theory of life is correct, our lives represent something of unimaginable beauty, for we live them under what can sometimes be extremely trying and difficult conditions, and do so all in pursuit of our self-improvement through deeper understanding. No words of mine can do any justice to how incredible and beautiful that is, and it would stand embedded in the spiritual foundation of the life of every single one of us.

That noted, it is wise to be careful with beautiful ideas, for all of us are motivated to make a comfortable home for ourselves inside the space of our own beliefs, and believing something like what has been proposed here allows us to do exactly that. The simple fact is that it would be one thing for us to have a very beautiful way of looking at our lives, and quite another for *that same way of seeing them to be true.*

---

[17] Except in the meta-level sense that the events all happen as part of the unfolding of the universe, and that the universe itself exists in order to reflect truths about being in a natural, causally independent and self-sufficient way.

Recall again then that while the picture proposed draws strength from the plausibility of values like understanding and autonomy as spiritual ends, it also suffers from at least one unmistakable problem, and that is the level of pain and suffering that exists in the world. Even if that problem can be offset by considerations like those presented, the level of experiential evil found here surely does extend beyond what most of us can countenance as being allowed for by any divinely-conceived system. Though we may assume that if god exists there is a completely satisfactory explanation for it all, or some better way of appreciating the values involved such that the problem itself disappears, it is a problem in itself to have to make those assumptions on the theory's behalf.

All we have so far, then, is a rather interesting theoretical possibility: that the spiritual meaning of life could be centered on the deepening of our understanding. Whether there are any good independent reasons to justify believing this is a question that needs further attention. Before we will address that matter, and in order to clear some of the way towards doing so, we will turn first to questions of religion and god.

Chapter 2
The Problem with Religion

He lives immured within the Bastille of a word.
—Thomas Paine (1739–1809)

It is pure illusion to claim that a notion that has passed from one
century to the next, from generation to generation, cannot be
entirely false.
—Pierre Bayle (1647–1706)

A Brief Overview

More than half the world's population believes that a divine being has
authored a book for all of humanity to read and live by. Within
Christianity that book is the Bible, a collection of writings most
Christians view not as a word for word dictation, but an "inspired text"
written by a number of different authors under divine guidance. Special
emphasis is given by Christianity to the Bible's New Testament, and in
particular to the teachings of Jesus, a first-century Jew believed to have
been the incarnation of god on Earth. Jesus's moral character is viewed
by Christians as faultless, and his resurrection after death is thought to
have made our spiritual redemption from sin possible. Tradition
maintains that Jesus is just one of three divine identities who jointly
constitute the single and unified being that is god. Those who do not
believe in god and live their lives according to his wishes risk eternal
punishment in hell when they die, while those who do what is asked will
receive an eternity of happiness in heaven.

Islam offers a notably simpler picture of the metaphysical order of
things. Central to Islam is the belief that there is one and only one god,
indivisible and uniform. His finest and last prophet was Muhammad, a
seventh-century Arab merchant who was chosen in mid-life to speak for
the divine. Just as how we might say that much of what it is to be a
Christian is to believe that Jesus was divine and died for our sins, much
of what it is to be a Muslim is to believe in the absolute oneness of god
and the prophetic status of Muhammad. Indeed, the Muslim declaration

of faith that you speak when converting to Islam involves nothing more than genuinely affirming the truth of those two propositions.

The principal holy book of Islam is the Quran, which is the literal, perfect, and timeless message to humanity that god sent down via the angel Gabriel to Muhammad some fourteen hundred years ago. The excellence of the Quran in its heavenly purpose can be seen in the fact that, after Muhammad died, no further acts of revelation were seen as necessary. So far as heaven is concerned, Islam completes the revelatory mission that god is believed to have initiated with Judaism and Christianity.

Like Jesus, Muhammad is regarded by Muslims as having set an ideal moral standard for people to live by. For this reason, to know the details of his life and teachings is to gain tremendous insight into the way in which one should live.

Unlike Christianity, Islam does not recognize "original sin"—that is, sin that has been inherited down through the generations as a result of the wrongdoing of Adam and Eve. The idea of sin still exists in Islam as the violation of god's teachings and commandments, however, and is committed by individuals on a case by case basis. Those who do not believe in god or lead good lives can expect to be condemned to hell when they die, while those who lead acceptable religious lives can hope for paradise.

So would go a short introduction to some of the immediate features of Christianity and Islam. From a philosophical perspective, of course, we must wonder whether their claim to represent and derive from god is correct. The best way to begin looking at this question is by taking a long step back.

A Second Look At Things

Suppose someone told you that god is a being characterized by infinite love, and that in an act of great wisdom and justice, he once condemned humanity for the actions of two people who ate fruit from a tree he had warned them from. Realizing a problem with this, god eventually came up with a plan to set the relationship between divinity and humanity right: he would go and live in the world and teach people how they should believe and behave. Thus it unfolded some two thousand years ago that the creator of all things was born in human form. Conceived through a miracle to a young virgin, god grew and matured into a man, walked upon a tiny corner of the world, performed all kinds of miracles and wonders, preached only the highest ideals and ethics, and eventually died by crucifixion at the hands of the authorities. The grave could not hold him, however, and he rose up from it to ascend into heaven. These events served a powerful metaphysical purpose, for his death made salvation from sin (including that most original of all sins) a possibility for us all. To achieve this we must devote ourselves to god in mind and heart, either with evidence or without it, and seek his forgiveness for whatever we do that is wrong in his eyes. Only by doing so do we stand a chance of being saved from his judgment, and that is coming.

Yes, god is going to return to the world once more. To one side of him will go those people who have believed, who have recognized their spiritual tendency to error, and who, after having prostrated themselves before him, are granted forgiveness. Their great reward will be an eternity of happiness and joy in heaven. To the other side will go the remainder. They will suffer terribly in a fire that lasts forever.

This must be believed, for something like it has happened already. God, having apparently seen no better way, once drowned nearly all of humanity by sending down a great deluge of rain from the skies. Only one family was forewarned of the cataclysm to come, and to them went a very important task: they were to build a great boat onto which they were to load pairs of animals from all over the world. It was from this preserve of life that the world was repopulated when the flood waters finally subsided.

Suppose this account was presented to you in all seriousness and conviction by someone unquestionably well-meaning. How should you think about it? Even putting aside its claims concerning the origins of human life and the geological history of the world, it is difficult to think that anyone needs to ask whether a just god would condemn all of the progeny of Adam and Eve for sins that were not their own, whether a wise god would kill himself to wipe clean the slate of human sin, or whether a good god would kill all but one family in a cataclysmic flood. We cannot, without the greatest of reasons to, believe that anything like this happened, yet for many people in the world, this is precisely what we must.

Unfortunately, the quality of being very difficult to accept upon philosophical reflection is something widely found in religion. If you analyze any of the major elements of Christian revelation, from the story of Job to the Resurrection of Christ, you will likely find things that cannot be sensibly believed. Consider the escape of the Israelites from Egypt for a single, salient example.

As the story goes, the Israelites were being held in slavery by the pharaoh of Egypt. Upon hearing the cries of his people—something that seemingly took a while—god decided that they should be set free. He therefore sent Moses on a divine mission before Pharaoh to demand their release. Not surprisingly, the request was refused, and god was left to resort to a show of force. The first punishments involved turning the Nile River into blood, making frogs, gnats, and flies cover the land, and striking dead many of the livestock of Egypt. Pharaoh was unmoved, so god ramped up the incentives by sending festering boils upon the people and the animals of Egypt. It was at this point that something odd happened (boils and gnats and frogs and flies aside). With Moses once again standing before Pharaoh to reiterate the demand, god hardened Pharaoh's heart so that he would not release the Israelites. Why? Because if they were freed then god would not have an excuse to send even more calamities upon Egypt, thereby denying himself an opportunity to further demonstrate his divine power and the unique spiritual status of the Israelites (Exodus 9:13–17).

As god continued to punish the Egyptians with hail storms, locust plagues, and darkness, so did he continue to harden Pharaoh's heart against the freedom of the Israelites. Finally, at the very last, god elected to kill all of the firstborn in Egypt, including even the firstborn cattle. The Israelites were told that they could avoid this fate by painting their doorways with the blood of a slaughtered lamb and eating its cooked meat. There were further rules to this. The meat had to be roasted over a fire not boiled, eaten inside and not outside, and consumed with special herbs and unleavened bread. Nothing was to be left until the morning; anything remaining was to be burned. Moreover, it had to be eaten with cloaks tucked into belts, sandals worn on feet, and staves ready in hand. Do this, god said, and the firstborn of each complying household would be spared. The rest in Egypt awoke the next morning to discover an unspeakable horror.

Hopefully you, like me, find more than a few crippling problems with this story. To speak to just three of them, for god to have hardened Pharaoh's heart so that he could have an excuse to carry on punishing the people of Egypt, rather than letting the Israelites be freed and averting further punishment, is morally inexcusable. To strike dead the firstborn of every family in Egypt is an outrageous act of collective punishment, and something that stands far beneath the divinity of god.

To include firstborn cattle in that punishment is simply bizarre. Finally, to require elaborate steps from the Israelites in order to avoid being caught up in the final punishment, like painting the doorways of their houses with the blood of a slaughtered lamb, is completely unnecessary and makes god an agent of superstition of the very worst kind. He might just as well have required them to chew their food only an even number of times or not think about a blue elephant for all the difference it would have made. Although the story itself ends appreciably with the freedom of the Israelites after years of enslavement, I can't see that it does anything more than make a rather devastating parody of the idea of god.

If the silliness of this religious story is far from atypical, why *aren't* we better at avoiding believing them? Why, for example, do people think it makes any sense for god to have had himself executed to save humanity from his own condemnation? I've been using examples from Christianity, but the question can very easily be posed more widely: in the general context of religion, why do things that are best thought of as resoundingly false come to be accepted as safely true by billions of people?

There is no single psychological or sociological explanation, of course, but one major part of it relates to the fact that most people acquire their core religious beliefs when they are young. This is a time at which we are acquiring a huge amount of information about the world, and evolution has seen fit to dispose us to mostly accept whatever we are told by people we trust. Not doing this would be difficult anyway, for much of the effectiveness of our critical thinking depends on our background beliefs, and when we are new to the world our background beliefs are still being filled in. As a result, those who are new to life aren't in a good position to critically evaluate the truth of what they are told—we may simply not know enough at that point to know any better. Moreover, not only is religion the most socially salient thing going when it comes to human spirituality—and hence what we are most likely to encounter and have structure our beliefs—we tend to seek the approval of our parents when we're young. In practice, this can mean believing whatever they tell us to believe—especially when religiously believing as they do is emphasized as extraordinarily important.

Another part of the explanation relates to the fact that things that have been believed by us for a long time and have been reinforced by trusted authority figures can seem entirely natural within our own field of view. This can result in absurd beliefs lying so close to our whole way of thinking that they escape our awareness as being that. Just as how a painting viewed too closely resists being seen for what it is, certain beliefs and assumptions can elude our scrutiny precisely because of where and how they sit in relation to our overall thinking.

If there is any solution to these problems, it surely being willing to subject even our most basic assumptions and accepted beliefs to questioning. As the philosopher Stephen Toulmin memorably put it, "There is only one way of seeing one's own spectacles clearly: that is, to take them off. It is impossible to focus both on them and through them at the same time."[1]

I would add that we can be helped enormously in that task by taking seriously the reasoned views of others who do not share in exactly the same assumptions, beliefs, and expectations as we do. The importance of other people to us can hardly be overstated, in fact, for what stands at first as very difficult for me to see or accept about my own beliefs may be blindingly obvious to you, and vice versa. Indeed, sometimes it may *only* be by listening to what others have to say that we can (with any promise of efficacy) look back upon our thinking in a truly revealing light.

For all the necessity of it, though, examining and questioning our most deeply rooted beliefs can be one of the most difficult things in life we ever do. Not only can we not examine all of our beliefs at once (we have far too many of them, and we need to hold onto some just in order to pose and answer questions about the others), questioning the most treasured aspects of our belief structures risks paying a high price. If we discover that certain elements within them are problematic, and if they cannot be satisfactorily modified in some way, great parts of what we believe may need to be abandoned. Therein lays a major problem, for our beliefs—and particularly those that are most pivotal to our understanding and identity—tend to matter a great deal to us. The inherent possibility of emotional and psychological distress that comes in questioning what we believe therefore acts as a natural deterrence to engaging in critical reflection.

And as if that difficulty wasn't enough, there can be tremendous social and familial pressures placed on people to retain their religious beliefs. Putting aside the most serious cases involving being attacked, imprisoned, or subjected to widespread social hostility for failing to believe, just imagine being the cause of angst for loved ones who believe

---

[1] Toulmin (1961)

that, by questioning religious truth, you have imperiled the fate of your soul.

For these reasons and more, it really shouldn't be too hard to understand how difficult it can be for people to critically examine the truth of the religion they believe in, or to experience their religion being criticized by others. Doing so is still important, however, for few areas of our beliefs hold greater consequences for our lives and how we experience them than what we believe spiritually.

Questioning the Authenticity of Revelation

In a very elementary way, both Christianity and Islam purport to be miraculous, for it is only by the action of god that we are to believe either has arrived in the world. On what rational basis might we accept this claim about them?

Much of what we have to go on, it seems, comes from reports allegedly given by people living many centuries ago that they were subject to some kind of special interaction with god. The religious experience that precipitated Saul's conversion is one of the most famous examples.

As the well-known story goes, Saul was traveling on a road heading to Damascus when a light from heaven suddenly flashed down all around him. Collapsing to the ground, Saul heard a voice ask why he was persecuting him. Revealing itself as Jesus, the voice told Saul to get up and go into Damascus where he would receive further instructions.[2] Though blind from his experience, Saul was able to make it into the city where his vision returned to him three days later. Going by the name of Paul and eventually becoming one of the most important figures in all of Christianity, letters he wrote now make up a significant part of the scriptural content of the New Testament.

So what do we have here? A case of testimony to the effect that a certain person, Paul, was subject to a dramatic religious experience of a kind that can be taken to confirm both the existence of god and the truth of Christianity.[3] But how can we know that he really did have the experience described? Should the word of someone alone be enough? Presumably not, for then we would have to believe every person who

---

[2] Acts 9:3-6, NIV.

[3] What we technically have is testimony from the writer of the book of Acts that Paul had those experiences, not Paul himself. To keep things maximally simple here, however, we can ignore that detail.

ever reported seeing or hearing from god, and not only are there very many of those, it would leave us vulnerable to being exploited.

Imagine if I was to tell you that god came to me last night and told me that I had been chosen to speak to the world on his behalf. Should you believe me? In the absence of any supporting evidence, the claim is simply too large to be believed on my say-so alone. After all, we know that much can be gained out of lying about such things, including attention, prestige, power, wealth, and political advantage. We also know that hallucinations are a very real cognitive phenomenon, that self-deception is an ever-present possibility for us all, and that we are all influenced in our reasoning and recollection of events by our preferences and expectations for what is the case. In short, there is a small mountain of reasonable doubt that needs to be overcome before we can justifiably accept the idea that someone was privately chosen to deliver a special message on god's behalf. While it's true that some level of justification might exist for a person who *actually undergoes* an experience like Paul's to believe in god, and perhaps even to believe in the truth of a particular religion like Christianity, that doesn't necessarily mean that they would be objectively right, or that any such justification automatically transfers over to other people upon hearing about it. [4]

Could public miracles offer a way around this problem? An example taken from 1 Kings illustrates the evidentiary value of miracles particularly well.[5] Urging those listening to believe in the existence of his god over all others, the prophet Elijah is said to have proposed a public demonstration: he and the priests of the god Baal would prepare wood for a sacrifice but would not light it. Rather, they would pray for their respective gods to set the wood alight for them. The priests agreed to this test of faith, and after having arranged their sacrifice they called upon

---

[4] Any such justification would be *prima facie* and *pro tanto* (i.e., initial and surmountable), meaning that it would serve to justify those beliefs only in the case that there are not counterweighing reasons known to the person in the body of their background beliefs, or as subsequently presented to them or learned by them, to cast sufficient doubt on the experience as genuinely spiritual or religious in nature. This comports with common sense account of justification. For example, you might see what you take to be an apple on a table in someone's home, but upon getting closer and picking it up discover that it was just a plastic imitation apple. We would say that you were justified in believing that there was an apple on the table, given that there was nothing known to you at that time to contradict that belief, right up until the point you picked it up and felt it, at which point you were no longer justified.

[5] 1 Kings 18:21–40. Salmon (1978) uses the same passage while discussing the evidentiary value of miracles.

Baal to ignite the wood for them. To their great disappointment, however, nothing was seen to happen. Cutting themselves in exhortation, they called out once again to Baal to set the wood on fire for them. Still, nothing was seen to occur. Next it was Elijah's turn. Gathering the people around his preparations and getting them to douse the wood three times in water for extra effect, he called out to his god to set the wood ablaze. Acting on his call, god struck the wood with a fire that consumed it in a blazing inferno. The people fell to their knees in belief, and Elijah had the priests of Baal seized and executed.

The killings aside, for fire to have fallen from the sky and struck at the exact place and time it was called would have been an extremely surprising event for anybody to see. To observe such a thing would have violated people's deeply held expectations about the natural order of things, and given the particular context in which it happened would have spoken very strongly in favor of the existence of the god Elijah claimed to be a special representative of.

It seems clear that public miracles *could* provide people with excellent justification for believing in a particular religion, then. Indeed, the more people who witness such an event, the more unlikely that event was to naturally occur, and the more religiously significant the context in which the event happened, the stronger their justification would seem to be for believing in god and the truth of some religious way of thinking about him.

So if miracles can justify religious belief in principle, what actually is a miracle, and how are we to know one when we see one? When I speak about miracles, I mean any intervention in the causal order of the natural universe by an external metaphysical being. Under this fairly wide definition, a miracle need not be something caused by god (since god is just one of an indefinite number of possible metaphysical beings) or be either noticed or noticeable as a miracle. If god caused an apple to fall from a tree at a rate one-ten-millionth slower than it otherwise naturally would have, for example, this would be a miraculous event. Nobody would be aware of such a thing happening, however, and so it would not impress anyone. Because of this, it will only be a subset of interventions in the natural causal order of the universe that we will be interested in. These will tend to be the ones that involve highly improbable events occurring in some kind of meaningful and observable public context. Given their improbability and their contextual significance, such events (it can be argued) have their best explanation in terms of the causal intervention of a being like god in the natural order of the world. When

Moses allegedly parted the Red Sea in order to escape from Pharaoh's soldiers, it was precisely because large bodies of water don't usually part down the middle when they are ordered to, and that they parted at the request of a man who claimed to have a special religious authority, that the event described stood to provide evidence for both the existence of god and for the validity of Moses's own religious authority.

The Bible and the Quran could both count as miracles under this definition if they actually happen to be from god. This could not be used as evidence in their favor without begging the question, however, for their status as god-given is precisely what is being questioned. In other words, it is precisely because we don't know beforehand whether either the Bible or the Quran really are the work of god that we need *some other reason* for believing this before we can call them miraculous.

The Quran happens to be especially interesting in this context, for it is widely believed by Muslims to be so beautifully written that its author could not possibly have been human. The Quran itself challenges anyone who questions its truth to "produce a work like it" or to believe; anyone who doubts its authenticity and yet is unable to produce something equal to it is swiftly reminded of hell (2:23–4). Since I can't speak or read a word of Arabic myself, I must concede the possibility that the Quran might be the most beautiful book ever written in a natural language, relative to that language.[6]

However, I remain skeptical of this for three reasons. First, not a single recognizable part of that literary miracle appears to have made its way into any English translation of the Quran I know of. While this could be because translation from one language to another tends to undo the literary qualities of the original work, might at least *some* of that unrivaled poetic achievement should have shown through (however dimly) in English translations?

Even if not, a second and more significant point is that the aesthetic quality of a work is partly influenced by the context in which we experience it. Seeing the Mona Lisa hanging in a magnificent art gallery and in perfectly adapted lighting is going to provide for a much richer aesthetic experience of it than seeing a print of it hanging on a poorly lit bathroom wall, for example. Background knowledge counts too. While knowing that a very famous artist painted a particular painting can cause

---

[6] Since the original language the Quran was written in was an old form of Arabic, and since the Quran is theologically believed to have existed timelessly in heaven before making its way into the world, calling Arabic a natural language is actually a bit problematic.

us to appreciate it more than we otherwise would have, learning that a particular painting is a forgery can cause a depreciation in our aesthetic enjoyment of it. While in either case the physical image remains exactly the same, in both cases our experience can vary.

It is worth asking, then: is it possible that believing you are reading the *very words of god* could imbue the experience of it with an aesthetic quality that just wouldn't otherwise be there? I have to think so. Indeed, if *anything* is going to make us stand more in awe of a literary work more than we otherwise would have, it is the belief that god was the one responsible for it.

Third and finally, it strikes me as rather odd that god would provide special assistance to a group of people in ascertaining the truth of Islam by providing them with a miracle of poetry in their own language, but not do something epistemically equivalent for any other group of people. Perhaps there should have been other miracles set aside for non-Arabic speakers as a way of providing them evidential compensation. To the best of my knowledge, however, god does not appear to have obliged.

There are of course many more orthodox examples of miracles to choose from in the Bible and the Quran. While Muhammad never performed any miracles himself, Jesus is famous for having raised the dead, healed the sick, transformed water into wine, walked on water, fed whole crowds from only a handful of items, exorcized demons, and having himself ultimately risen from the dead. Lesser known is Jesus's attitude towards miracles. Not only would he often swear people to silence about any miracles they saw him perform (e.g., Mark 1:43–45, 3:10–12, 7:33–37), sometimes he would just flat out refuse to perform any when he was not unreasonably asked to. He went so far as to tell a group of people at one point that no sign would be given to anyone of their generation (Mark 8:12). This was bizarre for two reasons. First, by the Bible's own reckoning a great number of signs were given to people of that generation (we just saw a list of them). Second, given the rather serious nature of the predicament he claimed people everywhere were in with god and the potential evidentiary value of miracles in establishing his identity as god's emissary, not providing them with miracles to overcome their perfectly healthy doubts was a tremendously counterproductive thing to have done.

Regardless, the problematic fact is that *we ourselves* were not witnesses to any one of these publicly performed miraculous happenings. Indeed, we find out about them only long after the reported fact, and in the very same books that claim to contain god's message. Moreover, other public miracles like them do not seem to be forthcoming. We are thus asked to judge the question of their occurrence ultimately as a matter of testimony, but it was public miracles that were hoped to rescue us from the problems surrounding testimony with private religious experiences in the first place. We're essentially right back where we started, then.

So why can't we just accept testimony of public miracles? Considerations include the fact that our perception and memory are fallible, that we are all subject to social influences that bias and pressure our interpretations, that some of us are quite willing to deceive others for personal benefit, and that our reasoning is capable of being swayed by our desires. (You only need to see how eagerly some people interpret water stains on highway overpasses or uneven burnt patches on toast as apparitions of the Virgin Mary to get a sense of how easily something completely trivial can come to be viewed as a miracle.) We also know that what gets counted as a miracle depends partly on what we understand as sitting within the capacities of nature, and that those who reported miracles in the Bible and the Quran lived in times considerably more ignorant and superstitious than our own.

The eighteenth-century Scottish philosopher David Hume viewed the problems surrounding testimony of miracles as epistemically severe, famously concluding that "no testimony is sufficient to establish a miracle, unless the testimony be of such a kind that its falsehood would be more miraculous than the fact which it endeavors to establish."[7] In other words, unless it would be *more* miraculous to believe that a person or a group of people had lied or had managed to get it wrong, we are without justification for believing on the basis of their testimony that a miracle actually took place.

While we don't necessarily need to be Humeans about the matter, there are still excellent reasons to be evidentially demanding when it comes to miraculous claims, and I am not aware of any considerations that come close to justifying our acceptance of the ones reported within the Christian and Islamic traditions.

Does this mean that it's *impossible* for a miracle to be accepted via another person's testimony? Not at all. In fact, it is quite easy to imagine how this could be done. If everyone in the world spontaneously levitated and heard a voice that said something distinctively religious back on a certain day in 1680, reports about this would provide those of us today with a rather compelling reason to believe in the truth of the associated

---

[7] Hume (1748).

religious tradition. It is something we could find reported in every cultural corner in the world, from New York to Mongolia and Papua New Guinea, and in everything from newspapers, diaries, and letters to oral traditions and wood carvings. It should hopefully be obvious, though, that isolated reports from two thousand years ago about the dead rising and the blind seeing again do not come anywhere remotely close to that in evidentiary caliber.

Adopting a different strategy, what if god revealed himself very widely to people, but also did so much more subtly through private religious experiences? An example might be someone experiencing a noticeable sense of inner peace coming over them at some terribly lost or battling point in their life while reading from the Bible or sitting in a church pew. Could something like that justify belief in the truth of Christianity?

Again, it seems a possibility, but we must remember that our brains are entirely capable of fooling us, and hence our experiences cannot always be taken as reliable reflections of reality. Psychologists have a seemingly inexhaustible supply of examples to give of this, but I'll make use of just one to illustrate how compelling those tricks can sometimes be.

It turns out that no matter where you are in the world, the Moon will appear larger when it is sitting low down close to the horizon than when it is sitting high overhead. You might imagine that the explanation involves something to do with the way the Moon's light travels through the atmosphere, but it actually has nothing to do with that. It doesn't even have anything to do with our eyes, in fact. The true reason is cognitive: our brains simply *make us* experience the Moon as though it is larger when it is low.

A good portion of people who aren't familiar with this will struggle to believe you when you first tell them about it. After all, if you can't trust your own eyes, what can you trust? Happily, everyone can verify the truth of it for themselves. How? The next time you see a full moon sitting close to the horizon, extend your arm out fully, and using either your thumbnail or an appropriately chosen coin, note how much of it is needed to cover over the sight of the Moon. Then, when the same full moon is further up in the sky, perform the same procedure again. In both cases you should find that the amount of thumbnail or coin needed to hide it from view remains the same, yet the size of the Moon as it seems to us appears to change dramatically between the two positions.

This particular illusion has been known about since ancient times, and it continues to be a source of major disappointment for amateur photographers seeking to immortalize the low full Moon's seemingly grand size in a photo. Of particular interest to us here is the fact that knowing the Moon is *not really* larger when it is lower in the sky does absolutely nothing to correct our misleading experience of it. The brain can be a stubborn and convincing illusionist, and doesn't care in such cases for what we do or don't know.

Now return to questions of spiritual and religious experiences. Is it imaginable that for reasons of metaphysical conviction, deep emotional or psychological need, or just plain old wishful thinking, someone might mistake themselves as having undergone a genuine private spiritual experience when they haven't? Just imagine the case of someone searching within themselves at a time of great personal anguish. Longing for assistance from anything out there, they might notice and then interpret subtle feelings of inner warmth and peace as having a spiritual origin. This might then cause those feelings to cascade and amplify under that interpretation into something much more intense, thereby erroneously validating the whole thing as authentically spiritual from the start. While no doubt very significant to that person, those feelings need not have any true metaphysical explanation. Indeed, you can probably bring about something somewhat like it yourself right now by just taking a quiet moment to introspectively look inside yourself and see yourself as the object of your own thought. And all this to say nothing of other, more elaborate causes of apparently extraordinary experiences, like extreme tiredness, dehydration, the consumption of toxins and drugs, or the fact that certain medical conditions (like some forms of epilepsy) are known to produce hallucinations and religious visions.

To be especially clear, nothing in what I have just said should be taken as suggesting that feelings of inner peace and warmth at painfully low points in our lives *can't* be authentically spiritual in origin, or that *every* seemingly spiritual experience people have is nothing of the kind. My point here is much more minimal: that what we interpret as spiritual need not be any such thing, and that reliably determining which if any of them are real may be a potentially very difficult thing for anybody to do.

You might think: but wouldn't the fact that someone's subtle private spiritual experience occurred in a special religious context (like while sitting a church or reading from the Bible) provide compelling evidence for the truth of the associated religion? Not if the same kinds of experiences occur for other people in competing religious contexts, and that is precisely what anthropological considerations lead us to believe. Moreover, since religions like Christianity and Islam require much more to be true than just the existence of a divine being alone, much more is evidentially needed on their behalf to believe in them than is needed to believe in the existence of a divine being alone. Even if someone's subtle private experiences do justify them believing in the existence of god, then, that doesn't necessarily mean those same experiences will justify them believing in a specifically religious way of thinking about him.

What if more striking spiritual experiences were privately used—could they do the epistemological job? That does seem to be a possibility once again. Imagine if a Jesus-like character appeared to you in your thoughts and gave you permission to ask him anything you liked, so long as you never told anyone else about it. Wisely concerned that you might just be hallucinating, and hence wanting to verify the authenticity of the experience, there would be no point in asking him anything that you yourself already knew. You might therefore decide to ask him questions that you did not know the answer to but could easily find out about. For example, you might ask him to describe everything that will happen in the next day's news or what the telephone number of your neighbor five houses to the right is. You could then go and check these things by buying a newspaper and knocking on a door.

By these and other more elaborate methods, it should be entirely possible to confirm the truth of at least some Christian propositions. In fact, should that not be possible, my first thought would be that there must be something wrong with the epistemological principles or evidential standards that are being used to assess things by.[8] Even so, it can hardly be overlooked that the scenario imagined involves something far more evidentially weighty than feelings of inner warmth and peacefulness at emotionally stressed times.

Even if we assume that god really has made a solid public effort to reveal himself and establish the truth of a particular religion, we must surely wonder why he did so in such geographically and historically limited ways. The problem was elegantly highlighted by Red Jacket, a nineteenth-century Native American chief, while conversing with a group of Christian missionaries.

---

[8] Someone might object "But couldn't the experience of asking your neighbor for their telephone number or reading the newspaper and seeing all the predicted news stories there be *itself* just an extended element of the hallucination, even though it is not experienced by the person as part of it?" Surely it could, but choosing to explain the success of the predictions in that way looks like a rather *ad hoc* way of trying to preserve the truth of the hallucination explanation over the religious one, and in doing so moves the hallucination explanation much closer into the area of unfalsifiability.

You say that you are sent to instruct us how to worship the Great Spirit agreeable to His mind. And if we do not take hold of the religion which you white people teach, we shall be unhappy hereafter. You say that you are right, and we are lost. How do you know this to be true? We understand that your religion is written in a book. If it was intended for us as well as for you, why has not the Great Spirit given it to us, and not only to us, but why did He not give to our forefathers knowledge of that book, with the means of understanding it rightly? We only know what you tell us about it.[9]

When believing in god and abiding by his commands is so important that those who fail must suffer the most severe and ongoing of consequences, it is simply incredible to suppose that he revealed himself only to certain individuals, in certain groups, and at certain times. One surely cannot have it both ways here—if the books of revelation truly are as important as they are imagined to be, we should have expected far more out of god in terms of their distribution than we have any reason to believe they did receive, if they received any at all.[10]

The structure and composition of the Bible and the Quran also raise significant doubts. The New Testament is made up of a number of letters and reports written by people who were allegedly divinely inspired to write what they did. As anyone who has ever read the Bible will know, though, just stringing together a whole bunch of different accounts and letters from different authors addressed to different people, about varying topics and themes, and without any scene-setting or introduction, doesn't necessarily result in the most systematic, coherent, and clear picture of what god actually wants from us.

And the Quran? While it benefits from the fact that everything in it came from the same person, its structural problems are no less pronounced. Composed of chapters (or *suras*) that are ordered neither chronologically nor by subject, but (with the exception of the very first) from longest to shortest, the result is something that can only really be described as a disorientating mess. Though it is no less true for the Bible, reading the Quran can feel a lot like you've just walked in on a

---

[9] Red Jacket (1805).
[10] The Quran makes a number of references to unnamed "messengers" who were sent before Muhammad to other groups of people around the world, thereby showing that it is at least aware of the need for some kind of theological answer to this question. However, nothing is ever offered to substantiate the claim and no further details are ever given.

conversation halfway done between two people you don't know, neither of whom bothers to stop and run you up to speed, and which flips at random between different topics.

The 111th sura provides a particularly powerful illustration. One of the Quran's shortest suras, it reveals in the complete absence of any context that a man called Abu Lahab was condemned by god to burn in a flaming fire, along with his wife, who will have a rope of thorns put around her neck. That's it; end sura. So what do we learn? That some guy we don't know and his wife were condemned to hell for doing something we're never told about. I'm sorry, but the idea that god could have actually wanted something like this for a book of timeless and universal revelation is extraordinarily difficult to accept.[11]

Returning to the Bible, it is reasonably well-known that Jesus did not write any part of the Bible himself, and that there is not a single account of his life or teachings in the New Testament that was written by anyone who knew him directly. While we might assume that those who did write the books of the New Testament and those who compiled them into a single collection were divinely inspired to do so, and in just such a way that the Bible came out exactly (or very nearly) as it was supposed to be, this is all very hard to believe unless you are already committed to the claim that the Bible is the word of god. In any case, it seems much easier for god to have simply done it all himself than to have done it like that.

Picking up where Jesus left off, Muhammad made no effort to carefully preserve god's revealed message either. Allegedly he could not, even if he had wanted to, for he is popularly said to have been illiterate. Islamic tradition therefore holds that this task was taken up by others by either memorizing or recording down the divine transmissions on scraps of paper, leather, and other materials. It was only after Muhammad died that the Quran was brought together as a single book, and—we are to believe—in precisely the way that god had always intended.

As for who really wrote the four Gospels of the New Testament, we don't actually know; the fact that they all carry the names of either disciples or close acquaintances of the disciples is rather misleading in that respect. As peasants, it would have been unlikely that any of Jesus's disciples would have been able to write, or if they could write, to compose pieces of writing as complex as those found in the Gospels. Moreover, the language used in the Gospels suggests that their authors

---

[11] Who actually was Abu Lahab, you wonder? He was Muhammad's uncle. According to tradition, his crime was to openly doubt the prophetic status of Muhammad.

were not the same as the people they were named after. When the Gospel of Matthew talks about the calling of the disciple Matthew by Jesus, for example, the author does not use first-person pronouns like "I" or "me," which is what you would expect if the author was the disciple Matthew (see Matthew 9:9. The same issue is found in the Gospel of John; e.g. John 21:24).

Whoever they really were, we do know that they wrote at least a couple of generations after Jesus died, and that the original copies of their works did not make it into the Bible. In fact, so far as we know, the originals no longer exist. What did make it through were copies that were produced at a later time by unknown people. Unfortunately, not only do all of the known copies contain copy-errors (which in most cases are harmless, but are in some cases significant to the meaning of the text), it appears that some scribes took it upon themselves to change bits and pieces of what they were copying to suit their own tastes.

The Gospel of Mark provides a good example, for the version of it that appears in the New Testament has a number of verses tacked on to the end that were not in the original document. How do we know? Because the verses in question do not appear anywhere in the very earliest copies of the Gospel that have been discovered. A natural inference to make from that is that someone at some point just wasn't too happy for Mark's account of the resurrection of Jesus to end with the women fleeing from his empty tomb, and so added in some bits and pieces about Jesus having made appearances to the disciples after his death to encourage them to spread the Christian message (see Mark 16:9–20). The much-loved story in the Gospel of John (7:53–8:11) of Jesus saving the life of an adulterous woman by proclaiming to those who would kill her that those without sin should cast the first stone is also a scribal addition that isn't in the earliest copies of the Gospel.

More scandalous still is the fact that whole letters are in the New Testament that are known to be forgeries. For reasons ranging from considerations of style and content to detailed forensic analysis of the language used, considerable scholarly agreement exists that Colossians, Ephesians, 1 and 2 Timothy, Titus, and 2 Thessalonians were not written by Paul, despite all claiming to have been. The fancy word for this phenomenon is *pseudonymity*, but polite words should not be allowed to disguise the philosophical significance of it: that forged letters could have ended up being included in what we are told is god's timeless revelation makes a strong case against the idea that any part of the Bible is revelation.[12]

What you have to try and imagine, then, is that god would be willing to go to Earth and live as a human, speak a great deal about the importance of believing in him and abiding by his message, and not write a single word of any of this down. Instead, he would have others do that for him. Not anyone who knew him personally, mind you, but people who probably lived at least a couple of generations after him, who lived in a different region of the world to him, who wrote their accounts anonymously, and who came up with their accounts on the basis of hearsay from others (or, perhaps—if you really insist—as intuited directly from god). Then, he would allow for the original copies of their accounts to become lost or destroyed, for the only remaining accounts to be copies of the originals, and for the scribes who made those copies to not only make mistakes in doing so, but to insert or delete what they liked. Lastly, as if all of that were not enough, he would allow for deliberate forgeries (in the form of letters written by people who were not who they were claiming to be) to make their way into the final compilation of revelation known as "the Bible." This story is many things, but plausible is not one of them.

Finally, it is worth assessing the books of revelation from an aesthetic point of view. I don't think it would be unreasonable to assume that the word of god would present a message to humanity in some of the most crisp, clear, and sublimely beautiful use of words imaginable. So seamless and powerful should that book's use of language be that it would capture and hold our attention simply in the way that it is written.

How do the Bible and the Quran fare by comparison? While the Bible certainly does have its moments, on the whole it is safe to say it is nowhere near that kind of book. And as for how the Quran reads in

---

[12] See Ehrman (2009) for more details on all of the historical points mentioned. It might be argued that the writers of the pseudonymous letters were inspired to write what they did, even if they did so deceptively by writing in the name of someone else. There are a couple of problems with this view, not least of which is the fact that the pseudonymously written letters sometimes straightforwardly contradicted the content of the authentic Pauline letters. For example, by declaring that the kingdom of god is not just around the corner and that it will in any case be preceded by a series of signs and events, 2 Thessalonians contradicts 1 Thessalonians, which says that the kingdom of god is coming very soon and will happen entirely suddenly and unexpectedly. Indeed, the fact that the two letters contradict one another is one of the reasons scholars have for thinking that Paul was not the author of both of them (people aren't *usually* so self-contradictory).

English, it would be being charitable to note only that it is a highly fragmented, confusing, and very difficult book to read. While it is surely better than the very worst of what some philosophers have managed to produce from time to time, saying so is hardly a compliment to it.

This issue holds epistemic importance in more than one way, for how people understand what god has revealed to them depends in part on the clarity and the accuracy of the language used. Since all natural languages evolve over time, however, and since translation between languages can be difficult and imprecise, there is a possibility that any divinely given message—if given only once—will have its meaning lost or distorted as it ages and disperses to the different corners of the world. Moreover, if someone (like a scribe) takes editorial liberties and adds or subtracts things to or from revelation, the intended meaning of what was set down will be compromised. There would seem to be a pretty clear need for god to ensure that the meaning of revelation does not become distorted or hijacked over time, then. This might include (but would not necessarily be limited to) monitoring how his revelation is recorded and interpreted, and following up on that wherever necessary with interventions designed to eliminate any inaccuracies, ambiguities, or falsehoods.

What we should ultimately expect revelation to be, then, is perhaps the most thoroughly readable, reliable, and comprehensible text ever written, and that should be the case in every language. Needless to say, neither the Bible nor the Quran qualifies as that.

But what if there was a special reason to not take that kind of care with revelation? For example, what if evidentially "unforced" belief in god is a critically important spiritual good? If books of revelation miraculously updated their wording every twenty years to suit the latest developments in the language of a community, I think it would be pretty obvious to all that something was up. This line of reasoning might even be extended to help explain why god revealed himself only very narrowly to a limited number of people at particular times and places. If every culture in the world recorded the exact same details about god completely independently of one another, the coherence of those independent reports would make a rather compelling case for his existence and involvement in the world. But that might also mean that belief in god was not being freely chosen but evidentially compelled.

Is this a good reply? Not in my view, for it isn't clear why free belief in god would constitute a profoundly important spiritual good. Nobody would argue that it is better to believe that water boils at one hundred degrees centigrade under normal atmospheric conditions just because we *chose* to believe it does one day, rather than because it is a scientifically established fact. Why should belief in god mark such a radical departure from this typical story about belief and evidence?

One might respond by saying that in god's eyes evidentially uninformed or underinformed belief in him (and only him) *just is* good, and that that remains the case even if we ourselves cannot see it. The problem with this is that there is practically no end to the number of actions and states of affairs that can be defended by appealing to some mysterious good tailored to suit them in justification.

Imagine that someone tells us they want nothing more out of life than to count blades of grass on a hillside. When we ask them why, they might tell us that it is not because counting blades of grass makes them any happier or relaxes them that it is good (though they are in fact made happier and relaxed in doing it). Rather, counting grass blades is a profound good simply for what it is *in itself*, and they plan to dedicate their lives to it entirely.

What could we say to them in response? Probably nothing. If counting blades of grass on a hillside really is a tremendously important intrinsic good, devoting one's life to it could make perfect sense. Most of us just aren't going to see it that way, though. The same can be said of the idea of free belief in god as a basic and very important spiritual good. While it is logically possible that god might take free belief in him as resoundingly important, unless we can understand something of why that might be, any argument that depends upon it for its persuasiveness will be unlikely to convince.

So where does all of this leave us in respect to Christianity and Islam? Well, not only does the idea of god only revealing himself most clearly to certain people within particular groups at specific historical times appear improbable, the testimony of people making claims to that effect does very little to justify anyone believing them. While the use of public miracles could help justify much wider religious belief in god, the reports of miraculous happenings recorded in revelation fail to provide for that. Moreover, if Christianity and Islam really do represent attempts by god to reveal himself and set humanity upon a straight spiritual and moral course, we are forced to think that he was not much interested in manifesting a sublimely beautiful, coherent, and readable book for people to read, or in protecting its meaning from distortion and manipulation over time. Given that we can reasonably expect exactly the opposite from god at each of these points, this all proves to be a rather significant problem for the truth of religion.

The Bible

Attributed by Christians to god, the Bible contains many ideas that, if read in any ordinary context and if interpreted as general "rules of thumb," deserve high moral praise. For example, the Bible lauds the peacemaker, the merciful, and the pure of heart (Matthew 5:7–9). It urges us not to follow a multitude to evil and to speak the truth (Exodus 23:1–2). We are encouraged to be just (Exodus 23:9), to not hate people in our hearts (Leviticus 19:17), to lay aside evil, malice, hypocrisy, and envy (1 Peter 2:1), and to do more than just wish others well (James 2:15–16). We are to be forgiving and kind (Ephesians 4:32), loving and peaceful, and refrain from doing evil when evil is done to us (Romans 12:17–20). It also contains a version of the Golden Rule requiring us to treat others as we would have ourselves treated (Luke 6:31, Matthew 7:12).[13] In themselves these are all fine ideas, and they are worthy of respect and appreciation.[14]

That is not the complete story, however, for there are many other passages in the Bible that bear nothing of the same moral resemblance. It tells us that those who work on the Sabbath must be put to death (Exodus 35:2), as must those who curse or hit their parents (Exodus 21:15–17, Mark 7:10) or commit blasphemy, incest, or bestiality (Leviticus 24:16, 20:11–20, and 20:15 respectively). Death also goes for adulterers (Deuteronomy 22:22, Leviticus 20:10), homosexuals (Leviticus 20:13), witches (Exodus 22:18), the promiscuous daughters of priests (Leviticus 21:9), and women who are a) found not to be virgins on their wedding nights and b) displease their husbands (Deuteronomy 22:13–21). Staggeringly, even engaged female virgins who are raped in a city are not spared heaven's call for execution (Deuteronomy 22:23–25). Just let the thought of that sink in for a moment: if you are a female

---

[13] The other way of rendering the Golden Rule is negatively—i.e., "do not treat others as you would not have yourself treated."

[14] It unfortunately becomes something of a different story when we are obligated to act in accordance with these ethical prescriptions at the penalty of being metaphysically tortured. If I tell you that you must be kind to others, and that if you're not then you will be tortured for it, this does not speak well for me, and that remains the case even if the idea of being kind to others is perfectly morally appreciable in itself.

virgin, are engaged to someone, and are raped, you must *die* for it. If you think that moral sentiment cannot be surpassed, brace yourself, for a truly remarkable thing must happen if the woman was *not* engaged at the time she was raped: her rapist must purchase her from her father and take her as his wife (Deuteronomy 22:28–29). And *god* said this.

He also said that women are beneath men in standing (Genesis 3:16, 1 Corinthians 11:3, Colossians 3:18) and if beautiful may be taken captive and raped during times of war (Deuteronomy 21:11–14; see also Numbers 31:1–54). Burdened with childbirth as a punishment (Genesis 3:16), wives are told to submit themselves to their husbands, for men sit at the head of women in the same way that Jesus sits at the head of the Church (Ephesians 5:22–24). Not only is it disgraceful for a woman to pray to god with an uncovered head (1 Corinthians 11:5),[15] women are not permitted to speak at any point during a service. If they have a question about something that was said, they should ask their husbands when they get home (1 Corinthians 14:34–35). They should dress modestly and adorn themselves not with jewelry or elaborate hairstyles but good deeds. They should learn quietness and full submission to males, and are not allowed to teach or assume any authority over men. If they have enough faith and love and holiness, in the end they will be saved through childbearing (1 Timothy 2:9–15). That said, they are still a problem reproductively, and when menstruating should be treated like they should be quarantined (Leviticus 15:19–30, 20:18). Consistent with a view of women as property, widows must marry their deceased husband's brother if the two brothers had been living together and the surviving brother doesn't have a son (Deuteronomy 25:5).

Though the practice of slavery is widely condemned in modern times, the Bible doesn't reflect the same attitude. In fact, in many ways, it supports it. The Bible declares that if a man sells his daughter into slavery, she can never go free as a male slave can (after seven years), and that if a slave owner gives his male slave a wife and they have children together, they are both to be considered the property of their master. Neither the children nor the wife should be freed when he is. If the man refuses to go when his term of slavery is up, his ear is to be bored through with an awl (a kind of long pointed spike) and forced to remain a slave

---

[15] Paul's (or god's) reasoning given in 1 Corinthians 11:6 for why an uncovered female head is shameful when bent in prayer is almost comical: for a woman to pray to god without her head covered is, Paul says, pretty much the same as for her to pray to god with a shaven head. But if it is a disgrace for a woman to have a shaved head, so it must also be a disgrace for a woman to pray to god without her head covered. QED.

forever (Exodus 21:2–7). Though Israelites were prohibited from selling themselves into slavery out of financial desperation, it was perfectly fine to purchase and keep slaves of other nationalities (Leviticus 25:39–46).[16] Slaves can be beaten and killed so long as they do not die immediately after being beaten, for they are the property of their owners (Exodus 21:20–21). As for slaves themselves, god commands them to obey their earthly masters with respect, fear, and sincerity of heart (Ephesians 6:5–8, Colossians 3:22, Titus 2:9–10), regardless of whether their masters are good or cruel (1 Peter 2:18).

While the Bible regards homosexuality as a sexual perversion (Romans 1:26–27), its views on heterosexuality are hardly what one would call positive. While it's true that married couples are told not deprive one another of sex except by mutual consent and only to pray, that this is prescribed at all is nothing more than a concession to human weakness. As the Bible makes clear, it would be far better if everyone just lived perpetually celibate and unmarried (Matthew 19:10–12, 1 Corinthians 7:4–8). While divorce is prohibited, should it ever occur, the divorced are not allowed to marry anyone else but their former partners again (1 Corinthians 7:10–11).[17] Indeed, according to Jesus, anyone who marries a divorced woman aside from the original husband commits adultery (Matthew 5:31–32). Famously, the Bible even goes so far as to say that anyone who looks at another woman with lust while married commits adultery in his heart (Matthew 5:28).[18] Given the Bible's views on adultery, this is a very serious crime to be guilty of.

---

[16] Given that the Israelites were a people god had liberated from slavery in Egypt, it would have been unseemly for them to resell themselves. The Bible does appear at one point to condemn slavery by saying that those who enslave a man should be put to death (Exodus 21:16). However, if this instruction only applied to the enslavement of Israelite males, rather than to males generally, this can be made sense of in a way consistent with what else it has to say on the subject.

[17] Cf. Matthew 5:31, which admits one justifiable reason for divorce: adultery.

[18] The ruling presumably applies to women in relation to men, but that isn't explicitly stated. Just in case the problem with that proclamation isn't completely obvious, I can find nothing morally wrong in being sexually *attracted* to people other than one's own spouse. It might not be desirable from the point of view of the relationship itself, and it may be acutely detrimental if actually acted upon, but it certainly isn't beyond being part of a normal and healthy human reaction to see other human beings as sexually attractive. Moreover, as there is no reason to think that attraction to others would stop upon marrying someone, and it's far from clear that being attracted to people is something we have direct control over. Jesus's moral proclamation, therefore, burdens people with an impossible demand and sets them up to fail. More than that, though, it proposes to judge and convict us for what amounts to a thought crime.

As for unbelievers, they are sinful (Hebrews 3:12) and suffer from the wrath of god (John 3:36). God lets it be known that those who don't believe are fools with darkened hearts (Romans 1:21–22) who cannot please god with their good deeds (Hebrews 11:6). He sternly warns that the accursed will be cast into the furnaces of hell (Matthew 13:41–42) where they will experience everlasting destruction (2 Thessalonians 1:7–9), be tormented with brimstone (Revelation 14:10–11), and suffer eternally (Matthew 25:41–46; John 5:28–29). As bad as hell is, god has "closed the eyes" and "deadened the hearts" of some so that they will never believe in him (John 12:37–41, Isaiah 44:18, 2 Corinthians 4:4). Only those who are like children (i.e., credulous and subordinate) will avoid hell and enter the kingdom of heaven (Matthew 18:2).

What about god himself? According to Christian revelation, he is the maker of the world who rules in heaven (Acts 17:24). Loving and kind (Psalm 100:5, 1 John 4:8–12, Romans 2:4), god is all-knowing (Romans 11:33) and all-powerful (Psalm 115:3). Although he cannot be seen (1 Timothy 6:15–16), he is everywhere (Jeremiah 23:24), and all good and perfect things come from him (James 1:17). Untiring (Isaiah 40:28) and unchanging (Malachi 3:6), he favors no group of people over any other (Romans 2:11), and exercises kindness, justice, and goodness (Jeremiah 9:24). While unforgiving to the unforgiving (Matthew 6:14–15), god is still compassionate, gracious, and slow to anger (Exodus 34:6). The only one in existence who is good (Mark 10:18), in god is only light (1 John 1:5), and he urges us to accept one another (Romans 15:7). His desire is that we should rid ourselves of all bitterness, anger, slander, and malice (Ephesians 4:31), and says that we should even love our enemies (Matthew 5:44).

God is also stern in judgment (Romans 11:22) and disciplines us in the way that a father would discipline his children (Proverbs 3:11–12). Despising oaths (Matthew 5:33) and hating gossip (2 Timothy 2:16), god will punish anyone who gives themselves over to sexual impurity or passionate lust (1 Thessalonians 4:3–7, Romans 1:24–27). Viewing strong family ties with suspicion (Matthew 23:9), he promises anyone who abandons their family for him a great reward (Matthew 19:29). Filled with wrath (1 Thessalonians 1:10) and consumed by jealousy of the worship of other gods (Exodus 20:5, Exodus 34:14), he demands to be worshiped and loved (Matthew 4:10, 22:37). Indeed, anyone who does not god is cursed (1 Corinthians 16:22). We are to be thankful to him for every circumstance of life we might possibly find ourselves in, regardless of its hardship, and pray constantly (1 Thessalonians 5:16–18).

If we do not acknowledge and repent our sins, he will cast us into the furnace of hell (Matthew 4:17).

At times impatient, intolerant, and coarse (Matthew 17:14–21), god dislikes foolish and stupid arguments, for they lead to quarrels (2 Timothy 2:23). We are told not to love the world or anything in it, for if we do, we do not love god (1 John 2:15). Calling judgment upon those who label anyone else a fool (Matthew 5:22), he asks that we submit ourselves to worldly authorities, for he has appointed them over us (1 Peter 2:13). Indeed, to rebel against them is to rebel against god (Romans 13:1). Capable of rage, rebuke, and name-calling (Matthew 23:13–39), god is an agent of torture (Revelation 9:3–6) and ruthless in violence and punishment (e.g., Matthew 11:20–25, 13:47–50, 25:31–46). Repeatedly mentioned, one of the most central messages of the Bible is that we should fear god (e.g., 1 Peter 2:17–18, Proverbs 3:7–8, Revelation 14:7, Psalm 111:10.).

Miscellaneous Biblical commands include not being permitted to wear clothes made of two kinds of cloth (Deuteronomy 22:11), plant a field with two kinds of crops (Leviticus 19:19), make fire on the Sabbath (Exodus 35:3), boil a baby goat's meat in its mother's milk (Exodus 23:19), get tattoos or cut one's beard (Leviticus 19:27–28), plough fields with an ox and an ass together (Deuteronomy 22:10), or attend church if one's penis and/or testicles have been damaged (Deuteronomy 23:1). Beyond that, god tells us that he punishes the children, grandchildren, and even the great-grandchildren for the sins of the father (Exodus 34:7), that those who are not with him are against him (Matthew 12:30), and that those who love their parents more than him are not worthy of him (Matthew 10:37).

As you can see from the above, while some of the content mentioned merely vacillates between the comical and the strange, other passages are genuinely abhorrent in their suggestion and should leave us thoroughly shocked.

If we turn our analysis from questions of morality to logical consistency, we can note that the Bible exhibits a number of internal contradictions and discrepancies. [19] I'll limit the vignette to four examples, beginning with a discussion between Jesus and his followers in the lead up to his arrest and crucifixion.

As the Gospel of John recounts it, Jesus and his Apostles shared a final meal together not long before Jesus was arrested by the authorities

---

[19] See Ehrman (2009) for an extensive treatment of this issue.

and crucified. Whereas the Gospels of Matthew, Mark, and Luke all have Jesus take bread and wine at this meal and give it to the Apostles (telling them that it is his body and blood), the Gospel of John mentions nothing about this. Instead, and uniquely to that Gospel, Jesus washes the feet of the Apostles. After doing this, he tells them that he is going away soon, and that they should love one another as he has loved them when he is gone. When he is asked by Peter where he is going, Jesus responds by telling him that where he is going they cannot immediately follow, but that they know the way (John 13:33–36, 14:4). After Thomas notes that since they do not know where he is going, they do not know the way, Jesus changes the subject and talks about something else (John 14:5–6). It comes as some surprise, then, when only moments later, and at the very same meal they were at all along, Jesus questions his followers why none of them had bothered to ask, "Where are you going?" (John 16:5). That is precisely what they had asked him and what he had chosen to avoid answering. Since it seems rather unlikely that Jesus could have overlooked something like this, it stands out as an internal inconsistency in the narrative.

Next we have Judas and his betrayal of Jesus. According to the account given in Matthew (27:3–10), after trying to return the money he was paid by priests to betray Jesus and being refused, Judas threw the money down on the floor before them, went outside, and hanged himself. The money was collected up by the priests and used to buy a field that was set aside as a cemetery for any foreigners who died while in Jerusalem. Because the field was bought with blood money, the field was known as the Field of Blood. In the book of Acts, however, a completely different story is told. For one thing, instead of being bought by the priests with money that Judas had tried to return to them, Judas purchased the field directly himself. Moreover, instead of hanging himself there in shame and regret, Judas died by falling "headlong" in the field such that "his body burst open and all his intestines spilled out." It was for this reason that the field came to be known as the Field of Blood (Acts 1:18–19).

Not even the biblically critical story of the empty tomb is exempt from problems of consistency. One of the most pivotal events in all of the New Testament, the story goes something like this: after Jesus's body had been taken down from the cross and placed in a tomb, a group of women went to it in order to anoint it with spices. Who went? It depends on which Gospel you read. It was either Mary Magdalene and another Mary (Matthew 28:1); Mary Magdalene, Mary the mother of James, and

Salome (Mark 16:1); an unspecified group of women (Luke 24:1); or Mary Magdalene all by herself (John 20:1). When whoever it was got to the tomb, which had either been left guarded (Matthew 28:4) or unguarded (Mark, Luke, and John), they found either that the stone covering the entrance had already been rolled away (Mark 16:4, John 20:1, Luke 24:2), or that there was an angel there to roll it away for them (Matthew 28:2). In the reports given in Matthew and Mark (16:5) there was a single angel at the tomb. However, in Luke there was two (24:4), and in John there was none. For the three Gospels in which there was an angelic presence, the women were either told to go and tell the disciples that Jesus would meet them in Galilee (Mark 16:7), to tell the disciples just that he had risen (Matthew 28:7), or to remember the fact that Jesus had told them while they were in Galilee that his death was necessary (Luke 24:7). Since there were no angels in the Gospel of John to issue instructions, Mary Magdalene is reported as having gone on her own initiative to tell the disciples that the tomb was empty (John 20:2).

Finally, consider the otherwise tiresome genealogies provided for Jesus in Matthew and Luke, which are relevant to us here for three reasons. First, genealogies are chastised elsewhere in the Bible as a waste of time and something that should be avoided (Titus 3:9). If that is so, it's not clear why god would bother to provide them for Jesus. Second, the genealogies given in the two Gospels are mutually incompatible. The genealogy in Luke (3:23–38) gives a total of fifty-five generations preceding Jesus from Abraham, for example, while the genealogy found in Matthew (1:1–17) gives only forty. Third, the whole idea of a giving a genealogy for Jesus extending back patrilineally through Joseph and King David to reach Abraham is, in light of Mary's supposedly virginal birth, a waste of time. Having been conceived via a miracle rather than by sexual intercourse, Jesus had no biological connection whatsoever to Joseph. Not only does it not make any sense why god would denounce genealogies while offering two of them for Jesus, then, it's not clear why he would give two different genealogical accounts of that, or why he would bother to give any at all, given Jesus's supposedly miraculous appearance on Earth.

The importance of discrepancies like these does not come from their details but from the fact they exist at all. The Bible is supposed to be the word of god, after all, and it is difficult to believe that contradictions and discrepancies of any kind would be found within it. Yet that is what appears to be the case with the Bible.

The list of problems highlighted here is by no means exhaustive, but it is intended to show that there is a very real problem confronting the idea of the Bible as the revelation of god in light of its moral and logical character.[20]

The Quran

As noted at the start of the chapter, the Quran is traditionally understood by Muslims to be a word for word account of revelation received by the prophet Muhammad over the course of twenty-three years. Recorded in various ways and brought together as a single book after Muhammad's death, the Quran gives ringing endorsement to many morally excellent ideas. It tells us to be forgiving and kind (3:134, 4:36), to do good and avoid evil (2:195, 11:85), to combat evil with goodness so that our enemies become like our friends (41:34), and to be staunch in justice, even when this is costly to us (5:8, 4:135). We are instructed to help the needy and the poor, the sick and the unfortunate (22:28), to live peacefully with those who disbelieve (43:88–89), to be honest (22:30), to avoid stealing (4:2), to not kill others (4:29), and to refrain from forcing the religion of god upon people (2:256). Just like the Bible, however, there is a much darker side to the Quran.

It announces that men have authority over women, for women were created a degree below men and must submit themselves in obedience to men (4:34). Women are told to remain faithful and chaste, to keep their gaze lowered, to cover themselves in public, and to avoid stamping their feet (lest the sight of their ankles and legs be revealed; 24:31). A woman's value as a witness is half that of a man's (in the case of

---

[20] To be clear, all that morally and factually problematic content in revelation most minimally shows is that *those* specific passages were not set down into revelation by god. That doesn't strictly show that nothing else within it could have been from god, however. That said, to maintain that the rest of revelation *apart* from that which is most morally problematic about it really is from god, you'd need to argue something to the effect that "everything that is morally good is from god, and everything that is morally terrible is not." Not only does this not explain why god would allow so many morally terrible things to be inserted by others to sit alongside what he said, it is about as *ad hoc* an explanation for why the rest of revelation can be trusted as you'll ever find. Needless to say, just because a particular passage is morally benign or virtuous does *not* mean that god must have said it. Short of a convincing explanation otherwise, then, evidence of morally harmful content within books which purport to be from god does constitute evidence for their wholly non-divine status.

recording debts, at least; 2:282), and they are entitled to inherit only half of what a man is (4:11). The use of violence by men to correct women is also permitted when other recommended steps have failed (4:34). Sexually speaking, women are associated with uncleanliness, and a man may not pray if he has recently had sex (just as he cannot when drunk or dirty; 4:43). Menstruating women should be avoided for the length of their menstruation (2:222), but at all other times they may be used for sex by their husbands (2:223). "Lewd" wives may have their dowries revoked (4:19), and the taking of females as slaves in times of war is acceptable (33:50; other passages, such as 24:33, at least encourage the freeing of slaves as a virtue, and, where owned, not forcing them into prostitution; see also 90:12–13).

God's sense of justice is strangely compatible with the framework of tribal ethics dominant in seventh-century Arabia, and he accordingly mandates acts of retaliation to an equal degree between tribal social units in cases of murder: the free for the free, a slave for a slave, a woman for a woman (2:178). Recompense for an injury is also an injury equal to it. Thus if you were to accidentally blind someone, god gives them permission to blind you in return. God does also say, however, that forgiveness is preferable to retaliation, and anyone who forgives is promised a reward (42:40–43). Adulterers, both male and female, are to be lashed with a whip one hundred times (24:2), while the punishment for stealing is having one's hands cut off (5:38; the verse immediately after notes that if they repent they will be forgiven by god, but it is unclear whether they get to keep their hands). Lewd women are to be confined to their houses until death (4:15).

While the Quran declares that there is no compulsion to religious belief (2:256), it also states that there is nothing more unjust in the sight of god than those who do not believe in him (6:21). Indeed, for all else that might conceivably qualify, those who reject god are literally the worst of all creatures (8:55). Among other things, they are ignorant (43:20), unsuitable for friendship (5:51, 9:23, 4:89), and unloved by god (30:45).

Given how much god despises unbelief, it is dumbfound ding to learn that god has set a seal upon the hearts of some in order that they will never believe in the truth of Islam (2:6–7, 14:4, 39:23). Since we know how severe the metaphysical consequences waiting for those who do not believe in god are, it is strikingly unjust that these people should be condemned to hell through no fault of their own.

The Quran does an interesting job with the ideas of heaven and hell. Characterized as a magnificent garden with plenty of shade, food, drink, and couches to sit on, those who succeed in making it to paradise will share their eternal time with "wide-eyed" young virginal girls as company (4:57, 2:25, 3:15, 78:31–34, 76:5–20, 52:20). Hell, in contrast, is a place of eternal punishment and humiliating torture with fire (4:14, 4:168–169, 5:36–37). Those who reject Islam will be dragged by chains placed around their necks through boiling liquid while being taunted (40:70–76). Their skin will be burned off by fire and then replaced, all in order that their torture can endure forever (4:56). They will be made to drink boiling water (6:70) and will not be able to extinguish the fire from their faces and backs (21:39). They will wear clothing made of fire, their skin and organs will melt, and they will be impaled on iron hooks (22:19–22).

Against a backdrop of eternal reward in paradise, eternal punishment in hell, and a hatred of unbelief, a message of violence can be placed. Restrictions governing warfare and its initiation are raised many times in the Quran. God makes it repeatedly known that peace is to be sought over war, and that war is only allowed in response to being attacked (for he does not love the aggressor). Fighting is not allowed in the mosque in Mecca (unless fought there first), nor during the holy months, nor against those who repent and surrender. When and where these conditions are satisfied, however, violence and persecution is urged (persecution of one's enemies rather than slaughter is preferred, as persecution is regarded as worse; 2:190–192). A man who fights for Islam is a holy warrior, while a man who dies fighting for Islam is a holy martyr. Whether slain or victorious, he will receive a great reward (4:74). While some argue that the historical context of the time at which the revelation took place restricts the applicability of the passage in question to a quite specific set of people, the Quran states that unbelievers with whom no treaty is held are to be slain where they are found, besieged, and taken captive (9:1–5). Indeed, unbelievers who have been shown god's message yet fail to believe are to be fought against until they pay tribute and are brought into a state of subjection, for their disbelief and greed is perverse (9:29–34). God shows little sympathy for Muslims who dislike violence, emphasizing that preparation for war and participation in it when called is ordained, whether they like it or not (for as god says himself, he knows best, you don't; 2:216). At one point he even goes so far as to mock a group of Muslims who feel reluctant to engage in warfare after having a revelation "sent down" to them instructing them to fight. He rebukes them for being afraid and for having "sickness in their hearts," and threatens them that it would be much better to be obedient to god's commands (i.e., "fight when I tell you to, or else"; 47:20–21).

What more does the Quran reveal about god? Despite being beyond the possibility of being defined or comprehended (43:82, 6:103), god is a supremely wise (22:52), kind (22:63), and loving being (85:14). One and absolute (4:87), there is nothing that god can be successfully compared to (112:1–4). Ruling everything and never sleeping, he is eternal, self-existing (2:255), and knows all that is in our hearts (64:4). Indeed, not a leaf falls without his knowledge (6:59). The source of all righteousness and forgiveness (74:56), god encourages us to goodness (5:48), is exceedingly merciful (3:16), and is the best of all judges (10:109). Capable of everything (24:45), he is the creator of both humans (15:26, 16:4) and angels (35:1) and is closer to us than the veins in our neck (50:16). Strong (22:74–75), rich (35:15), and needing nothing (64:6), god is the light (24:35).

God is also ruthless (35:37) and demands to be worshiped (53:62, 4:36, 2:21). In fact, to worship god was the sole reason we were created (51:56). Wrathful (6:147) and quick in retribution (6:165, 24:39), god is severe in punishment (59:7). Indeed, were he to punish everyone according to their sins, no creature would be left to walk upon the earth (35:45). A proponent of collective punishment (65:8), god tests believers with hardship, fear, hunger, and loss (2:155–156, 76:2), and strikes dead whoever he pleases with thunderbolts (13:13). He utterly condemns anyone who places something spiritually alongside him (17:39); indeed, those who do will never be forgiven for it (4:116). Even just to question whether or not there is an afterlife, or what it might possibly consist of, is to disobey god and deserve a place in hell (13:5).

Guiding believers along the right path but leading the wicked astray (6:39, 22:54, and 14:27), god is responsible for any blessing or curse that happens to us in life (16:53). A cause of both laughter and weeping (53:43), he ordains the ritual sacrifice of animals in honor of himself (22:35–37). Everything that happens in the world occurs only by the will of god (64:11). Thus whether you cut down a tree or leave it standing, it happens only because divine will aligns with that outcome (59:5).

Maker and designer (59:24), it is god alone who sustains the continued existence of Earth and the Moon (35:41), and who gave Earth stabilizers so that it would not shake (21:31). His creation contains many signs of his existence, including: that there are mountains and rivers, that there are two of every kind of fruit, and that day and night run in series (13:2–

3); that some plants and fruits taste better to us than others (13:4), that the sun and moon are beneficial (16:12), that there are colors (16:13), that so many generations of people before have been destroyed (20:128), that so many things in the world are useful (45:13), that ships move across water (31:31), that there is love and romantic partnerships (30:21), that people sleep (30:23), that there is fear-inducing lightning (30:24), and that birds fly (16:79; interestingly, birds fly not because they physically *can* fly, but because god holds them up in the air).[21]

Regardless of the evidence or the lack of it, one of the most central messages of Islam is that god is to be worshiped, obeyed, and feared (2:278, 3:130, 5:2, 16:51, 24:52, 33:1, 39:20, 49:1, 53:62, 57:28, and 59:18). Indeed, those believers who experience fear at the mere mention of god's name are called true believers (8:2).

As for Muhammad himself, revelation extended him a number of special privileges and requirements. The instructions of god's prophet were to be treated as special by Muslims, lest they suffer a very painful punishment (24:63). If he needed to be conversed with, it was good to give something to charity before doing so, if one was able (58:12). Sensitive to rejection, god comforted Muhammad that those who rejected his message weren't really rejecting Muhammad *per se*—they were rejecting god (6:33). Unlike other men, he was allowed to marry practically any believing woman he wanted. Indeed, he could have an unlimited number of wives (a privilege he alone was granted; 33:50). As for his wives, heaven ruled that nobody was permitted to marry them after him, and that they had to remain secluded from the sight of other men in their homes (33:53). In practical terms, this meant that visitors to Muhammad's house could speak to his wives only if they were behind a barrier or curtain. While his wives were promised a great reward for their sexual loyalty and good behavior, they were also threatened with double the normal punishment for any sexual impropriety (33:30).

One passage of revelation is particularly interesting in this context, but to see why first requires some background. After he began receiving

---

[21] What Muhammad needed to evidentially show wasn't that *some* god exists, but that his *particular* god exists, and that he was a prophet for it. Just arguing for the existence of a god responsible for the design of the universe does nothing to establish the truth of the latter two points, and raises questions about why the Quran (as universal revelation) spent so much time arguing in that way. It's possible that Muhammad simply failed to apprehend the logical distinction between propositions concerning the existence of *some* god and the existence of *his* god, or that he just ignored the distinction in the hope that, by doing so, others would as well.

the revelation of god, Muhammad took several wives and divided his time between them equally. This system appears to have worked well until one night when he was discovered in bed with one of his concubines. Given that the night in question belonged to his wife Hafsa, she became infuriated at this, and when news of the event spread to the attention of his other wives, they banded together and barred him from having any sexual contact with them.[22]

Taking note of the situation, god intervened with a special revelation dedicated to resolving it. Announcing that he had revoked the oath that Muhammad had made to his wives, god expressed puzzlement as to why Muhammad had (up until that point) refrained from having sex with his concubines when they were lawfully his for that purpose. Warning his wives that Muhammad was protected by both god and by angels, and threatening them that he might decide that Muhammad should divorce them and take more submissive wives in their place, he finished by reminding them that hell is a very warm place (66:1–6).[23]

Just like the Bible, the Quran comes with number of apparent internal contradictions. For example, the Egyptian Pharaoh of Exodus fame was both drowned by god (17:102–103) and spared by him (10:90–92), drinking alcohol is both permitted (16:67) and not permitted (5:90), and Muhammad was the first Muslim (39:12) and Moses was the first Muslim (7:143). In terms of factual inconsistencies, the Quran makes the mistake of agreeing with the Bible that god put the universe together in just six days (7:54, 25:59). The Quran talks of stars as missiles that drive devils away (67:5). As for mountains, they were created by god to stop the earth beneath from shaking (21:31, 78:6–7).

Just as before, what is listed here is not intended as a complete account of what is objectionable or problematic about the Quran. What it is intended to show, however, is that Islam, much like Christianity, bears all the marks of the period of its inception, and that it comes off all the worse for that. Indeed, the sheer number of times that the Quran mentions the shameful doom and humiliation awaiting unbelievers makes a startling impression, and certainly not a favorable one.

Of course, not everything that is said in the Bible or the Quran ends up actually being believed by Christians and Muslims. While it could be hoped that what is accepted is divinely guided to believers by some mystical intuition or inner voice, this strikes me as too much of a wishful

---

[22] Ibn Warraq (2003).
[23] This kind of thing is hardly unique to history. It has been the misfortune of males to use the gods, spirits, and ancestors as a way of aiding themselves in dominating women.

thought to be taken seriously. After all, why would god go through the trouble of setting up a book of revelation that includes such things, only then to go back through and tell people by way of softly spoken intuitions that this part over here is to be believed, this part over here is more of a rule of thumb, this thing over here is not to be understood literally, and this thing here isn't to be believed at all? Why the two-stage process, and why such a fallible one? Is it not more reasonable to think that this is simply a way that people have thought up to justify ignoring some of the worst moral and factual content of a book they are otherwise required to believe is the Word of God?

Some Anticipated Objections

There could be a few objections building up at this point, and it may be worthwhile trying to address some of the more expected ones now before moving on.

Objection: *Contrary to criticism, the picture of god that emerges from revelation is an exceedingly positive one. God is described there as wise, powerful, knowing, loving, beneficent, just, merciful, and compassionate, and all to an extent we cannot comprehend. How can you say that religion promotes an extremely poor picture of god, then? This could not be further from the truth.*

It is certainly correct that many glowing things are said about god in revelation. However, nothing more needs to follow from this fact than a conflict between god's *description* and his *depiction*. We can easily imagine a person like Joseph Stalin being described in wholly positive terms by state-run newspapers and Communist party officials, but would that mean that those descriptions of him are true? Surely not; Stalin's actions spoke a different story.

I would argue no less that many of god's supposed virtues as listed in revelation are emptied of their meaning when you consider what he is otherwise presented as being. These descriptive offerings to god, like the burnt offerings of old, are part of a natural and expected attempt to venerate god, and they need not be taken as anything more substantial than that.

That said, it isn't even true that *only* positive things are said about god in revelation. The Bible tells us that god is jealous (Exodus 34:14), for example, while the Quran tells us that he is wrathful (6:147) and severe in punishment (5:2).

Objection: *But what about all the good parts of Christian and Islamic revelation? While you have mentioned some of these, isn't it biased to draw attention to the most morally unbecoming passages? Though that content exists, it is neither representative of those religions as a whole, nor what they actually mean to most people who identify with them.*

Is it an exhibition of bias to search through revelation and pick out passages that affirm a morally negative view of it? While it might certainly be bias that leads someone to do that, given that our interest here is a philosophical one relating to the question of religious truth, being focused on those negative parts is appropriate. The reason why is simple: we learn more about the origins of a book claiming to be revelation by finding that it has morally unbecoming content in it than we do by finding it has morally praiseworthy content. Other things being equal, the former is much more challenging to the idea of its divine authorship than the latter is confirming of the same.

I entirely accept that there are many genuinely admirable moral ideas promoted by Christianity and Islam—ethical notions that, in themselves and all other things being equal, are worthy of our highest moral regard. If believers need to hear that affirmed before they can contemplate some of the ways in which other parts of revelation might be deplorably bad, consider it openly accepted and acknowledged.

Objection: *In interpreting the meaning of revelation literally, critics show themselves to have the same lack of sophistication that religious fundamentalists/extremists have. The meaning of revelation is (largely) metaphorical, not literal.*

One of the goals of this objection, I presume, is to make critics who take a literal approach to revelation feel uncomfortable for sharing something of the same intellectual space as those who might blow themselves up in crowded marketplaces, stone people to death, or advocate for the subpersonal status of women. After all, both groups of people understand the meaning of revelation as intended largely literally. Doesn't that speak to the wrong-headedness of literalism?

Honestly, no. In short, it is hardly just *obvious* that so much of what is put forward in revelation wasn't intended literally, and therefore isn't best interpreted in that way. While a more in-depth look at the merits of nonliteralism will be examined later in the chapter, for now we can note that there are no warning stickers or prefatory notes to either Christian or Islamic revelation indicating that their contents should be broadly interpreted nonliterally. Rather than displaying a shared fault on the part of both religious critic and fundamentalist, then, it just as easily supports error on the part of those who embrace nonliteralism because it enables them to escape the literal meaning of some parts of revelation.

Objection: *The god you describe from revelation is not the one that I religiously believe in, and I don't personally know anyone else who does. It would be fair to say that I no more believe in such a god than you do. Accordingly, you fail to address the religious beliefs that I (and most others of my faith) actually accept.*

While this could certainly be a good thing, it doesn't follow that the most rational approach to revelation doesn't require us to believe in such a god. Simply put, there are understandable reasons why most people would want to avoid believing the totality of what Christian and Islamic revelation each tell us, and the fact that most do avoid it doesn't reveal how we *should* believe. Religious worldviews as they appear in the minds of believers can be a vast improvement over how they are laid out in text-theoretical form. Christianity and Islam are both excellent examples of this, for they are in many ways far better as practiced and believed in by the majority than they are as written down. If the question we're interested in concerns the *truth* of a given religion, however, then presumably we will need to take what is written down in its revelation seriously, for it is there that the message of god is said to reside. Moreover, if we are in fact best to avoid interpreting certain passages as literally true, we will need to know what rationally justifies us in doing that.

Objection: *Critics of Islam routinely point out examples of violent content in the Quran, yet Islam is a religion of peace, not war. Even the word Islam itself means peace. Violent extremists represent only a small fraction of the overall Muslim population, and it is grossly unfair to judge the fruits of any religion by the beliefs and actions of its worst apples. Drawing a connection between Islamic revelation and* *violence mistakenly yields to a harmful misrepresentation of the true Islam, and perpetuates that false image even further.*

A survey published in 2013 by the Pew Research Center found that 7 percent of Muslims in Indonesia, 13 percent of Muslims in Pakistan, and 15 percent of Muslims in Turkey believe that suicide bombing in defense of Islam is "sometimes" or "often" justified. Support for this proposition was found to be significantly higher in other Muslim countries, with 26 percent of Bangladeshi, 29 percent of Egyptian, and 39 percent of Afghani Muslims holding the same opinion. Asked whether they agree with adulterers being stoned to death, 9 percent of Muslims in Turkey said they did. Yet for Indonesian Muslims the figure was 42 percent, for Egyptian Muslims it was 80 percent, and for Pakistani Muslims it was 86 percent. Views concerning the execution of people who abandon their belief in Islam were similarly alarming. 16 percent of Indonesian Muslims were found to support the death penalty for apostates, as do 58 percent of Malaysian Muslims, 75 percent of Pakistani Muslims, and 88 percent of Egyptian Muslims.[24]

While it is wise to treat survey findings with a level of caution,[25] it seems safe to say that a significant subpopulation of Muslims face an issue with violence at the level of their beliefs and attitudes.

The question we may then reasonably ask is: is there any meaningful causal connection between the religion of Islam and these beliefs and attitudes? The issue is clearly sensitive and sharply disputed, and I think it is too often discussed with insufficient causal complexity in mind. While a full treatment of the question cannot be given here, some of the most important considerations worth making can be outlined.

A good place to begin from is with the counsel of history. In his book *Humanity*, Jonathan Glover examines the following question: what brings ordinary people to commit moral atrocities? What was it, for example, that led to the deaths of millions of people in Communist Russia and China, the Rwandan genocide, the massacre of Vietnamese villagers by U.S. soldiers at My Lai, or the concentration camps in Nazi-occupied Europe?[26]

---

[24] See Lugo, Cooperman, Bell *et al.* (2013), appendix Q92b, Q92d, and Q89.
[25] Surveys can ask questions that are so poorly phrased or coarse-grained that they end up being of only limited value for understanding what people's true attitudes and beliefs are.
[26] Glover (2001)

Take the mass execution of Jews in the village of Jozefow, Poland, at the hands of a German Police Battalion in July 1940. As Glover outlines, members of the unit were given the choice at the start of the day of not participating, but only a very small number took up this option (twelve out of five hundred). While more did drop out as the day proceeded, a full 80 percent continued through until the end. All in all, some fifteen hundred Jews were killed. What factors brought these men to engage in a prolonged act of systematic murder?

Unsurprisingly, there isn't just one explanatory factor. What occurred obviously had something to do with their indoctrination by Nazi ideology, the acutely negative characterization of Jews within that ideology, and the role of trusted experts and authority figures in establishing and maintaining those views. This was only part of the story, however. For example, a strong deferential attitude had been instilled in members of the unit as part of their training. They understood themselves as there to follow the orders of their commanders, and they internalized that as part of their identity. They were also concerned with their reputations within the unit, and feared negative repercussions from others if they chose not to participate. Also problematic was the fact that, in order to defect from the task, they would need to do so in a way that was highly visible to others. This made it much more challenging for them to acquit themselves from what was taking place.

Though brief, this example helps illustrate the way that different causal factors can combine and amplify one another to produce something morally catastrophic.

If we take that same kind of moral-analytical lens and apply it to the question of Islam and violence, what stands out as being of concern? My suggestion is that all of the following do:

- The Quran is widely understood by Muslims to be the literal and infallible word of god. While some are likely to report believing this for essentially honorific reasons, others will genuinely hold it to be the case. This is problematic, for believing that the Quran is both literal and infallible makes it more difficult to avoid any morally objectionable content within it by resorting to metaphor or mistake.
- Obedience to god is venerated and demanded within Islam. At the axiological core of Islam resides the normative ideal of submitting oneself wholly to god as a fundamental good and goal in life. Much of what it is to live a good life just is to be devoted to god in an unfailing and resolute way.

- The Quran contains a considerable amount of content that either describes or normatively recommends violence under certain circumstances. For example, it talks in great detail about the kinds of tortures that await people in hell, it imposes corporal punishments like the cutting off of hands for theft and lashing people for adultery, and it permits "an eye for an eye" tribal justice. To its credit, intergroup violence between Muslims and non-Muslims is framed in most cases as justified only defensively in the Quran. However, the willingness of Muslims to engage in warfare is religiously obliged, whether they like it or not (2:216), and those who run from battle are told that they incur the wrath of god (8:15). God is said to adore those who fight for him in an orderly and disciplined fashion (4:95, 61:4), and he promises those who do a tremendous reward, whether they live or die (4:74). Unfortunately, and against the grain of the usual defensive constraints, there are a handful of passages in the Quran that risk appearing to advocate open violence against unbelievers, with one of them citing an explicitly religious reason for doing so—namely, the perversity of disbelief (9:29–31; see also 9:123).[27] While these are exceptions to the general case, and while they may have been intended to be limited by the defensive restrictions set out at the beginning of the sura (9:1–5), or perhaps aimed *specifically and only* at the unbelievers who were present in Mecca at the time when the revelation was received, believing this comes only at the cost of an extraordinary failure on the part of god to take complete care with revelation on matters pertaining to violence.

- Islam encourages both obedience and deference by exploiting powerful metaphysical incentives. While the obedient can hope to enter paradise when they die, the disobedient are promised nothing less than eternity in hell. It hardly needs to be said, but belief in the possibility of hell for oneself constitutes an enormous consideration in the question of how one is best to live. Islam's treatment of the idea of heaven is particularly interesting for the fact that it is framed in a highly sexualized way. Believers (really here, *male* believers) are told to expect a bounty of virginal women awaiting them after their righteous deaths. Because sex and the relationships that facilitate it motivate most people very deeply in life, we can justifiably expect

---

[27] Their greed is also cited as a reason for killing them in 9:34, but that does not morally improve things.

that the thought of acquiring what amounts to a metaphysical harem is a tantalizing idea for many men, and therein acts as a powerful motivation for them to strive for spiritual success.

- Significant social pressures exist in many parts of the Islamic world in favor of religious conformity. The desire to conform is a general feature of human psychology, of course, and not something that is specific to any religion, much less Islam. Yet by monitoring religious expression and behavior, and by issuing punishments for any deviation from what is deemed to be religiously acceptable, the problem of that pressure is massively compounded. In some parts of the Muslim world, it can even translate into physical harm or death for those who commit sins like blasphemy or apostasy (abandonment of Islam).

- Islam has embedded within it a variety of mechanisms intended to insulate it from external criticism. For example, the Quran provides spiritual and moral explanations for why some people fail to believe in its truth. The interesting thing about these explanations is that they do not cast Islam's critics in any favorable light—indeed, critics and criticism are condemned. This is significant, for by encouraging Muslims to take a dim view of those who question Islam's truth, a psychological barrier is built up against anything that they might have to say against it. After all, how easy is it to truly hear the arguments of people you have religious reasons to think want to subvert you to hell, and are more than willing to lie in order to do it? Better still, should an argument with any persuasive bite be produced against Islam, it can simply be discarded as involving some form of hidden deceit.

- Islam promotes tribalism in ways aimed at its own advantage. Those who believe are placed squarely against those who do not as marking out a fundamentally important division between people, and one that is especially concerning to god. This distinction is made worse by the fact that those who do not believe are described in acutely negative terms. They are vilified, in fact, as ignorant (43:20), the worst of all creatures (8:55), unloved by god (30:45), unsuitable for friendship, marriage, or allegiance (5:51, 2:221, and 9:23), and as worthy of suffering extraordinary punishment in hell (98:6). All of this is troubling, for when the view we hold of others is poor, or when the picture we have of them sits at a great distance to our own positive self-conception, it can become that much harder to be moved empathetically in concern for them.[28] Whether that was intentional or inadvertent, there do appear to be passages in the Quran that were intended to undermine extensions of empathy to nonbelievers in specific circumstances. The Quran reports that, following a particular battle, it was not the Muslims who had taken part who had killed the nonbelievers, but god invisibly (8:17). This is not a metaphor for some more esoteric truth—god really was supposed to have landed the killing blows. The goal, presumably, was to help minimize any feelings of guilt or remorse, for if it was god who had done the killing then those who had fought need not feel bad about it. Indeed, if god would act in that way again, the same would hold in the future. When you're trying to get devout but morally sensitive people to wage war for you, stories like this come in handy.

Now, none of this proves that Islam makes a causal contribution to the emergence or maintenance of objectionably violent beliefs, attitudes, and behaviors in people. However, it also wasn't intended to. The most I would argue is that, taken together, these considerations build plausibly towards the case for Islam's causal involvement with violence in that regard.[29] This case is given further support by the empirical fact that many Muslims who either engage in or support morally objectionable violent behaviors report doing so for explicitly religious (i.e., Islamic) reasons.

It is worth noting that even if Islam is one element of the overall explanation, that doesn't *necessarily* mean that it is morally blameworthy. That might sound odd, but the reason why is straightforward: there can be many causes behind an event or pattern, and not all of them may stand out culpably. I might cause someone to cry by inadvertently referring to something that reminds them of a childhood trauma, for example, but most people would not say this puts me at moral blame. There was (or so we are assuming) no way for me to know that they had had such an experience, or that saying what I did would trigger their recollection of it. This is merely a technical point, however, and I suspect there is little room in it to defend Islam from the kinds of criticisms made about it in this regard.

---

[28] See chapter six for more on this feature of our moral psychology.
[29] I should emphasize that violence can come in many different forms, and we shouldn't limit ourselves to thinking about it just in terms of intergroup conflict.

A more significant point is that identifying that Islam makes a positive causal contribution to violence does not tell us about the *size* of its causal effect, and there could easily be factors other than scripture that play a much larger role in determining whether someone accepts violent beliefs or attitudes, or engages in violent behavior.

Lastly, it is critical to note that there is much in the Quran that appears to work *against* violence and intolerance of various kinds, and perhaps most especially in relation to intergroup conflict. For example, hell and the hypocrisy of it ignored, god says that there is no compulsion to religion (2:256, 50:45), and that Muslims are not responsible for what disbelievers believe or do (6:107). Though Muslims must fight in the way of god when they are called, they must not begin hostilities, for god does not love the aggressor (2:190). More than that, if the enemies of Islam incline to peace then Muslims should seek it with them also (8:61). As the Quran records god having said to the Jews, for he who kills a person, it is as though he has killed the world entire, and for he who saves a person, it is as though he has saved the world entire (5:32).

Unfortunately, what counts as a defensive justification is not carefully defined beyond references to things like attacks by enemies upon Muslims, war upon Muslims, persecution of Muslims, breaking oaths or treaties with Muslims, and, in one concerning instance, attacking the religion of Islam itself (see 22:39–40, 4:74–75, 8:38–39, 2:190–193, 9:12–13). This sets up a problem, for what should count when these short instructions are applied to the real world? Should Israel's inhumane treatment of Palestinians count as justification for violence? Since the Quran makes it clear that those who support one's enemies are to be considered one's enemies as well, what about the economic and political support given to Israel by the United States? What about drawing cartoons that depict the Prophet Muhammad in a negative light? What about drawing cartoons that depict the Prophet Muhammad in any light whatsoever? What about countries that enact or propose enacting legislation that bans Muslim women from wearing the burqa or niqab in public places, or that prevent the construction of new mosques? What about those who criticize values that are widely found in Islam, such as sexual conservatism and the subordinate standing of women? What about simply questioning the truth of Islam, the revealed status of the Quran, or the prophetic standing of Muhammad?

There will be different answers that different Muslims might give as we move down the list of questions, but for those with the greatest sensitivity, most or all of them might qualify. Moreover, with incentives like paradise and the special favor of god on offer for those who do fight for Islam, there is reason for some to *want* to come to such issues with more than a little sensitivity about them. After all, a world where Muslims face persecution, insult, and oppression at every turn is a world that provides ample opportunity to alleviate one's anxiety about hell and secure a glowing standing with god through violent conflict.

As you can see, a picture of some complexity is beginning to emerge. On one hand, Islam's revelation does things like exalt peace as a virtue loved by god, repeatedly depict intergroup violence as justified only defensively, and characterize the religious beliefs of others as a matter over which Muslims hold no personal responsibility. On the other, it does things like savagely libel nonbelievers, glorify the use of violence against them on less than completely well-defined defensive grounds, and offers tremendous rewards and punishments depending upon whether one heeds the call to violence or not. This reality leads to the necessity of a choice—to let the more violent side of Islam sit foremost within one's own religious attention, or to see it theologically minimized by focusing more peaceful aspects of scripture. Indeed, the existence of such a choice helps explain why the vast majority of Muslims reject the kind of violence that extremists within the religion promote and set forth.

In light of this, how might we understand the relationship between Islam and violence? A useful analogy may be to compare Islam with a bar rotating centrally around a point: while the rotation causes some people standing on it to end up more closely aligned with the peaceful and tolerant end of the behavioral and attitudinal spectrum, it also causes others standing closer to the opposite side to end up even more closely aligned with violent and intolerant ways of being, and all in the same swift theological action. And, as best as I can tell, this is essentially what we should expect. After all, I'm not aware of any reason to think you can say the kinds of things that the Quran says, and do so in the voice of god, and expect nothing bad to come from it when averaged out over the minds of billions of people.

It is important to be clear about what this claim means and what it doesn't. For example, nothing said so far should be taken as implying that Islam alone is responsible for where people religiously end up. The phenomenon in question is undoubtedly sensitive to many variables, including the psychological makeup of individual people, the political and social situation they find themselves in, and the availability of reasons for holding grievances against out-groups. All other things being equal, we can expect that the less moral aversion a person has to harming or killing others, the less absurdly it strikes them that god would command violence through his religion, the more satisfying they find staunchly aggressive postures, the more readily their situation allows for enemies to be made out, the more genuinely they believe in the literal truth of the Quran and the requirement that they follow it to the letter, the more eagerly they wish to edify themselves in the role of a cosmic warrior, the more anxiety they feel about their fate beyond life, the more consistently they have been exposed to others of their own faith who maintain and promote violent outlooks, and the tighter their social links with them, the more they may be inclined to accept violent beliefs, attitudes, and actions.

At the same time, there are reasons for thinking that Islam is still *one* of the causally relevant factors involved with the instantiation of objectionably violent beliefs, attitudes, and actions found in some Muslims, including those that specifically relate to intergroup conflict. While it is far from unique in this regard, it does appear to me to have features of special significance in relation to the promotion of violence, and which are, at the end of the day, completely unnecessary from the point of view of spirituality or truth.

This is anything but a pleasant conclusion to arrive at, for Islam is incontestably precious to the hearts and minds of billions of people. At the same time, accepting this view does not commit us to believing that Islam is the *only* factor causally involved with religious violence (it isn't), that Islam makes a *major* causal contribution to the manifestation of violence of certain types (it may or it may not, but that is a largely empirical question),[30] or that it can't simultaneously work to produce more tolerant and peaceful attitudes in other people within the same population (it very likely does, though here again not in isolation of other relevant causal factors).

Objection: *We know that the vast majority of Muslims don't actually engage in or support the most graphic and notorious forms of intergroup violence, like terrorism. Doesn't that prove that Islam is innocent of all charges?*

---

[30] See Bloom (2012) for a summary of empirical evidence looking at the causal effect of religious belief on moral thinking.

Almost all Muslims are better than the totality of the worst of their religion, and are so for the same reason that almost all Christians are better than the totality of the worst of theirs: because there is an overwhelming moral need to be. However, this alone does not mean that Islam has nothing to do with how its most violent adherents morally end up.

Consider another causal illustration: it is accepted that contracting syphilis can cause paresis, a form of paralysis of the limbs, but this only occurs in a small percentage of untreated cases. Does this mean that syphilis is not a cause of paresis, or that a person's contraction of syphilis doesn't subsequently help explain their development of paresis? No; it need only mean that there is more to the development of paresis in cases of syphilis than the untreated contraction of the disease.

Similarly, surveys highlight that only a small percentage of Muslims express open support for terrorism in defense of Islam. However, the fact that the number is small doesn't necessitate that Islam had nothing to do with the causal explanation of how that subset got there.

Seeing Religion Nonliterally

So far I have been interpreting the Bible and the Quran in the same way that the majority of people who are religious interpret them: as largely reality-aiming, literal reports about what was and is the case.[31] It might be argued that this is the completely wrong approach to take, however, and that what we need to do is to interpret them as either significantly or wholly nonliteral in their meaning.

Now, this isn't necessarily as crazy as it might first sound. We all make use of metaphors and similes to help us convey meaning, and we could barely get by in social life without being sensitive to their use. Just consider the kind of mayhem that would be caused if we all took a rigidly literal stance towards expressions like "it's raining cats and dogs" or "I'm so hungry I could eat a horse."

The Bible and the Quran are no exception when it comes to the use of metaphors. A famous example from Jesus is found in his claim that it

---

[31] A 2011 Gallup poll of American respondents found that 30 percent of Americans regard the Bible as "the actual" word of god, 49 percent regard it as "the inspired" word of god, and 17 percent regard it as a "book of fables/legends." Catholics were more likely than Protestants to see it as the inspired word of god rather than the actual word of god, as were those with greater education. See Jones (2011).

is easier for a camel to pass through the eye of a needle than it is for a rich man to enter heaven (Mark 10:25). Since it is obviously physically impossible for a camel to pass through the eye of a needle, we are left to infer that his meaning was metaphorical and that it is simply very, very difficult for the rich to enter heaven. Interestingly, the Quran makes use of the same camel-needle metaphor but switches the subject from rich people entering heaven to those who either deny or are arrogant about the signs of god's existence in nature (see 7:40).

Jesus was actually pretty fond of allegorical language and often used parables to convey spiritual truths. Curiously enough, those parables could be very opaque in meaning and tended not to be understood by those listening to him (e.g., Matthew 13:36). While he found the need to explain himself frustrating, and even stooped at one point to making snarky comments about the intelligence of the people he was speaking to (Matthew 15:15–20), given how cryptic his parables could be I really can't say that I have any sympathy for him. Worse, when he was asked why he didn't just speak plainly, his explanation renders his annoyance completely baffling: he used cryptic parables, he said, because it enabled him to conceal his true meaning, thereby preventing the masses from understanding it (Matthew 13:11–15).

Of course, the mere fact that metaphors appear in revelation does not mean we're free to interpret just whatever we might like as a metaphor. We should no more do this than we should interpret just anything that others say as nonliteral. Yet even the most literally-minded person should admit that the books of revelation cannot be approached *absolutely* literally.

It's not hard to understand where much of the temptation towards religious nonliteralism comes from, though, for adopting it would offer a number of concrete benefits. For one thing, it would enable us to avoid many of the factual and moral problems that arise with literal approaches. If god is *not really* commanding us to go out and execute adulterers and blasphemers, then whatever else he might be saying, it probably isn't going to be as deplorable as that. Equally, if revelation isn't really suggesting that god created the world in six literal days before resting on the seventh, a pretty crucial piece of Christian theology doesn't have to look ridiculous when compared with the modern scientific view of the age of the universe.

However, as with so much else in life, things here are not that easy. While nonliteralism is capable of eliminating many of the most morally devastating and factually absurd propositions expressed in revelation, it is unlikely to make the truth of religion much more likely than it was. To see why, consider the following story from Imre Lakatos. It begins with

...an imaginary case of planetary misbehaviour. A physicist of the pre-Einsteinian era takes Newton's mechanics and his law of gravitation, *N*, the accepted initial conditions, *I*, and calculates, with their help, the path of a newly discovered small planet, *p*. But the planet deviates from the calculated path. Does our Newtonian physicist consider that the deviation was forbidden by Newton's theory and therefore that, once established, it refutes the theory *N*? No. He suggests that there must be a hitherto unknown planet *p'* which perturbs the path of *p*. He calculates the mass, orbit, etc., of this hypothetical planet and then asks an experimental astronomer to test his hypothesis. The planet *p'* is so small that even the biggest available telescopes cannot possibly observe it: the experimental astronomer applies for a research grant to build yet a bigger one. In three years' time the new telescope is ready. Were the unknown planet *p'* to be discovered, it would be hailed as a new victory of Newtonian science. But it is not. Does our scientist abandon Newton's theory and his idea of the perturbing planet? No. He suggests that a cloud of cosmic dust hides the planet from us. He calculates the location and properties of this cloud and asks for a research grant to send up a satellite to test his calculations. Were the satellite's instruments (possibly new ones, based on a little-tested theory) to record the existence of the conjectural cloud, the results would be hailed as an outstanding victory of Newtonian science. But the cloud is not found. Does our scientist abandon Newton's theory, together with the idea of the perturbing planet and the idea of the cloud which hides it? No. He suggests that there is some magnetic field in that region of the universe which disturbed the instruments of the satellite. A new satellite is sent up. Were the magnetic field to be found, Newtonians would celebrate a sensational victory. But it is not. Is this regarded as a refutation of Newtonian science? No. Either yet another ingenious auxiliary hypothesis is proposed or... the whole story is buried in the dusty volumes of periodicals and the story is never mentioned again.[32]

---

[32] Lakatos (1970).

In short, all observations depend upon some level of background theory. To go out and look for the undiscovered planet in the first instance, it had to be assumed that the telescope was working correctly, that the calculations and the assumptions made by the physicist in determining the planet's location were all correct, that the telescope itself was of a kind appropriate to the task of detecting the planet, and so on. Not finding the planet didn't necessarily mean that the extra-planet hypothesis was false, for there could have been an error somewhere in the calculations or a fault with the equipment.

The implication of this is that it is not necessarily logically inconsistent of someone to continue to maintain a pet hypothesis in the face of negative observational results—all they need to do is fault something else that was used in conjunction with their hypothesis to arrive at the failed predictions. Whether this can be done *reasonably*, though, and for all lengths of time, is another matter. There often comes a point when we think it would be better to just admit the error of even our most cherished ideas rather than to continue on with them in the hope that they are shown right. Indeed, continuing to uphold the truth of a hypothesis by faulting everything around it can quickly become an increasingly unreasonable and dogmatic way to proceed.

The moral of this astronomical story is important in the context of discussions about religion, for the choices we make in dealing with theological problems can have ramifications that extend well beyond the range of what we were most immediately concerned with. In short, in trying to solve those problems, we can end up only causing more for ourselves, and some of the new ones may be just as serious as what we were originally concerned with fixing. I take this to be exactly what happens when we adopt broadly nonliteral approaches to revelation in the hope of avoiding the moral and factual problems it contains.

The claim of both Christianity and Islam is that god has revealed his existence and his expectations for humanity in a book. Yet we find on any sober reading of those texts that they are deeply at odds with what can reasonably be expected to have come from the mind of a divine being. One option we have open at that point is to reinterpret their problematic content in a metaphorical or allegorical way, and to do so wherever needed in order to get a picture of things that is more consistent with our expectations for god as a divine being.

Deciding exactly what nonliteral meanings to give different parts of revelation may require considerable imagination and ingenuity on our part. When the Old Testament commands us to kill homosexuals, for example, perhaps what it is really commanding us to "kill" is homosexuality *as a category of sexual inclination and/or behavior*, and where "killing" it means something like overcoming it. That would allow us to escape the morally deplorable idea of killing people because of their sexual orientation, which is a moral gain of a kind.[33]

Unfortunately, this solution generates its own problems. The most obvious of them relates to the idea of god once we have decided that he hides metaphors in *prima facie* literal statements. Are we really to believe, as by implication we must, that god would plant far-from-obvious metaphors in statements that, when understood literally, encourage appallingly immoral actions? That god could find no better way of talking about homosexuality than by cloaking his views against it in a command for execution? The idea that he was so starved of ways to express himself that he had to resort to this, and over and above simply speaking plainly and clearly, is not to be taken seriously; we end up making god ridiculous to save him from being monstrous.

This is just a single illustrative example, and other passages may lend themselves more readily to metaphorical interpretation than the one I've highlighted. Moreover, I certainly don't wish to claim that the use of metaphors in revelation is always dangerous or problematic. It does seem clear enough, however, that for a particular range of religious statements—and perhaps most especially those that are in greatest need of reinterpretation—that reading them nonliterally causes significant problems for the truth of religion.

A second method for explaining away problematic scriptural content involves framing it as the result of a mistake in translation or transmission, a change in the meaning of words over time, or manipulation of the original text by others. After all, we know that the meaning of words can change over time, that translation between languages can be difficult, and that it is quite possible for the content of revelation to be manipulated by people inserting or deleting verses to suit their own interests.

Aside from the independent evidence that would be needed to support claims like this, they all raise further questions concerning the importance of accuracy and clear understanding in matters of revelation. In short, strong responsibilities undoubtedly owe on god in setting forth revelation to ensure that the meaning of his message is accurate, and

---

[33] Though certainly not a complete one. After all, what is morally wrong about homosexuality?

imagining that it became distorted or corrupted soon after entering the world without him doing anything to correct it only serves to undermine the case for him having had anything to do with it in the first place.

A third option is to argue that some parts of revelation need to be assessed and understood only from within their particular historical contexts. To put that another way, we must understand that certain parts of revelation were given a long time ago to people in vastly different circumstances to our own. Do that and we should find that what seems wrong to us today cannot be said to have been wrong all the way back then.

Take the destruction of the Midianites. As the Bible tells it, Moses was instructed by god to destroy the Midianites. After defeating them in battle, Moses learned that some of the Midianites had been taken captive rather than executed. Enraged by this, he ordered that they must be put to death immediately: men, women, and children all (with special exemption given for any female virgins, for reasons that once again need no explanation; Numbers 31:1–54).

However shocking we might find these reports, someone might argue that Moses and his people lived in times radically different to our own, and given their historical circumstances, it wasn't appallingly wrong to kill, rape, and enslave people by the tens of thousands. Moreover, because of the historical context we should be very careful before drawing any wider normative lessons for ourselves today.

Problem solved? Well, hardly. After all, what features of that historical context could have justified god, Moses, and the Israelites doing what they are said to have done?[34] Any divine being worth its salt would surely stand far above the likes of rape and genocide, and practically irrespective of any plausibly-occurring worldly situation.

But let's suppose that the destruction of the Midianites really was morally justified within the constraints of that particular historical context. We would still expect god to take extreme care with how that was recorded in revelation so that nobody got the wrong idea afterwards. This is especially so given that a lot of other things in the Bible do not appear to be tightly contextualized. When the Bible says "love your neighbor" and "do not follow a multitude to do evil," these do not appear to be time- and place-sensitive requests, and most people don't interpret them that way.

---

[34] Scholars don't actually believe that the events described took place—they are myths rather than history—but that is immaterial to the point.

And it is not as if notifying future generations of the special circumstances surrounding god's instructions for genocide would have been an especially difficult thing to have done—he could have simply said something like, "Please take note, this commandment to enslave, rape and kill people applies only to you and your people at this moment, Moses, but not afterwards. Now, proceed with your bloody and awful task." We can therefore wonder why, in a book of otherwise unrestricted normative scope, god chose to include instructions of very narrow application, of potentially great moral significance if misunderstood, and without any indication of its special historical status.

He wouldn't, of course. While the desire to try and cauterize off the worst parts of revelation to the savage and blood-soaked past from they came is perfectly understandable, the various tactics someone uses to achieve that may end up getting them nowhere in relation to the question of religious truth, and that is something that all should be conscious of.

Religious Non-realism

Besides literalism, a second major assumption built into a lot of criticism of religion is that the books of revelation were intended to provide us with a "picture of reality." That is, they aim to tell us something about the way things are—about reality, its structure, and its contents. Not everyone holds this assumption.

If revelation isn't about reality, though, what could it be about? It depends on who you ask, but one set of answers would be that it embodies, symbolizes, crystallizes, makes salient, exemplifies, induces, inspires, or reinforces a range of important human values, desires, hopes, aspirations, ideals, or emotional and conscious states. For example, one point of revelation might be to use stories to focus our attention upon virtues like compassion and charity, thereby making them much more obvious and understandable to us. Alternatively, the point of revelation might be to aid us in manifesting an increased sense of awe, mystery, beauty, or transcendence about our lives, thereby enriching how we feel about them.

Taken in this way, revelation does not represent a *theory* of how things are—it is not a collection of statements about fact that may or may not be true—but an assemblage of stories we engage with and respond to in some desired way. By seeing revelation as something quite different, critics like myself could be accused of having made a somewhat serious and embarrassing error. I suppose it would not be unlike criticizing a fantasy movie for its detachment from reality when it is clearly intended to do no more than entertain. I mean, what would we say to a person who criticizes a fairytale because kissing a frog *won't actually* transform it into a handsome prince? Nothing, probably; their criticism is almost too detached from the point of a fairytale to bother with. Is criticism of religion for its failure to provide an accurate picture of reality just as wrongheaded?

You can probably already tell from this chapter's existence that I think the answer is no. First, let me say that religious non-realists—i.e. those who think religion's fundamental goal is not to present a true picture of reality as such—certainly have something right in noting that religion is deeply connected with our emotional and psychological responses to the world. However, that alone does not mean it has no other function. Indeed, there is nothing about seeing religion as a theory of reality that precludes it from aiming for an important emotional and psychological role in people's lives. Many of the most inspiring stories are true, after all, and are so precisely because they are firmly rooted in reality. Adopting a realist interpretation of revelation is not inconsistent with the idea religion serving deep emotional and psychological needs, then.

Nor are religious realists required to interpret everything put forward by religion, or in religious language, as intending to say something about reality. A Muslim might exclaim "God willing!" in one context to express their support for a proposed idea, but in another context might say the same sentence to highlight the Islamic belief that nothing can happen outside of the will of god. In short, there is nothing about seeing revelation as centrally concerned with conveying factual truth that prevents realists from accepting non-realist intricacies.

Moreover, it certainly *looks* as though both Christianity and Islam are very concerned with the representation of factual truths. Not only is the Bible full of what outwardly appear to be claims about reality, it reports that the evidence of god's existence is so well displayed in nature that those who disbelieve are without excuse (Romans 1:19–20). Jesus himself routinely assured people that he spoke only the truth, and he is reported as having worked many miracles in order to convince them that he was who he said he was. In one interesting case Jesus revealed to a woman "everything she ever did" as a way of convincing her of his spiritual authority (John 4:39–40), while at another time the heavens did so much as to announce through a cloud to a group that Jesus really was the son of god (Matthew 17:5).

The Quran also reads as deeply concerned with reality and the acceptability of claims made by Muhammad. We are told that Muhammad was neither misled nor was astray, that he did not merely say what he desired to, and that the Quran is inspiration sent down to him (53:1–5). It tells us that Muhammad would have been tempted to corrupt the message, but that he was fortified to resist that temptation by god, and that if he *had* corrupted it he would have been punished in both life and death (17:73–5). It affirms that it could not have been invented (11:13), that it is confirmation of what came before it (10:37–38), and that it is beyond doubt (2:2). It goes on to assure us that it was impossible for anyone to change the words of the Quran (18:27, 6:34, 10:64), and that if it had not come from god it would have been filled with incongruity (we're already supposed to believe that it is not filled with incongruity; 4:82). Given the choice between realism and non-realism, it seems more natural to fit these features within a realist framework.

Suppose revelation really is best understood in a non-realist way, though. If so, this seems like exactly the kind of thing that should be openly and universally known about it; there really shouldn't be any mistaking the fact. Perhaps labels should have been printed on the covers of the Quran and the Bible, or warnings written into the first few pages of revelation, so that everyone would understand the correct way to interpret their content—not as reports about reality, but as stories aiming to embody important human values and attitudes (or whatever the particular non-realist vision of their purpose might be). That would have helped avoid the confusion of hopelessly lost realist onlookers such as myself, at least. Yet if scripture and the majority of people who believe in it are anything to go by, at the heart of religion is a *realist* concern—to successfully capture and describe the objective truth of reality, both worldly and metaphysical.

True enough, nothing forces us to adopt a realist perspective on religion if we don't want to; with skill and creativity, the non-realist can simply interpret everything mentioned before in non-realist terms. Yet it is interesting to note just how contrary that way of thinking is when compared with virtually every other corner of human life. Be it reports about tomorrow's weather, contamination in the local drinking water, our favorite sports team's wins or losses, election results, scientific discoveries, or stock market reports, we understand what other people say in a committed realist fashion. We simply don't take a sunny forecast on the nightly news to be a covert statement about the value of fortitude or optimism in the face of difficulty, and we're right not to. Why should matters of religion be so different, then? Why should this otherwise pervasive human concern for information about reality suddenly give way at religion's door?

This question is especially pressing given that religion is probably the last place you would expect to find non-realism from most people. Why? Because the objective truth of many core religious propositions (like god's existence or our metaphysical continuity beyond death) would be such positive and comforting things to believe as a realist would believe them.

Let's assume that non-realism about revelation just is the most sensible approach, though. For argument's sake, let's say that the function of religion is to give people easy access to desirable values and attitudes by framing them in stories that can be easily digested and shared. In doing this it makes those values and attitudes more concrete and obtainable by holding them up before people's eyes. If that is what religion is all about, where is the harm?

Nowhere, really, so long as the values and attitudes it promotes actually are good ones. The obvious deep concern would be that not all of the values and attitudes embedded in religious stories actually are good; indeed, many of them appear to be straightforwardly inimical to human wellbeing. Moreover, because the values and attitudes found in religious stories come to us grouped up in narrative packages, bad values and attitudes can easily ride parasitically upon the back of good ones in their transmission and acquisition.

A quite legitimate concern, then, is that the stories that religion offers us just aren't the very best ones that we could be looking toward (just think of the horrible tale of Abraham taking his son out into the wilderness in order to make a sacrifice of him for a single grizzly and slavish example). Children's stories, novels, and movies could all do a far better job in bringing praiseworthy values and attitudes forward to our attention.

Insofar as I can imagine that the problem of packaging might be avoided—such as by concentrating upon and retelling *only those* stories in revelation which exhibit wholly commendable values and attitudes—I see no problem in a non-realist stance towards religion. Yet this doesn't change my view that this isn't how most people actually *do* approach religion, or, for both theological and psychological reasons, how most people ever will.

Language, Meaning, and Underdetermination

Returning to religious realism, if god really did send down a book of revelation for everyone to understand and live by, it will be pretty important to know what its true meaning is. But how should we determine that? What *is* the true meaning of the various passages of revelation? In fact, what is the meaning of anything? This might strike you as a strange question. After all, words and sentences just mean whatever they mean, don't they? As you read this sentence, for example, a meaning will arise in your mind without any great complication. What could be the issue in working out what Biblical and Quranic passages mean?

The issue is this: it is a seemingly unavoidable fact about natural languages that the meaning of sentences can be underdetermined by their syntax and the meanings of the words they are composed from. As a result, it can be possible to interpret their meaning in multiple ways. Steven Pinker gives a number of funny examples of this in his book *The Language Instinct*, but my two favorites would have to be the real life newspaper headlines "Squad Helps Dog Bite Victim" and "Drunk Gets Nine Months in Violin Case". As you can see, their meaning really does depend on how you read them.

Two different theses of particular relevance to this book might be constructed from this issue concerning the underdetermination of the meaning of scriptural sentences.

The weak thesis: some sentences, including some religious sentences, can have two (or more) equally rational interpretations taken of their meaning.
The strong thesis: all sentences, including all religious sentences, can have an indefinite number of equally rational interpretations taken of their meaning.

While the weak thesis implies that the meaning of some sentences can be ambiguous, such that we may not be able to decide which of two (or more) possible meanings is the most rational, the strong thesis goes much further. It states that all sentences are semantically underdetermined to such an extent that any and all interpretations of their meaning are equirational with every other.

Of course, if no interpretation of a sentence is rationally superior to any other, and if for any sentence an indefinite number of interpretations can be taken of it, it's hard to see how any sentence could be said to have an intrinsic meaning. But if that is so, what determines the meaning we come up with in our heads? Here it may be suggested that it is our interests, biases, and prejudices that do the heavy lifting—we adopt interpretations to suit our own interests and existing understandings.

The relevance of this issue should be obvious when it comes to religion and religious criticism. Since books are just long collections of sentences, and since the Quran and the Bible are both books, we are left to infer from the strong thesis that neither the Bible nor the Quran have any essential or intrinsic meaning. And if that is the case, there are no grounds on which they might be faulted for what they say, for what they say is wholly dependent on us.

It's not hard to understand the kinds of motivations that might lie behind this view about language and meaning, especially in the context of religion. After all, if texts like the Bible and the Quran don't have an essential meaning that we must endeavor to draw out of them, we are free to walk away from anything we don't like in them by simply changing our interpretation. This would mean that people don't have to be locked into one particular way of understanding them, and therein could opt for less violent, more compassionate, and more tolerant interpretive approaches (and also more violent and more intolerant approaches, depending on the individual and what they want).

The strong thesis isn't just desirable because it is theologically liberating, though. It may also appear to some as a logical consequence of the discussed fact that meaning doesn't objectively exist in words and sentences, but is in some sense bestowed upon them in the act of interpretation. Ergo, the strong thesis must be true (or so the chain of reasoning may go).

The problem is, focusing on the absence of meaning in sentences overlooks what seems to me to be thoroughly obvious. Although sentences don't literally possess meaning in and of themselves, we can't explain their existence and structure without referring to a meaning that was originally intended for them by their creators, and it is that meaning that we're interested in.[35] The whole reason why you would bother to try and understand the meaning of the Bible is because you want to try and connect with the message that was intended for it. If you just wanted to

---

[35] Well, one of two things we might be interested in getting at, for one might also be interested in the most reasonable interpretation to take of any given sentence, even if we knew (for some other reason) that the writer or speaker actually intended something quite different for it.

think your own thoughts however you want, free from the constraint of having to follow another person's mind, you don't actually need an elaborate device like a book to do it. You could just sit alone and think whatever you fancied. This isn't what we do, though, for we understand that even though words and sentences don't independently possess meanings, they *do* act as vehicles for it, and that is what we're interested in getting at.[36]

Moreover, the problem of semantic underdetermination is not insurmountable in many cases. Consider as a working example the sentence "She ate the pear out of the box." There are at least two different ways of reading this on first glance. On the first interpretation, it expresses the claim that 'she' (whoever she may be) ate the pear that was in the box and which she had gotten out of the box. On the second interpretation, we read it as saying that 'she' ate the pear, wherever it may have come from, while standing in (or sitting in, or otherwise being in) the box. With more than one possible interpretation, the sentence is strictly ambiguous.

Does this generate a hopeless dilemma for us? Surely not, for we can make use of our background knowledge to help us decide which is the most reasonable interpretation. For example, how often it is in the normal course of things that people eat pears they have retrieved from boxes, as opposed to eating pears while standing in (or otherwise being in) boxes? Surely the former possibility occurs much more frequently than the latter, making it more likely to be the meaning intended, all other things being equal. Similarly, because a child would be more likely to eat a pear while standing in a box than an adult, knowing the age of the person in question could also help. If 'she' is a 40-year-old woman, one may guess that she probably didn't eat the pear while standing in a box.

These two examples should be enough to illustrate that by considering norms of language and expression, what kinds of things are normally believed by people (and hence are more likely to be expressed in the first place), social and cultural taboos, idiosyncrasies or nuances on the part of individual speakers, the wider context in which a sentence appears, and so on, we equip ourselves with tools to narrow down the various possibilities for what was most likely intended and arrive at the

---

[36] Indeed, this is the whole reason why language exists in the first place. It didn't arise as a way for us to echo our own minds back to ourselves, but so that we could connect with others. In this sense, the strong thesis is not just an abuse of language, it is a denial of others.

most reasonable interpretation of a sentence's meaning.[37] If at the end of all of these methods the correct meaning of a sentence still befuddles us, what we might have is nothing more dramatic or exciting than a case of bad writing (or speaking, as the case may be).

Imagine that the strong thesis is simply right, though. If so, we might expect to hear from directors that film critics only ever had the nicest things to say about their films, from politicians that they never received any opposition to their proposed laws, and from lawyers that the judge's decision supported them in every case they ever argued. After all, if all interpretations of the meaning of a sentence are equally rational, it is in everyone's best interests to take the most flattering interpretations possible.

While this would be a strange world to live in, it would be a morally problematic one as well, for it is not just verbal language that is subject to the implications of the strong thesis. To give a single worrying example, it would be completely legitimate for a rapist to say that by pretending not to notice him as he watched her at the bar, his victim was actually flirting with him. This continued as she turned his advances down and pretended to be unaware of him as he followed her home. And when she screamed no while hitting and scratching him? Well, that was simply more evidence (on his freely chosen and rationally legitimate interpretation of her body and verbal language) that she wanted him too. We could say nothing to fault his interpretation in such a world, except to say that our interpretation of the meaning behind her words and actions is far different—which of course means nothing.

Moral concerns aside, the truth of the connection between meaning and language confronts us anytime we attempt to express ourselves. The ideas we convey may not always be precise in terms of what they are, of course, for sometimes they possess a certain conceptual fuzziness which prevents them being thought about exactly. Even so, we generally strive to use language in ways aimed at anticipating and resolving possible confusions in others, and we justifiably expect others to do the same in return. All of that effort would be pointless if people are free to adopt whatever interpretation of our expressions they like. Indeed, I can hardly think that god would have bothered to reveal himself to humanity if any interpretation we might take of his meaning was as good as the next. What possible point could there be to his doing so?

---

[37] Sometimes sentences can have multiple intended meanings, or no true meaning intended for them at all (as one sometimes finds in some song lyrics), but these can be set aside as exceptions to the normal situation.

Lastly, consider the delicious irony lurking here. The strong thesis can be seen as a mark against critiques of religion (like mine) that assume that revelation has something more or less definite and rationally discernible to say. In order for that to count as a point against me, however, I must first be taken as having had something concrete to say myself. But as we all know by now, the strong thesis tells us that what I am interpreted as saying is not a function of what I have written, but of what I am taken as having meant by others—which, again, is decided entirely outside of the sentences themselves.

In other words, I cannot be criticized for being wrong here, because what I have said is not wrong in itself, but is made to be that by the interpretations that others choose to take of it. It follows that anything I have said that is false, offensive, or stupid is entirely the reader's fault.

The Poverty of God, So Conceived

On the morning of 23 August 1973, Jan-Erik Olsson walked into a Kreditbanken branch in Stockholm armed with a submachine gun. Demanding that his friend Clark Olofsson be released from prison to join him, Olsson took four bank clerks hostage and barricaded himself in the 3.3 by 14.3 meter bank vault.

What psychologically unfolded for the hostages over the next six days would later be called "Stockholm syndrome." Even though their lives were directly threatened, the hostages appeared to bond with their captors, and did so to the point of no longer wanting to be rescued. As one of them said to police, "This is our world now… sleeping in this vault to survive. Whoever threatens this world is our enemy."[38]

Since then psychologists have sought to identify the causal preconditions necessary for Stockholm syndrome to occur. One of the most widely cited requires that all the following conditions are true: 1) that those taken hostage perceive a genuine threat to their own survival, 2) that the hostages are isolated from the perspectives of anyone other than their captors, 3) that the hostages perceive some element of kindness, however small, on the part of their captors, and 4) that the hostages feel powerless to control their situation.[39] It is thought that under extreme situations such as this, victims may begin to identify with

[38] Namnyak, Tufton, Szekely, *et al.* (2008).
[39] See Graham, Rawlings, Ihms, *et al.* (1995) for discussion.

their abusers as a self-protective mechanism and way of managing their terror. Concerningly, religion appears satisfies all of these same criteria.

In *What's So Great about Christianity*, bestselling author Dinesh D'Souza claims that what really sets Christianity apart as a world religion is that whereas other religions grant people a limited form of control over whether they achieve salvation, Christianity completely denies this. No matter how much good someone does or what actions they might undertake, they do not deserve—and cannot alone achieve—salvation.[40]

The problem stems from human sinfulness. As D'Souza describes it, sin is not something we occasionally do, but a tendency that sits right in the heart of human nature. We sin so much, in fact, that we aren't even aware of all the ways in which we do it. This makes it strictly impossible to atone for sin because nobody could ever be sufficiently aware of all the ways they sin in order to make spiritual amends. Moreover, since nothing less than moral perfection will do in the eyes of god, it is entirely right and justified that he should punish us. Our only way out is for god to freely forgive us. That is something he can do, thankfully, but only because of the profound sacrifice he made as Jesus when he died for our sins.

This metaphysical account would seem to represent an almost perfect recipe for inducing Stockholm syndrome. After all, not only does it give god every reason in the world to judge and punish us, our inherently sinful nature means that there is nothing we can do to avoid presenting him with that justification. Moreover, we should feel incredibly grateful and indebted towards god, for he died by crucifixion just so we could be forgiven. Finally, since by definition god is the ultimate knower and perfect judge of all things, whose opinion besides his own could really matter? Surely none. This checks off every item in the Stockholm syndrome checklist: threat, powerlessness, kindness, and isolation.

If Stockholm syndrome is a cognitively real phenomenon, it seems eminently plausible that at least some Christians are affected by a metaphysical variant of it as a result of their religious beliefs. In other words, the intensity with which at least some believers accept and identify with the truth of Christianity is a partial product of the emotional and psychological trauma they experience as a result of accepting core religious postulates concerning god and the nature of humanity. And just think of it: if Christianity really is right, not only are we all trapped in god's cosmic bank vault, and not only are there not any police waiting

---

[40] D'Souza (2008).

outside to rescue us, we are continually and inescapably doing things that we deserve to be profoundly punished for.

This view of existence is nothing less than tragic, and the goal of this chapter has been to show that we believe it needlessly, for there are a number of major philosophical problems standing in the way of religion in its claim to represent the truth of god. While the focus has been very much on the evidential case *against* religion, the reason isn't bias. The fact is that whatever other considerations might be rallied to the side of religion in support of its truth, they will need to outweigh the totality of what stands against it. Given the extent of the case against religion, however, this would appear to require nothing less than a miracle of evidence.

As it is, I am not aware of anything that comes remotely close to qualifying. Indeed, if such a thing did exist, I'm sure it would be impossible to go through life without hearing about it. One is left to think from this and other considerations that, whether interpreted literally or nonliterally, there just isn't any good reason available to believe that the Bible and the Quran are true.

Accepted or not, this conclusion and the arguments underwriting have the potential to be very unpleasant for believers to experience, and could lead to negative emotional and psychological states like anger, resentment, anxiety, existential worry, guilt, fear, offense, and hostility. While there is nothing about religion that makes criticism of it uniquely capable of doing that, I find myself very affected by this as a consideration, and if I knew of some way to highlight the depth of religion's problems without making anyone feel worse for it, I wouldn't hesitate to take it.

Still, while it brings me no happiness to be the source of someone else's upset, I also believe that room for open and honest criticism of religion—of a kind accepted and practiced in relation to just about every other idea out there—is needed. This is the case not just because it respects other people as rational agents who are capable of handling and deliberating on the truth, but also because it is a key ingredient in what is needed if the world is to finally leave religion behind.

Recognizing a role for religious criticism doesn't mean that there aren't problems attached to it. Far from it, in fact. While I want to be honest and appraise the philosophical issues confronting religion both accurately and fully, for example, I also want to be sensitive to the enormous emotional and psychological investment that billions of people have in the truth of what they religiously believe. Unfortunately, those two goals exist in a state of tension, for we don't tend to embrace arguments that seek to undo our most deeply held beliefs, nor listen particularly well (or for long) to those who would draw them to our attention. Get the balance between criticism and compassion wrong in your message and you run the risk of being too emotionally jarring, offensive, or challenging for people to accept what you say.

Compounding this difficulty is the fact that we tend to try to avoid having to think less of ourselves, and discovering errors in our beliefs may strike some people as a reason to do exactly that. This is a problem, for if being wrong about some important issue x means in the lens of someone's own interpretation that they are silly, bad, stupid, gullible, harm-causing, or cognitively unreliable, then this will give them an extra reason not to recognize any error in the first place. The prospect of changing one's religious beliefs is already daunting enough as it is, though. Indeed, for some people, abandoning their religion could be one of the hardest things they ever do.

Moreover, if accepting error in relation to some of our beliefs means boosting the self-esteem, confidence, or social status of a person or group arguing against us, and we really don't like that person or group (perhaps through perceptions of arrogance or the lurking sense that any error we acknowledge will be held against us long after being admitted), this too will act as a reason to be reluctant to do that. Social status is a currency that can be gained or lost, after all, and we tend to want to deprive people we find unlikeable from having it.

Lastly, research in psychology indicates that how persuasive we find an argument is open to being influenced by a wide array of non-epistemic factors, including the physical attractiveness of the arguer, whether the argument is fear based, whether the arguer has the same ethnic or racial background as us, and one's own emotional state or mood (positive or negative). It is highly plausible that how benevolent, trustworthy, and competent an arguer is perceived as being also affects our receptiveness to their arguments. Unfortunately, religion teaches that the efforts of some to usher people away from religious belief is something that, if not directly motivated by dark forces, at least coincides with dark interests. For the most devout and literal of believers, then, religious criticism is little more than an exposition in the very thing one should avoid at all costs. This is especially so given the belief that god hinges our metaphysical fates upon our worship of him. While my own view is that this grossly misunderstands the nature of god as a divine being, even just to make that point to a devout audience more or less requires that I am afforded a basic level of intrinsic goodness, and that is precisely what religion advises believers to be wary of about me.

As these few examples demonstrate, the situation with criticism and religion is very complex. While there probably is no *one best way* of going about it, though, that doesn't mean there aren't better and worse approaches. In the hope of leaning close to the first of those two possibilities, and in an effort to lessen any pain my criticism may be responsible for, let me emphasize the truth of a number of additional things I believe just as deeply as anything else so far said.

First, no matter how our understanding of the world is formed, we can benefit greatly in being open to receiving critical feedback, for one of the most effective ways to more fully grasp the nature and implications of our own beliefs is to be challenged on them. Indeed, it is possible to end up knowing far more about one's own position by taking the reasoned arguments of others seriously than we were ever likely to learn on our own. This doesn't mean that criticism of things we're invested in the truth of is pleasant to experience, of course, but it still helps us in the cause for truth to hear what others have to offer in critique.

Much of the explanation why has to do with a major deficit in human reasoning, and that is that we tend to find it easier to critically examine things we don't want to believe, or which oppose our existing beliefs, than we do with what we already believe, or what we would like to believe. In being open to others and listening to them, we help ourselves overcome the partiality of our focus and make the best of the vision of others. In contrast, choosing to see the reality of human efforts aimed at understanding as an "us vs them" situation where one faction of belief faces off against all others in a shouting match about who is right is tremendously unhelpful and overlooks the collaborative dimensions of inquiry and criticism that exist on a higher level. And just to be especially clear, this goes just as much for me in my own spiritual and philosophical views as it does for anybody else.

Second, I don't think there can be any reasonable expectation placed on a person to abandon or modify their core beliefs immediately upon encountering what appear to be weighty objections to them (should any such objections actually exist). It may not be satisfying from the point of view of those doing the criticizing, but we are all entitled to have time to think, reflect, and explore the problems confronting our beliefs, and time again to adjust our beliefs to meet those problems where necessary. This is the case not simply because it treats other people with empathy and respect, but because it makes room for the epistemic reality that the most effective time in which to think about a new and challenging idea is not in the first moment we encounter it, but later when we have had time to reflect upon it in a cooler manner.

Third, it is vitally important to distinguish between religion as an abstract set of beliefs, principles, and practices, and the people who actually incorporate those things into their lives under religious instruction. While the subjective experience may appear to indicate otherwise, to attack religion as harmfully false is not necessarily to hold enmity towards the billions of people who believe contrarily. Indeed, so far as I see it, at least, believers and nonbelievers are just me through other eyes—me, if I had been born at a different latitude and longitude than the one I actually was. It seems ridiculous to me to let a contingency like that obscure the fact that we are all in this world together, and we need each other.

Fourth, all manner of obstacles make it challenging to see religion for what it is if you already accept it as true. These include (but are not limited to) a biased tendency on our part to seek to confirm beliefs and hypotheses rather than challenge them, a common failure to distinguish clearly between different metaphysical possibilities, the sometimes high risks attached to the rejection of socially dominant religious beliefs (such as upsetting loved ones, being alienated from one's family, being ostracized by one's community, and being physically harmed), and our manipulation by metaphysical threats and rewards. Indeed, by working to morally castigate criticism and disbelief, and by identifying belief with virtue and goodness, religion actively suppresses critical treatment of itself amongst believers. This isn't to say that internal criticism of religion doesn't exist, but that it is discouraged, moralized, and penalized.

The point is that it's not by pure luck that Christianity and Islam have come to be so successful. As complex systems of beliefs and ideas, they work in powerful ways to shield themselves from questioning and rejection. With all of that going on and more, it is hardly surprising that so many people do accept the truth of one or another of the world's religion. Indeed, I'm positively sure that, had I been born at most other times and places, I too would have accepted religion.

Finally, while I appreciate that it can be painful, religious criticism really can come from a place that wishes only the very best for other people, without any nastiness or desire to elevate oneself over others. Those higher intentions may be hard to find when actually experiencing the religion you believe in criticized and challenged, and I don't envy the task of believers to find them where they do exist. Still, the truth is that nobody sees it all entirely by themselves, and none of us gets everything right. Accordingly, what matters most is not ever getting beliefs wrong, but what we do along the way to identify if and when we have. And, as I have said, one of the very best things we can do there to help is to listen to the reasoned positions of others who do not share all the same beliefs and assumptions as we do.

In that spirit, I put forward the following suggestion: while the books that sit at the heart of Christianity and Islam are responsible for a number of incredibly meaningful and important goods within the lives of billions of people, openly and unselectively read they also represent within themselves some of the cruelest, darkest, and most savage ideas we have anywhere. Bringing together factual truth with egregious error, moral wisdom with appalling travesty, and moments of beauty and sublimity in a sea of otherwise lifeless text, the Bible and the Quran simply do not read in a way that is consistent with their having been written or inspired by a divine being.

Unfortunately, a great deal of harm occurs when we believe otherwise. One of the most destructive claims that religion makes is that we are all spiritually broken, ugly, and sick, and that if we do not do as we are asked, we will suffer eternally for it when we die. While this metaphysical proposition might seem thoroughly ordinary within the context of theology, its normality is masking, for it leaves religion guilty of exercising quite literally the most widespread and well-accepted of all forms of terrorism found in the world.

And it's not just human beings who pay the price for our conceptually impoverished ways of thinking about the divine. Every year for the Islamic festival of Eid al-Adha, Muslim families who can afford to will, in pretenses to piety, sacrifice a religiously acceptable animal by reciting a prayer and cutting its throat. The theological basis on which this sacrifice occurs is utterly stupefying—it is a symbolic re-enactment and reaffirmation of Abraham's willingness to sacrifice his own son for god, a story celebrated within both Christian and Muslim traditions. That some of the meat is handed out to the poor afterwards is, to my mind, an utterly underwhelming reconciliation with anything praiseworthy or noble. Needless to say, anyone who would be willing to kill their own son or daughter at god's inexplicable request, or who applauds the willingness of others to do the same in their own case, has abandoned themselves to the very worst of revelation. Like so much else with religion, this tragic spectacle is symptomatic of an impaired way of thinking about god, and one that speaks in turn to a profound human spiritual failing.

Happily, it is entirely possible to be nonreligious about spirituality and believe in a divine being who has no name, who has begotten no sons or prophets, who stands without any trifling need for worship, and who promises us no final day of judgment. Religion's roots may be deep in the world, but no length of time can alter its standing as a terrorizing, archaic, and ultimately vastly implausible system of spiritual ideas. Finally recognizing this will help to heal the injury that religion has done to the idea of god, and through that, to humanity as well.

Chapter 3
The Idea of God

If god created us in his own image, we have more than reciprocated.
—Voltaire (1694–1778)

The Divine Tragedy

Religion attaches a number of ideas to god that are detrimental to human wellbeing and happiness. To give but a few examples, the idea that homosexuality is a sexual perversion, that women are subordinate to men, that human beings are continually offending god with something called "sin," and that we all stand to be judged and punished for doing so, are all deeply negative beliefs to hold, and contribute to a manifestly tragic way of looking at god.

To appreciate just how far the religious picture of god sits from divinity, though, it is worth considering three stories. The first comes from the book of Revelation and involves a famously esoteric description of heaven. Heaven, we are told, is a place where god sits upon a throne of lightning and thunder. Around him are seven blazing lamps, symbolizing the seven spirits of god, a rainbow, and something that looks a lot like a sea of glass. In his general vicinity are four strange creatures—one like a lion, another like an ox, a third like the face of a man, and a fourth like a flying eagle. Blinded in his presence, day and night these creatures relentlessly pronounce god's glory—"holy, holy, holy, Lord God Almighty, which was, and is, and is to come." There are a further twenty-four thrones placed around the throne of god, and upon them sit elders. Every time the creatures proclaim the glory of god, the elders fall down before him, place their crowns on the ground, and tell him to the limits of all eternity that he is worthy to receive glory, honor, and power.[1]

The second story comes from the book of Acts and details god's expectations in relation to faith and devotion. Moved by their religious message, Acts speaks of a man called Ananias who decided to sell his

---

[1] Revelation 4:2–10.

farm and donate the money to the apostles to further their holy cause. Unfortunately for Ananias, he decided to keep an undisclosed portion for himself and his family. Bringing his gift before Peter and setting it at his feet, the apostle could somehow tell that some of the money from the sale was missing. Though it was by any reasonable standard an otherwise remarkable gesture, Peter scolded Ananias for not being completely selfless in his generosity. Rebuked, poor Ananias fell down dead on the spot, presumably killed by an act of god.[2]

The third story is an anecdote concerning a Communist party conference held in the Moscow district in Soviet-era Russia. At the conference's conclusion, a tribute was called to Joseph Stalin. As expected, all in attendance rose to their feet and began clapping in rapturous applause. Minutes began to tick by. First it was two, then it was three, then four, then five. Even though hands and arms were beginning to tire at this point, no one dared to be the first to stop. Doing so would have shown disloyalty. In what must have been a quite extraordinary scene, then, the clapping of the audience simply continued—six, seven, eight, nine, and then ten. Finally, at the *eleven-minute* mark, a paper factory director sat down. With relief, so too did everyone else. Arrested that night to be incarcerated in the gulags, the man's interrogator coldly reminded him that one should never be the first to stop clapping.[3]

My claim is this: if the sentiment you're left with from the first two stories comes uncomfortably close in your mind to the third, it is for good reason. The notion that god would strike a man dead for not being completely selfless in his devotion to him, or that he might (metaphorically or otherwise) exist in heaven surrounded by a circle of kings eternally proclaiming his glory and telling him he is worthy of great power, is perfectly consistent with some of the very worst examples of power and vanity found in human beings. So far as I can tell, and as the first two stories would tend to indicate, the god described by Christianity is an unpleasant collision of incompatible ideas, and the fact that he remains credited with infinite love for humanity does nothing to change that. Indeed, if Stalin had truly loved those who suffered and died as a result of his despotic rule, I think that would have only made his character more diabolical, not less.

---

[2] Acts 5:1–11. Ananias's wife, who came along later and chose to lie about whether all the money from the sale was gifted, also fell down dead, therein suggesting that the reason for Ananias's death was indeed supernatural and not simply coincidence.
[3] Solzhenitsyn (1975).

If we really want to understand the kinds of conceptual problems that can arise out of religion in the way that it understands the idea of god, though, it won't be enough just to look at the most direct or obvious statements and implications of revelation.

Consider Christianity. According to the nineteenth-century German philosopher G. W. F. Hegel, Christianity is problematic in the fact that it places god in a timeless and perfect world above and ourselves in an imperfect, temporary, and corrupted world below. This arrangement causes us to feel as though we don't truly belong in the world, and therein alienates us from our physical existences.[4] Another nineteenth-century German philosopher, Ludwig Feuerbach, agreed that Christianity induces a sense of alienation. For him, though, the alienation exists not in relation to the natural world but to ourselves. Feuerbach maintained that the idea of god emerges when we project the essence of ourselves onto reality. In doing this we give god all of our most positive qualities, such as love, wisdom, and goodness. The more we do that, though, the less we see ourselves as possessing them. This leaves us alienated from the very best of what we are.[5]

A number of well-known ancient philosophies evidence this same pattern of self-depreciating thought in sacrifice to an ideal. According to Plato, reality has two aspects. The first is the world of ideas, a perfect and unchanging heavenly abode of archetypal templates for everything that exists. Breachable by the study of subjects like geometry and mathematics, philosophers could act as intermediaries—priests or prophets of a certain philosophical kind—between humanity and this ideal level of reality. In contrast, the world of flux is where we find ourselves, and it is an ever-changing and constantly decaying place of shadowy copies of those ideal or perfect ideas.

Like Plato, Aristotle also divided the world in two, but unlike Plato, he did it at the more terrestrial level of the sublunar and superlunar spheres (i.e., below the Moon and above the Moon). Everything in the sublunar realm was understood to be composed of combinations of four different substances: earth, fire, air, and water. The superlunar realm was different because it consisted of a series of concentric crystalline spheres made of "aether," an exotic substance that housed the planets in their eternal motions across the sky. Whereas things in the sublunar region move in straight lines towards their "natural place" (i.e., heavier things

---

[4] The fact that Christianity frowns upon sexual pleasure unsanctioned by marriage is a clear illustration of the point.
[5] See Singer (1980), Armstrong (1993).

towards the center of Earth and lighter things further out), the nature of the aether was to move eternally in perfect circles. While the level of existence we find ourselves was imperfect and ever-decaying, the aether was conceived as pure and incorruptible.

It's clearly not just religious modes of thinking that can drive us to depreciate ourselves and our place in existence, then. I also should say that religion cannot be accused of being uniformly or absolutely alienating, for there are clear ways in which religion stands to make the world *more* familiar to us, not less. At least part of the appeal of ancient animism and polytheism, for example, was that it reduced the overall sense of anxiety people felt about the powerful and mysterious natural phenomena surrounding them. Why did storms, floods, wildfires, earthquakes, droughts, and diseases occur? Because a god (or other sufficiently powerful supernatural entity) willed them to happen. Explanations like this represented a way to both understand and humanize an otherwise bewildering and threatening world. It also represented a way of gaining a limited form of control over it. If our ancestors could successfully avoid doing the things that angered the gods—indeed, if they could get on the good side of the gods by making sacrifices and engaging in worship—they could indirectly make the world a more pleasant place to live for themselves. Though they are both monotheisms, Christianity and Islam have inherited at least some of that same psychological function, for not only do they help explain why good and bad things happen, they open up an avenue for us to petition god for more favorable treatment and intervention on our behalf.

Despite this, I think there is something to the idea that religious conceptions of the divine can generate problems for how we come to implicitly see ourselves and our place in the world. Moreover, in the same way that the brightness of the Sun obscures its dark spots from our view, this particular fact may be something that is very difficult for believers to notice.

One may well wonder how religion ended up with such a poor overall conception of divinity in the first place. The full answer undoubtedly has many parts to it, but one of them is quasi-Feuerbachian and relates to the limits of human imagination.

In short, we have been very eager to ensure that god possesses all manner of virtues and excellences. After all, it is in the notion of what god is that he would be the embodiment of such things. As a way of accentuating and emphasizing the greatness of god as much as possible, though, we went and did something very unhealthy: we pushed ourselves and everything in our vicinity conceptually down so that god could stand up even higher in contrast. We said things, such as that it is only because of god that anyone can be good, and we reminded ourselves that while we are contingent and fallible, god is necessary and infallible; while we are corrupt and spiritually sick, god is perfect and without bound. As for the world, it is but a stage on which our lives play out, and one with no real future except to be annihilated. It is a place of temptation, sin, and doubt over our metaphysical fate. It has even been religiously maintained that the world is so frail in its existence—so utterly incapable of continuing on its own—that it requires a constant miracle from god in order to not simply vanish. Think about that: so weak and imperfect is everything aside from god that reality needs divine intervention just to make it into the next moment. It goes without saying, but if the universe were to cease existing, we would go with it.

A second part of the answer likely derives from early attempts to deal with an age-old philosophical problem: if god is a supremely powerful, knowing, and good being, why are our lives affected by so much pain and suffering? Why is life so unpleasant and hard? There were at least three somewhat obvious philosophical possibilities available to people.

The first was to say that god exists but is not *simultaneously* supremely capable, knowing, and good. If he is not all three of these things at once, we would have a ready-made explanation for why life is so painful—it could either be that the world was the creative error of a less than supremely capable being, that god just doesn't know that people are suffering, or that god does know but just doesn't care. Since it is very hard to drop one of those three key properties without completely undoing the idea of god, though, that wasn't necessarily a very attractive problem solving method for people to take.

A second option was to adopt a Gnostic approach and suppose that the world had not actually been created by god—even though god does exist—but by either a) an evil deity, or b) an imperfect, secondary deity. If this was the case, the pain and suffering in the world could be explained as the result of the imperfections of that lesser being, or as something an evil deity intentionally included in the world by design. Since death would release us from that undesirable situation and teleport us to a world created by the truly perfect supreme being, Gnostics viewed death as a kind of liberation from the suffering and misery of the world.

Though this philosophical option managed to preserve the perfection of god, it has a distinctly polytheistic flavor to it, and that would have made it unpopular with anyone intent on believing that there is just one god-like being in existence. Aside from that, it did not explain why the supreme being did not proactively rescue us from our earthly prison, why it would have allowed this world to exist, or how we ended up here in the first place.

A third possibility was to hold that the world contains pain and suffering not through indifference, mistake, or oversight, but as a punishment for sin. On this way of reading it, it is divine justice that properly explains so much of the hardship that is found in being here. Accepting this required people to adapt their sense of justice so that punishing people for being sinful fell within the moral domain of divinity, and it also required postulating the existence of sin itself. However, this seems to have been something that many were quite comfortable with. After all, the connection between pain and punishment would not have been too hard to find. The association could be clearly seen whenever parents punish their children for misbehaving, for example, and it is only a short imaginative leap to suppose that the pain and suffering of adults' lives was punishment from god (the "spiritual father") for their spiritual disobedience and misbehavior.

While a natural inference to draw back then, it nevertheless represents a deeply mistaken and unhealthy way to see life and god. That it continues to be central to many people's understandings of reality today is problematic, for we have seen that there is at least one alternative way of tackling the problem of evil that retains divine predicates like omniscience and omnipotence, and does not require the debasement of either god or humanity for its explanatory success. On that more sophisticated account, the presence of pain and suffering in the world is not punishment for sin but a necessary part of what it is to seek spiritual enlightenment in a universe that exists as a causally independent, natural system.

All of this makes the practice of deferring our spiritual thinking to people who lived thousands of years ago that much more perplexing. In no other area of contemporary human knowledge—be it art, history, medicine, logic, biology, mathematics, chemistry, engineering, music, or physics—would we dream of doing such a thing. Yet when it comes to one of the single most important questions we can ever ask ourselves— the meaning of life and the fundamental truth of the universe—billions of us are perfectly happy to trust that at least one ancient group managed to get their views there almost exactly or nearly right. It is long past time for us to recognize how precarious this assumption is.

Mysticism and the Transcendence of God

One claim not infrequently put forward by mystics and theologians is that god is a radically transcendent being. To say this is to hold that god goes entirely beyond all things, including all means of analysis and description such as logic, reason, language, and conceptualization.[6] We could not say that god is "loving," "powerful," or "wise" in any way like we understand the meanings of those terms, for example, because god is entirely beyond such things. We could not even say (as some mystics and theologians do indeed warn against saying) that god "exists," for as a wholly transcendent being he is above classification as either "existent" or "nonexistent." Our question will be: is this claim about god right? Is god really best thought of as a radically transcendent being? And if he is, what would it mean?

As a preliminary, let me acknowledge that we are limited in what we are capable of thinking about. Most people (including most physicists) can't imagine what the four-dimensional spacetime region we call the universe looks like, for example, presumably because our brains haven't evolved with any need to grasp how things look four-dimensionally. Nor we can we easily imagine what the behavior of particles is like at the quantum level. To give you an illustration of the latter difficulty, imagine taking Earth in your hands and spinning it around 180 degrees so that the North Pole is where the South Pole was and the South Pole is where the North Pole was. If you were to then spin it around another 180 degrees again, Earth would be back to how it started, right? It turns out that electrons behave differently. If you could take one in your hands and spin it around 180 degrees and then 180 degrees again, it would *not* be back to how it first was. In fact, you would need to spin it around a further 360 degrees (so 720 degrees in total now) before it would return to its original quantum state. While this defies my imagination, physicists assure us that that is just how things are at the smallest scales of the universe.[7]

If the physical world can so easily frustrate our ability to think about it, why should we expect god to be any different (especially when it is god who allegedly created the universe)?

---

[6] Radical transcendence can be contrasted with more modest claims of transcendence, such as that he "transcends" space and time, but not logic and so on.
[7] At least insofar as we can bring ourselves to adopt a realist stance towards the picture of the world provided by quantum mechanics. See Davies (2006).

There is an appreciable point to this. Any being capable of conceiving of and then bringing forth into existence something as incredible as the universe is probably going to be a pretty spectacular thing itself, and not necessarily straightforwardly open to us in our comprehension. This alone will not justify believing that god is a radically transcendent being (or nonbeing? or non-(being/nonbeing)?) that cannot be described, known, or thought about, however.

Moreover, the difficult-to-describe character of many mystical experiences doesn't provide a compelling case for god's transcendence either. After all, there are plenty of things we experience in the course of ordinary life that are, strictly speaking, beyond description. For example, what is the experience of redness like? Nobody can say, for there is no way of putting the experience of redness into words such that those who have never experienced it could gain insight. Simply listing examples of things that are red won't help, for this only tells us what kinds of things bring about the experience of redness. Nor will connecting redness with light at a certain wavelength be of any value, for this does not reveal what the experience of redness is subjectively like. The same thing is true for all other tastes, sounds, smells, tactile sensations, and so on. The fact that mystical experiences reputedly of god might have unique and indescribable qualitative features to them is not by itself immediately relevant to the question of whether or not god is transcendent, then.

This is just as well, for it turns out to be philosophically problematic to say that god is radically transcendent. To see why, we will go circuitously via the example of Immanuel Kant, an outstanding eighteenth-century German philosopher.

Kant was deeply troubled by the arguments of David Hume that questioned (among other things) how we can be justified in accepting inductive conclusions. Inductive reasoning involves inferring *non-certain* conclusions from the truth of premises. For example, one might inductively reason that because the Sun has risen every day in the past, it will most probably rise again tomorrow. Hume's problem with induction goes like this: what justifies us in thinking that simply because the Sun has risen every day before now that it will do so again tomorrow? There doesn't seem to be anything about the Sun's consistent rising every day up until now that makes it certain that it will rise again tomorrow. Why should we think it will, then? Tomorrow might be the first day that it doesn't.

One might be tempted to say that our confidence in inductive reasoning comes from the fact that most times in the past when we've used inductive reasoning, the conclusions we have drawn have turned out to be true. On the merits of its past success, then, it just seems like induction *works*. If so, we can have confidence that induction will probably continue to work the next time we use it. Hume was smart enough to realize that this line of reasoning just raises the same problem all over again: there is nothing about a particular pattern of inference working most times in the past that guarantees it will work again in the future. The struggle to justify our confidence in inductive reasoning is probably the single best-known problem in all of philosophy, and Kant was eager to find a solution.

Kant's attempt at an answer would involve metaphysically dividing the world in two. His proposal goes like this: there is this thing—a wholly unconditioned side to reality that lies entirely beyond the reach of our senses and reason. Call it the *noumenal* realm, and think of it as the metaphysical floor of everything. Because it is transcendently beyond us, we can never know anything about the noumenal realm. There is also a *phenomenal* realm, however, and it makes up the domain we actually experience. The fundamental difference between them is that whereas one represents the world as it really is *in itself* (the noumenal realm), and the other represents the world as it *appears to us to be* (the phenomenal realm). Importantly, the phenomenal realm only comes about when the mind imposes what Kant called "categories" of thought and various preconditions for its experiencing onto the noumenal realm.

That's quite a mouthful, so let me explain. According to Kant, a category is a basic concept that underlies all of our thinking. In fact, being necessary to thought, it is only in terms of such concepts that we can think at all. Take the idea of being single: just to recognize something as singular (e.g., *one* banana, *one* tablet) requires that we are first able to conceive of what something's being *single* might be. Since concepts like that are required for thinking before thinking itself can begin, Kant argued that they cannot be learned from experience. Instead, we must already have them within us somehow.

Now, the important thing to note about Kant's categories of thought is that they only applied to things *within the world of experience*. It followed from this that we could only ever have knowledge of what lies within the phenomenal world, and only there because the phenomenal world is brought into agreement with what the mind requires in order to engage in thinking about it. This is the reason why the noumenal realm was transcendently beyond us—nothing from the conceptual library of what we need to think about things applies to it.

Kant believed this metaphysical construction allowed him to answer Hume's problem. How can we trust in induction? Because the mind guarantees that the world *we experience* (not the world *as it is in itself*) is formatted in such a way that it can make sense of it, including by inductive means.

This had the curious consequence of making the world we experience a phantom of the mind, somewhat like a holographic image shining from a light, but Kant wasn't upset by that. He spoke about the noumenal realm as consisting of *things-in-themselves*—things as they are beyond all possibility of thought and experience. It was always going to be tempting to wonder what the noumenal realm might really be like, deep down. For example, what is an apple *really like* beyond the particular way in which we experience it? For Kant the answer was unequivocal—we can never know.

Complex and mind-bending though Kant's system was, in hindsight it was also a spectacular failure. For one thing, the idea that the mind imposes itself onto something that is by definition entirely beyond itself is impossible to understand. Like singularity, causality was one of those conceptual categories that were basic to the requirements for our experience. As such, it was something that should have only had an application *within* the phenomenal world. Why does a twig breaking cause the apple to fall? Because the mind generates its experience of reality such that events like that are connected in sequential order. But how then are we to understand the idea of the mind bringing the preconceptual, pre-sensible noumenal realm into conformity with what it requires for its intelligibility, therein giving rise to the phenomenal realm? It cannot be any sort of causal process, for to say that much is to immediately contradict what has already been asserted about causality—that it only applies *within* the phenomenal realm (not *to* the noumenal realm). But then what kind of relationship does the mind have with the noumenal realm when giving rise to the phenomenal realm? A good answer seems hard to find. In fact, even just by using the term things-in-themselves Kant appeared to go beyond what his own theory allowed, for *plurality* was a conceptual category just as much as *singularity* was, and so it could not have been said that there were *things* (plural) beyond the world of experience.[8]

---

[8] Another German philosopher, Arthur Schopenhauer, recognized this problem and refused to speak of the noumenal realm as consisting of anything other than the *thing-in-itself*. That was no better from a Kantian point of view, however, for singularity was just as much a category of thought as plurality was.

The point of this story was not to bore you with details of eighteenth-century German philosophy (even if that is an easy thing to do, given that topic). Rather, it was to illustrate just how incredibly tricky the idea of transcendence can be, and how it can trip even the unquestionably brilliant up with what they want to say.

With that in mind, think about the claim that god is transcendently beyond the grasp of any logical, linguistic, or conceptual system that is now and ever will be at our disposal. If you've been paying careful attention, you might notice that what this claim does is *noumenize* god; it says that there is nothing cognitively about us that applies to god in his divine transcendence. Yet to experience god (mystically or otherwise) surely requires *some* kind of conceptual framework to stand over that experience and cognitively organize it for us. How else could it be experienced or recalled as an experience if not under the aegis of concepts? If nonconceptual experience is impossible, it will be incoherent to claim that god is both radically transcendent and has been mystically experienced, for the former logically prohibits the latter.

A second issue has to do with the value of the idea of god after he has been deemed radically transcendent. As mentioned, if god truly is like that then no thought or statement would be true of him, for he would be beyond being limited by the content they express.[9] But what value could the idea of god possibly have if nothing can be cognitively assigned to it? It renders it completely meaningless, and in that, effortlessly discardable as well.

If radical transcendence is so problematic, why is it enthusiastically attributed to god? I can think of several possible motivations. The first is that *transcendent* seems like a pretty venerating thing to say about god—right up there with calling him omniscient, omnipotent, and infinitely loving. This may bring some people to say that god is radically transcendent, and to accept that claim when it is put forward by others, without necessarily thinking all the way through to what it philosophically leads to—the emptying of the idea of god of any value or point.

A second possibility has to do with the fact that if god is not subject to evaluation by rationality, logic, and reason, then any claim a mystic or

---

[9] You might be thinking: but isn't transcendence itself a property, and therefore, won't it be contradictory to say that god is wholly transcendent and still attribute something known to him—namely, his transcendence? The reply that might be given is that transcendence is ascribed only in the negative, i.e., it is the fact that no other properties apply to god that his transcendence becomes descriptively applicable.

theologian might wish to make about him cannot be criticized. This could be very convenient if you're a mystic or theologian yourself. After all, as providers or advocates of special truths, it's not necessarily in their best interests that others could come along, subject their claims to critical analysis, and then either accept or reject those claims on the basis of that. That would be to treat those claims as though they were ordinary, but truths about god are not supposed to be like that—they are supposed to be deep and highly meaningful, cutting to the heart of reality, and potentially achievable only by a very special process of insight. If the status of the mystic or theologian as a supplier of special truths is to be preserved, it will potentially be to their advantage that god's radical transcendence eliminates the basis upon which rationally guided criticism of their claims might proceed. But what about the fact that mystics and theologians are still insisting upon making claims about a being that, in principle, no positive claim can ever be made about? Chalk that up to just another of the many transcendent mysteries of god, perhaps.

A third possibility is that by treating god as transcendent, he is set up as a source of tremendous awe and mystery. Since some people might find those things intrinsically very pleasurable and enriching, they may be drawn to the idea of god as a radically transcendent being.

Fourth and finally, some people might be inclined to embrace the idea of god as transcendent out of moral concern. If we can never really know anything about god—indeed, if we can only ever mystically experience some sort of deep transcendent mystery—then god himself cannot be used as a tool to justify injustice and oppression in the way he historically has been. While this would also mean he couldn't be used to justify more positive things too, this may be something that some are willing accept in light of the moral history of the idea of god.

Of course, the fact that some people are motivated to see god as radically transcendent wouldn't mean he can't be. In light of the philosophical problems that attend to that claim, though, I can't see it as something we should seek to ascribe to him.

I should also say that although I have argued against the idea of god as radically transcendent, I'm not against mystical or spiritual experiences *per se*. After all, what *a priori* reason is there to think that truth can only come by way of the physical senses, introspection, memory, ordinary intuition, and reason? I suppose it to be at least possible that by ingesting certain compounds, going without normal amounts of food or water for days, engaging in certain meditative, supplicative, or religious practices, or just sitting quietly on one's own, certain states of consciousness could be entered into which make spiritual insights possible.[10] Whatever the merits of mysticism in providing access those truths, though, we should be wary on the topic of god and transcendence.

So What is God?

Two philosophical problems haunt human attempts to think about god. The first is a tendency to do so anthropocentrically—that is, to build into our image of god the thing that we are most intimately familiar with—ourselves. The problem was rather memorably captured by Xenophanes when he remarked that if horses have gods, they would be in the image of horses. While animals may not worry about such things, we must worry that our way of thinking about god suffers from a humanizing distortion, and in just such a way that how we end up thinking about divinity looks all too human (on reflection) to be taken seriously.

The second danger comes about almost as a reaction to the first, and involves taking god to be as transcendently different or "other" as we can find words to declare. If this means denying any common ground between humanity and divinity, either in terms of substance or the means by which we understand, think, and reason, then so be it.[11]

In trying to avoid these two undesirable extremes, I think the wisest approach is to aim for a *conceptually minimal* understanding of what god is. That is, we should aim to keep our idea of god as minimal in terms of content as possible while retaining its philosophical meaningfulness and usefulness.

The virtue of this course of action is reinforced by two epistemic facts. First, saying less is usually to our advantage where true beliefs are concerned. Just ask yourself: what is the probability that there is someone in Rome right now wearing a red hat? Pretty good, one would think. Even if it is currently nighttime there, Rome is a big city with a large population, and I would think that some of its inhabitants will own

---

[10] It was suggested in the first chapter that there is value in the universe's independence, since that allows us an unhindered pursuit of ourselves in being and knowing. That in itself would not necessarily rule out the possibility of people having mystical and spiritual experiences, however.

[11] Needless to say, just because we possess a particular trait does not mean that god must lack it, and just because we can comprehend something does not mean god must be beyond either it or the means by which our comprehension was achieved.

hats, some of those hats will be red, and at least one of those red hat owners will be wearing their red hat right now. What about the probability that someone is in Rome right now, wearing a red hat, and standing still on one leg? Now we have three conditions that need to be satisfied. I don't know what the probability of that is, but it is surely less than the probability that there is someone in Rome right now wearing a red hat. Finally, what is the probability that there is someone in Rome right now, wearing a red hat, standing still on one leg, humming a happy tune, and thinking about anchovies? I wouldn't like to bet on it; the probability is probably negligible. And so on it goes: the more independent claims we make with our hypotheses, the less likely it is that they will be true, all other things being equal. The idea of god is no exception, in that the more we choose to say about him, the less likely it is that our description will be the bearer of unqualified truth.

This aside, reason by itself just is less powerful than experience for illuminating the details of things. While experience could easily tell us the color of god's shoes—if it made any sense to think of god as shoe-wearing, that is—unless there were reasons based on what else we knew to expect that he would wear a certain color over others, reason is comparatively powerless to say. If we're taking reason as our guide to the divine, then, what we can justifiably say is naturally more limited anyway.

So what should a minimally-aiming conception of god look like? Here's one approach: god is a conscious and intentional being marked out by supreme or ideal (in the sense of unsurpassable) capability, rationality, intelligence, knowledge, and goodness. Assigning these properties allows the idea of god to function as an explanation of the universe, yet with the exception of the attribution of goodness, does not say more than what is needed in order to do that (in accordance with the minimal-property constraint).[12]

---

[12] Why is goodness an extended attribution? Because while god does need to be supremely rational, capable, and knowing to create a universe remotely like ours, and does need to be conscious and intentional in order for the explanation to be classically teleological, he doesn't *need* to be supremely good. As we will see shortly, however, there is at least one independent reason to see god as good rather than evil (which is why I include it as a property here). Also note that the theory of life advocated in this book requires god to be supremely good, where that specifically includes the valuation of things like autonomy, understanding, and independence in being, for they are (on this account) integral to making sense of both the meaning of life and the nature of experience found within it.

Naturally enough, this isn't the only way to define god. Here's a second possibility: instead of referring to a single being with the aforementioned divine properties, the word "god" could refer to the set of all entities that exist in a divinely-propertied state. Monotheisms like Christianity and Islam won't be comfortable with this suggestion, but if a divine state of being is an existential possibility for any conscious agency, there is nothing obviously limiting the instantiation of that state by none, one, or more than one conscious entity. Moreover, if there is more than one being whose state of being can be described as divine, it could well make sense to speak of the *class* of those beings as god. To talk about god's existence in that case would be to say that there is at least one (but not necessarily just one) divine conscious agency, and to speak of god as having created the universe would be to say that members of that class acted in such a way to be causally responsible for it.

A third possibility is to talk about "god" not as the set of all things that are divine, but as a segment on a continuum of conscious being that is marked out on one end by divinity and extends down from that point some finite and imprecisely defined distance. That might sound highly arcane, but the practical consequence is to allow for increasingly close approximations of a divine state of being to be grouped up in the meaning of the term "god."

So why should we be interested in the latter? One reason comes from the fact that the idea of god represents a kind of spiritual, moral, and existential ideal that marks out which state of being is the very best among all that are possible. By advancing very far towards that ideal, or at least sufficiently far along the continuum of being to indicate orientation, any beings approaching it would in some way represent that ideal and its value. Given that, it may well be beneficial to speak of them as belonging within the idea of "god," too.

There is another reason for being interested in the second and third definitions, and the argument for it begins in an unlikely place: with beavers. Constructed from wood, mud, and stones, beavers build dams across waterways to give themselves protection from predators and safe places to store food. Though dams require huge investments of time and energy to construct, their payoff for the survival of pairs or families of beavers working together is clearly large enough that evolution has seen fit to genetically encode beavers with something of a dam-building imperative. To be a beaver in the world is to be irresistibly drawn to dam flowing waterways, and given the role of the dam in promoting beaver survival, it seems fair to regard the dams as extensions of the beavers themselves. That is, the dams are as much a part of the beavers as their wood-gnawing teeth, paddle-like tails, and heat-insulating fur.

Biologists talk about this kind of thing under the rubric of *extended phenotypes*. Phenotypes are descriptions of the physical and behavioral characteristics of an organism. Opposable-thumbed hands, a large brain, and upright walking are all part of your phenotype, for example, while the possession of gills, sharp teeth, and fins are part of the phenotype of many shark species. An organism's phenotype is determined in conjunction with inputs from the environment by its *genotype*—the inherited genetic blueprint that sets out instructions for the body plan and behavioral tendencies of that organism. While the genes responsible for an organism's ability to smell are part of its genotype, then, its actual ability to smell is part of its phenotype.

The idea that the phenotype of an organism should properly include the survival-enhancing products of its behavior was argued at length by evolutionary biologist Richard Dawkins in *The Extended Phenotype*.[13] It simply appears to make little sense to limit how we talk about phenotypes to what is most immediately true of an organism's physical body. After all, spider webs, bird nests, and termite mounds all play an integral role in the survival of spiders, birds, and termites, and it seems arbitrary to say they are not a part of those organisms' phenotypes just because they are not physically attached to them as legs, beaks, and eyes are.

Something analogous is true at a philosophical level for human identity, for who we are can extend over things that are physically separate from us. Personal identity is all about mapping the boundaries and properties of the thing that is you—most typically, your mind, body, thoughts, feelings, beliefs, values, attitudes, preferences, tastes, aspirations, gender, race, job, social position, nationality, material wealth, fashion style, abilities and skills, personal history, and so on. What do you count as *being* you? What belongs as part of you and what doesn't? These are fundamental questions of identity. Note that the various elements that make up who we are do not need to be a) fixed or b) weighted equally. Who you are, and what you count as being you, can change over time, can be sensitive to context, and can involve elements that sit in a hierarchy of importance. In this respect, personal identity is

---

[13] Or more exactly, benefiting the *genes* which encode for those behavioral outputs. See Dawkins (1982).

rather like an onion, in that while some layers sit further out towards the surface, others reside in the very core of who we are.

With that as a background, consider someone who has unfortunately lost their leg following a nasty motorcycle accident. While this life-changing event might easily cause them to feel as though they have lost an important part of themselves, the loss itself can at least be functionally compensated for with a prosthetic leg. Indeed, they may become so dependent upon its use in day to day life that, after some time, the prosthetic leg is felt to be just much a part of them as their old biological leg was. And after all, what is the meaningful difference? The fact that the new leg is made from metal and plastic rather than flesh and bone hardly seems to matter from the point of view of its inclusion in their identity.

Alternatively, consider memory. Most people would say that their ability to remember is part of who they are. At a neurological level, of course, memories are just pieces of information stored in brain states. To be able to remember your middle name or birthday is to have information concerning that accessibly stored somewhere in your head. Yet we can imagine the case of someone who, having suffered a brain injury, now has a very hard time remembering things. With their ability to remember degraded, something that was formerly an integral part of them is now diminished. Yet memory too can be functionally compensated for. They might start carrying around a pen and notepad, for example, and write down anything they might need to remember as soon as they learn of it. They might then develop a practice of checking on the notepad throughout the day to see if there is anything they need to recall.

By replacing the memory function formerly handled by their brain, and by becoming so effective in using those items that it becomes second nature to them, it seems as though the pen and notepad become a part of this person. And again, what meaningful difference could there be between information stored neurologically and information stored on paper that is relevant to identity? Although the notepad and pen aren't located inside their body as their brain is, why should that matter? For all intents and purposes, the person has swapped part of their biological memory with something nonbiological, just as one can replace a biological leg with a prosthetic leg. In such circumstances, who they are extends to the pen, notepad, and the system of behaviors that enables them to use those objects to remember.

Replacing limbs and memory with nonbiological objects doesn't happen all that often, but nearly everyone will be familiar with the integral role physical objects play in their daily lives. We use watches to help tell the time, cars to get us where we need to go, cell phones and emails to communicate with other people, calendars to help us remember events, internet search engines to find answers to things we don't know, and GPS navigation to help us find our way. All of these things enhance our natural capabilities, and to the extent that we value and rely upon them for that, we may say that these things are all a part of us. If prosthetic legs can become part of a disabled person's self through the functional role they play, watches, cell phones, and the internet can surely become a part of the selfhood of nondisabled people by extending their functional capability beyond what is biologically default.

The takeaway from all of this is that identity is a rather amoeba-like thing, and the more we functionally integrate something into our lives, the more it can be said to be a part of who we are.

If you accept this much, the next step in the argument is straightforward: it needn't be just nonconscious objects in the external world that our identities extend over, but *other people* too.[14] Strange as that might sound, it follows from the importance of other people to our lives and the apparent lack of any meaningful distinction between conscious and nonconscious things when it comes to identity inclusion.

The most obvious example to give is the case of two inseparable lovers. Given the central role they each play in the realization of one another's happiness and wellbeing, we should think of them as a genuine part of one another, and in more ways than simply the poetic. Psychologically and emotionally depending upon each other, they get far more out of having the other in their life than they will ever get from having cell phones or watches. And what could it matter for who we are that the things we identify with includes other people? If cell phones and computers can be a part of us, other people can be too.

While extensions of identity over other people might be easiest to accept in romantic cases, the same goes in principle for non-romantic human relationships as well: if we depend on others for important non-romantic goods just as we depend on objects like cell phones and

---

[14] If it seems odd that something else which is living could be a part of you, consider the fact that the bacteria in your gut which help you digest food are a part of you, even though they are genetically distinct from you.

computers, then to the extent that we do, we may regard those people as a part of who we are.

I recognize that this may not be the easiest thought in the world to think. Most of us—especially those of us in the West—are accustomed to seeing ourselves as akin to Newtonian atoms scattered about in the void: there's you over there and there's me over here, and while we might occasionally interact and bounce off of one another, there is always something that is exactly and distinctly you and something that is exactly and distinctly me.

Setting aside that view's prevalence, my suggestion is that it is wrong, and that things are more uncertain and hazy than our naïve experience of the world would lead us to think when it comes to personal identity. Indeed, my own view is that, from a *sufficiently close point of philosophical inspection*, we bleed into one another through our mutual dependencies, just as the colors on a painting can bleed into one another along their edges. This doesn't mean that individual people don't exist, any more than the merging of colors on a painting means that distinct colors don't exist. The idea of individuality is a useful one, and it is important not to get carried away with monistic philosophies of being that proudly and mysteriously proclaim "everything is one." Still, if the issue is looked at closely enough, I should see that I am strictly incapable of telling myself *absolutely or perfectly* apart from you, or indeed you apart from me, and that for some people in our lives the extent of that blurriness can be far more considerable. To put that another way, human beings are neither completely one nor completely many, but some finer unity or division in between.

While this point might be accepted in principle, the extent to which overlapping human identity is seen as meaningful will depend on the person examining it. While one person might think it is quite meaningful to regard two lovers as at least a small part of one another, they may not think it is anywhere as meaningful to regard two strangers in a field as a much smaller part of one another, even if they admit that *technically* they can be. A different person, however, might see enormous significance in the principle that we are not atomically isolated in identity, even if the extent of that may only be slight in most cases. Regardless, it is only the philosophical principle that matters for my argument here, for it makes it strictly impossible to tell precisely where you stop and I begin. Just as how atoms appear to behave as Newtonian physics would describe until you experiment with them on the smallest quantum scales, you and I may be treatable as distinct and separate on the scale of ordinary life until we adopt a philosophical lens and zoom down deep into the details of things.

This finding has implications for the existence of a multiplicity of divine beings. If it's true that in some sense we extend over one another, it's hard to imagine this being any less the case for any divine beings, should more than one of them exist. While they wouldn't need each other in the same sorts of ways we do, need is not the only basis on which a relationship can be formed, and given their mutual exemplification of a divine state of being, it seems plausible to imagine them connected by divine love. The same point holds for any less than divine beings found in the segment on a continuum of being marked at one end by divinity: by being experientially significant to one another through an interrelationship of love, the same overlapping blurriness of identity would exist for them in respect to one another. This is naturally speculative, of course, but the idea that divine beings would hold love for one another, and that their experience of that love would be incredibly meaningful, seems entirely plausible on the face of it. Indeed, it would be rather curious to imagine it being different.

Once again, nothing about an overlap in divine identity should be taken as suggesting that there aren't individual entities in a divine class of beings. If the nature of their relationship to one another is such that they are in some way valuably involved with one another's experiences, however, then combined with the fact that they would all exemplify and represent a divine state of being, the use of the word god to refer to them all seems desirably useful. Indeed, it is possible to go so far as to include ourselves within that definition.[15] That all said, while the theory of life presented in this book is open to either of the latter two approaches, for simplicity's sake I will continue to use the word god as though it picks out a single, definite, and original divine being.

You may have noticed that defining god as supremely capable, knowing, and rational (and so on) doesn't actually reveal a tremendous amount about him. Suppose I told you that life was seeded on Earth three billion years ago by an ancient species of aliens known as *maglons*. Maglons, I explain, were an immensely powerful, knowing, and

---

[15] Why? Because one could argue that all points on the continuum of conscious existence would be interconnected (especially given the way that we may depend upon the idea of god for our experiences, and how god would be morally and causally invested in us and our highest good). In that case, we would literally be a part of god and god a literal part of us.

technologically advanced species, and they made it their mission to spread life to as many corners of the galaxy as they possibly could.

There are a variety of questions you might want to ask me about them. Where did the maglons come from? (I don't know, except that it wasn't from Earth or anywhere nearby.) Why did they set themselves the goal of spreading life throughout the universe? (Perhaps because they saw life as something that is essentially good and they aimed to make the galaxy a more beautiful, rich, and interesting place?) What did they look like? (I have no idea.) What did their spaceships look like? (I have no idea.) How did their spaceships work? (I have no idea.) Where are they now? (They could be still around, but I have no idea.) Though they have a name, a purpose, and a short list of identified properties, I haven't really told you much about the maglons at all. The situation with god is similar: just knowing that he has divine properties like omniscience and omnipotence and a spiritual reason to create the universe still leaves out a lot.

One response to this is to ascribe god a set of additional properties that are useful for conceptually filling out our picture of him, but are not necessarily committed to in terms of their truth. A precedent for this exists in science, where a distinction can be made between *detection* properties and *auxiliary* properties in the case of theoretical entities like electrons, quarks, and dark matter. Because detection properties define the causal nature of theoretical entities, they are appealed to when justifying claims about the objective existence of those entities. Auxiliary properties are different in the fact that they are not causally delimiting, and hence do not tell us anything discoverably different about how a particular theoretical entity behaves. They are still associated with the entity in question, however, because they enable us to think more easily about the theoretical entity in question than we would otherwise be able to.[16]

Though one is a scientific entity and the other a philosophical entity, both god and the electron are examples of theoretical entities: neither can be directly observed, both have their existence posited in order to explain a certain range of phenomena, and what can be said about each of them is limited by the fact that they exist at a significant epistemic distance to us.[17]

---

[16] See Chakravartty (1998).

[17] This is not to suggest that our confidence in the existence of god should be equal to that of our confidence in the existence of electrons. For one thing, our confidence in the existence of unobservable physical entities may be increased if they can be experimentally manipulated and caused to interact with other theoretical entities in

Now, just like electrons—or anything else, for that matter—god needs to be assigned certain properties if the idea of him is to be at all interesting or useful. Some of these will function as the philosophical analog of the electron's *detection* properties and provide the basis for his explanatory value. God needs to be supremely intelligent, knowing, and capable if his existence is to offer a good explanation of the universe, for example. However, not *every* property we attach to god needs to be taken as essential to the very idea of him, or indeed knowably true of him. So long as these properties are clearly marked out in our minds as existing for that reason, though, they can be ascribed to god in the auxiliary capacity of enabling us to more easily think and speak about him. We can choose to be *semi-realists* about descriptions of god, in other words, just as many physicists are semi-realists about a range of theoretical entities taken to exist in physics.

What we should want at the end of these philosophical pursuits is a conception of the divine that is explanatorily useful, that avoids the two extremes of anthropocentrism and radical transcendence, that is minimal in what it speaks to, and that can be successfully grappled with in thought. Beyond these goals, serious attention needs to be paid to the fact that, as a divine being, god would represent the very pinnacle of conscious existence—something that, I think, virtually eliminates any plausible notion of him being interested in praise and worship, regulating human sexual behavior, or punishing people (eternally or otherwise) based upon what they do or fail to do.

Unfortunately, doing away with outdated religious additions to the idea of god is not necessarily easy. To understand why, imagine that someone drew a swastika and placed it in front of you. The sight of it would no doubt call to mind a number of extremely negative conceptual associations, and all quite automatically and spontaneously on your part. You wouldn't have to consciously deliberate about the meaning of the swastika to find those connections—they would be right there for you in the sight of it, almost as if the symbol itself possessed those meanings.

Here is the interesting thing, though: the swastika's history long predates the Nazis' use of it. With roots in Ancient India, Greece, and Rome, and appearing frequently in the religious traditions of Hinduism, Buddhism, and Jainism, the swastika originally symbolized being well or good. Despite that, most of us in the West can't help but see it today as

---

predictable ways. For another, theories involving them may lead to predictions of novel and independently verifiable phenomena. Opportunities for doing this in the case of god don't seem to be especially open.

a symbol of fascistic totalitarianism, genocide, and an all-consuming pathology of thought.

The idea of god has suffered the same fate. That is, due to the long history of its religious misconception, god has come to have a number of extremely negative conceptual associations attached to it. Not only do these have no sensible place in the context of divinity, they make thinking about god in ways that are completely free of them very difficult, for they are what presently dominates over the basic idea of god. Importantly, they don't come about deliberately on our part, but subconsciously, and this makes them difficult to combat. Aside from emphasizing just how unreasonable and idiosyncratic religious conceptions of god happen to be, or coining a new word as a substitute for "god," I'm not sure how best to approach the task of combating this fact.

The Attribution of Goodness

Is god a divinely good being? Does he represent an existential pinnacle for things like love, compassion, and moral consideration? You might think that the answer to this question is clear. However, David Hume argued that if we are taking *the world* as our guide to the kind of being that god is, we are not justified in believing so. We might perhaps be justified in saying that god is a supremely powerful and intelligent being, for the universe is an astoundingly complex and intricate thing. Does the universe justify belief in god's divine goodness, though? Clearly it doesn't, said Hume, for it contains altogether too much pain and suffering.

A great thought experiment by philosopher Stephen Law draws out the bite of Hume's objection particularly well.[18] It starts by imagining another world that is nearly the same as ours except for one important difference: philosophers and theologians there speak not of god's supreme goodness, but of his supreme *evil*. With so much evil both possible and actual in the universe, they reason, how could its designer *not* be supremely evil? It is just the most sensible conclusion to draw.

As is always the case, not everyone there agrees. Critics point out that while life does indeed allow for great evil, considerable goods are possible in life too. For example, there is love, friendship, beauty,

---

[18] Law (2010).

success, compassion, and many different sources of pleasure. This objection is so well-known that it even has a name—*the problem of good*. If god is so evil, why does he allow so much good to occur?

Theologians and philosophers have developed a number of responses to the problem of good. One is to say that god allows just enough good into the world to maximize the overall level of evil. Perhaps god rejoices seeing people suffer from the death of loved ones, for example, or seeing people agonize over the misfortune of their friends. In order for either evil to take place, there first has to be the goods of love and friendship. Indeed, there appears to be no other way for him to realize those evils without allowing (or *tolerating*, if you like) those goods.

Another response is to say that god has given people free will, and this explains the existence of at least some goods. Why did he give us free will? Because it is so much more delightful for god to watch people doing terrible things to one another if they *freely* chose to do them. If people didn't have any power to avoid doing the evils they do, there is a sense in which those evils would be merely done *through* them, not *by* them. If in the course of living people freely choose to do good for one another, then that is simply part of the cluster of side-effects bound up in making freely-willed evils possible. It is recognized that this argument only explains the goods that people do in relation to another, and not the goods that result from entirely natural processes and states of the world (like the beauty of a crimson sunset or the feeling of contentment that comes after eating a fine meal). Still, it convinces many insofar as it goes.

What you can see here is how the imagined world inversely mirrors our own. In our world it is goodness and not evil that is ascribed to god, and it is the problem of evil and not the problem of good that exercises theologians and philosophers. Borrowing from Hume, Law's finely crafted point is that the world is too ambiguous for either claim about the moral nature of god to be justified on an empirical basis. In other words, the world contains altogether too much good *and* too much evil to justify calling god either wholly good or wholly evil on its account. What would be more justified, if anything, is saying that god has a mixed moral character.[19]

---

[19] It could also be said that god is simply not powerful enough, or knowing enough, to prevent all evils (or goods!) from occurring, but typically those who believe in god want him to have all three qualities of perfect power, knowledge, and goodness at the same time without sacrificing any for the sake of the others. This, therefore, is likely to be an unpopular move.

It's looking pretty bleak right now for empirically-justified belief in the goodness of god, then. If Hume and Law are right, the world as we find it no more supports belief in god's benevolence than it does his malevolence. But is there really nothing about the world that can provide a basis for justified belief in the divine goodness of god? I think there is, though to see it we will need to look a little closer to home.

If we were to trace the moral arc of history from ancient times until the present, could humanity be said to have undergone any moral development? More exactly, has there been any notable improvement in the overall moral situation (the morally relevant values, attitudes, beliefs, propensities of action, intellectual skills, and conditions that emerge from, support, and influence them) of a meaningful proportion of the total living human population? Much about this question depends on what counts as moral progress, and that is something that two people could disagree about. Moreover, the very notion of moral progress only makes sense if all ways of relating to one another are not morally equivalent. It needs to be possible for the life of Mahatma Gandhi to be morally superior to that of Genghis Khan, for example. If that is indeed the case, though, we can ask: is where we sit now better from a moral point of view than previous times?

Surely it is. Many societies have legislation protecting against illegal or arbitrary detention, torture, slavery, persecution, and discrimination based upon factors like sex, race, religious views, political views, and natural ability. Legislation also widely exists guaranteeing people the right to political participation, education, freedom of thought and association, political and religious views, social welfare, fair legal representation and process, employment, and security of life and possessions. Trace history back far enough and you will soon come to a point where very few of these protections and entitlements existed for anyone.

In addition to that, it is also true that, now more than ever, there are humanitarian and charitable projects aimed at causes ranging from feeding, housing, and educating people to vaccinating and providing medical treatment to those who would otherwise go without. It has been a long and grueling road, but the more we have gone on, the more we have learned about better and worse ways of relating to one another. We have quite simply gotten better at being better.[20]

---

[20] To be clear, greater understanding is not the only driver behind our moral evolution. Perhaps most obviously, we've also become much more effective in many countries at catching and punishing people for criminal behavior, and that acts as a strong deterrent against engaging in it.

Far too much violence, genocide, war, hate, greed, exploitation, intolerance, selfishness, cruelty, inequality, racism, and prejudice continues to exist in the world today for anyone to be satisfied with the way things are, of course, but that alone doesn't tell us whether any moral progress has been made; it tells us, at its logical most, that if any moral progress has taken place, it has not been *absolute* in scope—a thing we knew already.

One might worry that the course of human progress offers no generalizing inference about how time and understanding affect moral thought and behavior. Many science fiction stories have been premised on the idea of a very advanced and malicious alien species coming to Earth to kill everything in sight, for example, and some (including even some eminent scientists) worry about this as a possibility.

Personally, though, I doubt it is something we need to be greatly concerned with. The reasoning why goes as follows: if it is physically possible at all, the scientific and technological hurdles standing in the way of an intelligent species developing an efficient form of space travel appears to be nothing short of colossal.[21] Accordingly, the level of science and technology that any civilization would need to possess before it could accomplish that would have to be extremely advanced.

However, science does not exist in a vacuum. Instead, it sits atop a social, intellectual, and historical background, and depends very much on that for its efficacy and direction.

Knowing this, it is reasonable to assume that the same kinds of social and intellectual background developments needed for a civilization's science and technology to conquer space would also lead to significant developments outside of those areas as well, including when it comes to the moral development of that species. After all, how plausible is it that a species might unlock the deepest physical secrets of the universe, given all that demands, yet not unlock some fairly basic moral truths? That a species could advance that far *without also* coming by some pretty significant moral developments along the way seems unlikely—and at least, I would think, to the point that sentient species in other parts of the universe needn't worry about their own unprovoked destruction.

Call this expectation the *principle of benevolence*: the same background intellectual and social conditions that are needed in order to support a civilization's science in rising to a truly space-faring level of technology

---

[21] Though some species might be able to tackle these difficulties more easily than others due to a higher level of intelligence.

are also likely to result in some pretty significant moral developments, and to an extent that unbridled malevolence towards, or a complete lack of moral regard for, other forms of intelligent life is unexpected.

Incidentally, this expectation is supported by the fact that there are likely to be self-limiting factors involved with any advanced technology and moral development. To put it bluntly, intelligent species that do not morally progress sufficiently far and fast enough will, as their science and technology progresses, face an ever-increasing risk of self-elimination through intraspecies conflict—a threat which we ourselves have yet to overcome.

To be clear, nothing in this argument should be taken as denying the very possibility of a malevolent and technologically advanced alien species. It is entirely conceivable that an advanced civilization might be highly speciesist in their outlook, for example, such that it is only really members of their own species that they hold significant moral regard for (which, again, is something we ourselves still have an enormous way to go with). I would argue that a position like this is relatively unstable, however, and hence is unlikely to survive any real depth of moral thought and reflection for an extended period at the top end of intellectual and social development. Because of this, it is also unlikely to be found in the views of any space-faring species, all other things being equal. In any case, all that I am arguing is that asymmetrical advances in understanding in science and technology, requiring as they do a massive level of intellectual sophistication and social cooperation, and to the exclusion of positive developments in moral understanding, is, all other things being equal, improbable.

God can be treated as subject to a special case of the benevolence principle, for as a divine being he would have a number of properties that are directly relevant to it. He would have perfect access to all factual truths, for example, and given the way factual beliefs go toward informing moral reasoning, this would enable him to morally reason that much more reliably. He would also have an ideal understanding of the distinction between morally relevant and nonrelevant facts, and as a maximally rational agent, he would be as free as it is possible to be from bias and errors of reasoning. Further, he would be perfectly capable of imaginatively assuming the position of others—something that is, at least in our case, an important element in the generation of empathy—and could even be directly affectively aware of the experiential states of others as part of the reach of his awareness (and so on).

One result of this should be that god would have a moral character of the highest possible pedigree. We can call this expectation the *principle of divine benevolence*: god's idealized epistemic situation would make his possession of a morally exalted character highly likely.

This principle rests on at least two assumptions, both of which must hold true if we are to have any confidence in it: first, that not all moral positions are morally equivalent to one another, and second, that our own historical moral development points in the general direction of some nonarbitrary, morally optimal or ultimate position relative to the nature of conscious experience within the framework of existence.

The first assumption is obvious in its importance. If all ways of relating to each other are morally equivalent, there can be no overarching sense of right or wrong or any morally better or worse way of standing in relation to one another. In the case of the second assumption, we need to take it that the direction of our own moral development marks out some wider truth about the most optimal way of morally being—that the changes we have undergone over the course of centuries points in the general direction of morality's highest peak, so to speak. What we don't expect is for a being to reach a state of divinity and conclude that being either heinously evil (as we would call it from within our present moral vantage point) or morally indifferent is the best way to be.

If both of these assumptions are granted then we have an inductive basis for thinking that god would be divinely good. Hume was correct that the natural world around us does not in itself speak towards the goodness of god (or his evilness, for that matter). However, that is not the only place from which inferences about god's moral character can be drawn. Indeed, our own moral progress to date can be taken as evidence for the goodness of god (which, I would add, is rather ironic in the context of thousands of years of religion exclaiming that it is only because of god that *people* can be good.)

There are at least a couple of ways in which this argument isn't quite as simple as I have presented it, however. For one thing, there are differences between our moral situation and that of god's. For example, the importance of moral reciprocity as a motivation for treating others well is high for us; at least part of what motivates people to treat others in a morally respecting fashion stems from the expectation we have that, in doing so, we will be morally respected in return. Part of the reason we have for being moral, then, is simple self-interest—our lives tend to go better if we all agree to be more or less nice to each other. It is difficult to see how reciprocity could be relevant within god's moral thinking, though. After all, what possible harm could god be done by another?[22]

At the same time, though, reciprocity isn't *necessary* for there to be motivation to treat others well, and this shows through clearly whenever we donate money to help improve the lives of people who will never be in any position to reciprocate the good we do for them. Animals cannot reciprocate our moral treatment of them, either, for (with a few notable exceptions) they don't even see the world in moral terms to begin with. That shouldn't eradicate our desire to treat animals morally, however. Unless we are simply irrational to seek the good of those who cannot realistically return the favor, we needn't think that god would fail to hold moral concern for us simply because he is beyond the point of being harmed or benefited.

But what if god was without any moral feeling at all? What if god simply felt nothing for others? Then there could definitely be a problem. I can think of two replies, however. First, if god also happened to be directly affectively aware of the experiential states of others as part of his omniscience, there would be a direct self-interest contained within that for him to be positively concerned with the improvement of those states. Second, if at some point of spiritual enlightenment it just becomes abundantly clear that a deep unity exists among all things, or at least (and especially) among all conscious things, one result of that might be to make the distinction between oneself and others far less meaningful. In that case, concern for oneself might unavoidably spill over into concern for others, and all because of the way in which the boundaries between oneself and others dissolve in significance. This again is highly speculative, of course, but it would in principle overcome the problem raised by the rather unfortunate possibility of a morally unfeeling god.

---

[22] Those from a religious perspective might reply that the answer is sin. Sin, of course, is a crime against god, sometimes obviously overlapping with morality (e.g., do not commit murder) and sometimes not (e.g., do not work on the Sabbath; do not plough a field with an ox and an ass together). You will not be surprised to learn that I am unmoved by the idea that god is done a moral injury if we don't do everything he demands of us, or that murder is a crime twice over: once against the person murdered and once against god.

A Revolution of the Heavens Once More

In his efforts to account for the movement of the planets across the night sky, the second-century Greek astronomer Ptolemy put Earth at the center of the universe and the Sun, Moon, and five known planets in eternal rotation around it. His geocentric model agreed well with what was observed celestially at the time, but it soon became apparent as more precise observations became available that the model had problems accounting for some of the finer details of the planets' orbits. While other astronomers worked to try and solve these problems over the centuries within the Ptolemaic framework, this could only be done by making increasingly unlikely and complicated modifications, and this left it in an increasingly ugly state.

In the sixteenth-century, the Polish astronomer Nicolaus Copernicus boldly proposed to resolve the situation by doing away with geocentrism entirely. Putting the Sun at the center and having Earth move around it instead, Copernicus's heliocentric model was an extremely challenging idea for many people at the time. However, the core of Copernicus's theory was quite simply *right*—Earth and the other planets really do orbit around the Sun.[23]

Humanity stands in need of yet another revolution in our thinking today, and it emerges from religion's approach to life and god. From a religious vantage point, all of the following questions have the utmost importance: What has god said and done? What does he want from us? What are the earthly and metaphysical consequences of living in accordance or discordance with his expectations? How best can someone live in a way that god approves of?

However, none of these questions are sensible to ask in the way they are intended, for they are all predicated upon a dramatically mistaken understanding of what god is. What truly matters is not god and his will for us, but what we want for ourselves given the very fact we exist. By maintaining exactly the opposite of this, religion has gotten things almost entirely backwards.

It is tempting to want to say that this is a truth about god that, if not immediately apprehended by a person, cannot be easily explained to them—it's the kind of thing one could hope would be immediately

---

[23] Technically, the Sun and the planets share a common center of gravity known as the barycenter that can sit within the Sun but can also go outside of it, depending upon where the planets are.

evident in the contemplation of what it must be for something to be divine. This will not do any justice to how completely natural religious ways of thinking about god are for many millions of people, however.

More conversantly, then, let me say that the religious image of god is at overwhelming odds with what is best in us, and hence is highly unlikely to be true of god, should a divine being actually exist. To say this is not to engage in some kind of blind anthropocentric regurgitation of twenty-first-century liberal values onto god, but to make an inference about god on the basis of the progress we have made within our own way of thinking and being to date.

Removing god from the center of human spiritual attention would not eliminate him from spirituality, any more at least than the Copernican rearrangement of the solar system eliminated the ground that everyone stood on. The Earth remained, but it was then just one of several planets in a celestial system that correctly identified the Sun as being at its center. Equally, in revising our understanding of the relationship between god and humanity, god would still exist and would still be of spiritual interest. He just wouldn't be the focus—the thing through which everything else of spiritual value flows.

It's not hard to sympathize with how opposite and backwards my suggestion may appear when you consider that it is customary for millions of people around the world to thank god for the food they eat and for millions of others to bend their backs to him in mandatory prayer five times a day.

Still, nothing about the size of the challenge ahead reduces the need to realize that no such thing as worship or obedience is appropriate to god in light of what he conceptually is. It may be daunting, but even journeys of a thousand miles begin with a single step, and with time and effort world-changing shifts in thinking really can be accomplished. The Copernicans showed us as much.

Chapter 4
Life in the Universe

Life is an exploration of the unknown, and every human action presumes a wager with nature.
—Brian Skyrms (b. 1938)

The Nomological Character of the Universe

Consider where you live. Our planet, Earth, is the third planet out from an average-sized star that, together with as many as 200 billion other stars, make up a collection of celestial bodies known as the Milky Way galaxy. The Milky Way itself is part of something known as the Local Group, a family of about 50 other galaxies that in turn belongs to even larger galactic super-groupings.

Because light travels in the vacuum of space at a finite speed of almost 300,000 kilometers per second, and because the universe began with an extremely hot initial expansion around 13.8 billion years ago, we can only see as much of the universe as there has been time since the start for light to have reached us from those parts.[1] While this means we don't really know how big the universe is beyond the portion we can see, there are estimated to be anywhere from 100–200 billion galaxies in the observable region alone. However many more galaxies there might be beyond this, that by itself is a staggering fact. To help visualize what it means, it is commonly said that there are more stars in the observable region of the universe than there are grains of sand on all the beaches of the world combined.

While this is an enormous number, vast stretches of space separate stars from other stars and galaxies from other galaxies. The closest star to our Sun is Proxima Centauri, a red dwarf about 4.2 light years away.[2]

---

[1] Or more exactly, from a time about 380,000 years after the Big Bang happened, which was when matter in the universe had cooled down enough so that the first atoms could form and light could begin to travel relatively unimpeded across it.

[2] A light year is the distance that light can travel in a single year in the vacuum of space—about 9.5 trillion kilometers.

To put that distance in perspective, imagine shrinking everything down so that Earth was the size of a pea. On that scale, the Sun would be about twice the size of a basketball and the distance separating Earth and the Sun would be 54 meters. Since Proxima Centauri is only about one-seventh the diameter of the Sun, it would only be about the size of a large apple. While that is easy to imagine, what is not is that on this miniaturized scale, the apple-sized Proxima Centauri would need to be placed a whopping 14.4 million kilometers away from the double-basketball-sized Sun to correctly reflect their actual separation. Since a distance like that isn't imaginable, if we shrunk the scale down even further and made the Sun the size of a pea, Earth the size of a tiny fleck of dust, and Proxima Centauri the size of a pinhead, the latter would need to be placed 144,000 kilometers away from the pea-sized Sun. That is just a bit over one-third of the way to the Moon at the non-shrunk scale, or if you prefer, about 3.6 times around the world. This is an incredible distance, and yet of the billions of other stars out there in our galaxy, *that's the closest one.*[3]

And what about our galaxy? If we were to shrink it down to the size of the rim of a fairly typical frying pan, its largest galactic neighbor in the Local Group, the Andromeda galaxy, would be about twice its size and would be about 5.3 meters away from it. Now, 5.3 meters might not sound nearly as impressive as one-third of the way to the Moon, but when you consider how many stars Andromeda and the Milky Way contain, and the kinds of distances that separate those stars from one another, you can begin to see just how unfathomably massive the distance between the Milky Way and Andromeda must be. It is far enough that the light we see coming from Andromeda today had to leave the galaxy around 2.5 million years ago to make it here on time.

While the universe is incredibly large, what it is composed of is the very opposite. Everything we see around us is made up of atoms, units of matter so tiny that if you wanted to see one of the carbon atoms that makes up the ink in one of the periods on this page, you would need to enlarge a period to the width of a 100 meter running track to just barely make a carbon atom out.[4] So small are atoms, in fact, that there are vastly many more of them in your body than there are stars in the observable universe. Rather interestingly, though, only the tiniest fraction of the

---

[3] Not every star in our galaxy has that sort of distance separating them. Stars at the center of globular clusters or at the center of galaxies can be much more tightly grouped together, for example.
[4] Close (2004).

volume of an atom is what you might call "something." If the nucleus of the simplest atom (hydrogen) was blown up to be the size of an orange, its single electron would orbit at a distance of about 500 meters. The rest of the atom between the electron and the nucleus is empty. Somewhat ironically, then, most of what is, isn't.[5]

While the simplest atoms were created in the furnace of the early universe, the heavier atoms that make up our bodies were created in a very different place: in the cores of massive stars. It is only inside such stars that temperatures and pressures high enough to create elements like carbon, oxygen, calcium, phosphorus, nitrogen, and iron exist. Our Sun, for example, has a core temperature of around 15.7 million degrees Celsius, but this is not hot enough to produce elements beyond helium (which fuses from hydrogen at around 10 million degrees).[6] 15.7 million degrees is still very hot of course, especially when you consider that the range of temperatures experienced by humans in the course of an average lifetime might span from something like -25 degrees to +45 degrees, depending on where you are and how far you have traveled. When a mere 70 degrees separates the bitingly cold from the oppressively hot, 15.7 million degrees can be put into a better perspective. For all of that, it is still far short of what is needed to create the heaviest atoms in your body.

All life depends on carbon for its existence, and carbon is the next element synthesized by stellar nuclear fusion after helium. Carbon formation takes place in stars when the core reaches a temperature of 100 million degrees, and only stars much larger than the Sun are capable of generating that kind of temperature. Oxygen requires an even higher temperature of around 500 million degrees, while sulfur and phosphorous need something like 2 billion degrees. Iron, the means by which our bodies chemically transport oxygen in our blood, requires temperatures of about 3 billion degrees to form.[7]

---

[5] Which is doubly interesting for the fact that most of what materially exists in the universe isn't visible. Modern theories hold that "dark matter" (called "dark" simply for the fact that it is good at eluding being seen) makes up the bulk of the material composition of the universe. Indeed, only something like 4–5 percent of the matter that exists is visible to us.

[6] An isotope of hydrogen called deuterium does undergo nuclear fusion to helium at the much cooler temperature of 1,000,000 degrees Celsius. However, it is not anywhere near as abundant in the cosmos as ordinary hydrogen is.

[7] See Ryan and Norton (2010). Note that these temperatures should be treated as rough ballpark figures only, as the fusion reactions involved depend not just on temperature but also on pressure.

Temporally we sit at the tail end of about three and half billion years of evolution by natural selection on Earth, and about 600 million years since the first of the simplest animals developed through that process. If the life of an 80-year-old were to be represented as a 1 centimeter segment on a line on the ground stretching out to the horizon, the last of the dinosaurs (and so those that lived most recently to us, about 65 million years ago) would be 8.1 kilometers further back behind it. If we were to walk on this line back to the moment of the Big Bang, 13.8 billion years ago, we would need to walk for a little over 1700 kilometers. Given that a single stride or two would carry us beyond nearly all of the most notable achievements of humanity, I find this is an incredible thought. There is simply vastness everywhere—both around us, within us, and behind us.

Impressive as these things are, in recent decades something much more subtle and extraordinary about the universe has come to light, and that is the degree of "fine-tuning" it appears to exhibit. It seems that if the physics of the universe were slightly different in relation to a number of fundamental physical parameters and constants, life such as we know it could not have come about. Some examples will help to illustrate.[8]

Acting to bind protons and neutrons together with one another in the nucleus of atoms, the strength of the nuclear strong force has significant consequences for the stability of atoms. If the strong force had been slightly stronger than it is, for example, all elements heavier than hydrogen on the periodic table would have been eliminated. If it had been slightly weaker than it is, the stability of elements essential to the formation of carbon-based life would have been jeopardized. And if it had been either much stronger or much weaker then carbon formation could not efficiently occur in the core of stars, resulting in a relative scarcity of that element throughout the universe. Since life as we know it needs carbon to exist, this would have been a bad thing from the point of view of life's existence.

The rate of neutrino interaction is also important for the possibility of complex life. One reason why is because the rate of neutrino interaction establishes the ratio of protons to neutrons immediately following the Big Bang. This matters because the ratio of protons to neutrons in the early universe in turn establishes the ratio of hydrogen to helium, and the ratio of hydrogen to helium matters because it affects

---

[8] I rely here on discussions of fine-tuning in Collins (2003), Craig (2003), Davies (2006), and Rees (1999), (2003).

the length of time that stars live for. Since helium-burning stars exhaust their fuel much more rapidly than hydrogen-burning stars do, and since the evolution of life requires long tracts of time in which to operate, an early abundance of neutrons to protons would have meant more helium-burning stars and fewer hydrogen-burning stars, and that would have meant much less time for evolution to take place within.

A second reason why the rate of neutrino interaction is important is because it is integrally involved with the distribution of heavy elements in the universe. As mentioned, heavier chemical elements like carbon, oxygen, magnesium, and iron are all formed via nucleosynthesis in the cores of large stars. That presents a problem for life, for if that was where they stayed they wouldn't make it out to be part of planets and ecosystems. It so happens, though, that when a star of a sufficiently large mass comes to the end of its lifetime it can cataclysmically explode. Supernovas, as they are known, are among the most powerful events in all of nature, and stars that experience them can outshine the light of an entire galaxy for a brief period of time.

The chain of events leading up to a supernova begins when a massive star has used up the last of its available nuclear fuel. Unable to release any more energy through the fusion of atoms, the core begins to cool as the star leaks energy into space. This causes the core's pressure to drop, which leads to a shrinking of the core under the weight of the surrounding material. This in turn increases the density of the core, and thus so too the gravitational attraction it feels. Gripped more and more tightly by gravity, the core begins to shrink faster and faster, further reducing its volume while increasing its density. Soon a point is reached where the incredible pressure and temperature found in the core overcomes the protons and electrons of atoms and forces them together as neutrons. In less than a second, the star's core collapses down from something the size of the Moon to a sphere of neutrons just ten kilometers across.

Now, because of mass differences and conservation laws, the conversion of protons and electrons into neutrons works out unevenly. Nature is an exceptional accountant, however, and in the balancing of the mass-energy ledger, one of the things that get emitted is neutrinos. Neutrinos are very, very low mass particles that for the most part don't like interacting with much of anything. In fact, by the time you get to the end of this sentence, many trillions of them will have passed harmlessly from through your body. Socially introverted as neutrinos *normally* are, the innards of a collapsing star is no normal situation for neutrinos to find themselves in. Indeed, because there is so much matter compacted together there so tightly, and because so many neutrinos are emitted in the formation of the neutron core, some of them just can't help but collide with the matter of the dying star as they make their way out. The result is a neutrino pressure wave that emanates from the core and causes the outer layers to be violently shorn away into space at a speed of up to one-tenth the speed of light.[9]

The strength of the weak force is important for the extent to which neutrinos interact with the material of the star as they pass through it. Interact too weakly and the neutrino pressure wave will pass from the core into space without explosively liberating any of the heavier elements. Interact too strongly, however, and the neutrinos will interact too easily (and thus too early) with the innermost material of the star, and hence not enough with what lies beyond that, leading to the same non-distributive result. Since the possibility of life in the universe depends on the availability of heavier chemical elements in places outside of star cores, a change in either direction stands to negatively impact life's chances.

Another significant factor for the development of life is the uniformity of matter in the first few moments after the Big Bang. If matter was spread out too uniformly by the initial expansion, stars and galaxies would not have been able to gravitationally coalesce out of it, and this would have left the universe nothing more than a lifeless fog of hydrogen. If it was spread too nonuniformly, however, it would have been too clumpy and so would have been filled with little more than black holes. The rate of the initial expansion of matter is also important. Too fast and everything gets blown apart too quickly from itself for stars and planets to form, while too slow and the universe would have collapsed down to a point only an instant after the initial expansion.

The suggestion from considerations like these is that we sit atop a series of cosmological coincidences, a highly unlikely alignment of physical fortunes that have jointly seen our universe emerge as capable of bearing life. The kinds of figures floated around for the improbability of life are incredible. The chances of the strength of gravity being within a range suitable for the development of life, for example, has been

---

[9] Neutrino emission is not the only mechanism believed to drive supernova explosions; the "bounce" of infalling stellar material off of the neutron core after its collapse is also understood to be a factor. See Herant *et al.* (1997).

estimated in once instance as 1 in 10^{36}.[10] That is, one chance in a trillion trillion trillion. If we let each atom in a person's body represent one possible outcome for gravity, then assuming 7×10^{27} atoms in the average human body,[11] we'd need about 142 million people gathered together to represent the odds, and where just *one* of the atoms in *one* person's body represents the life-permitting value. When you recall that there are more atoms in a single person's body than all the stars in the observable region of the universe, you can get a sense for just how improbable that is.

Not every particular case of fine-tuning is so stunning, but since it's not one but many physical constants that all need to end up life-permitting at once, this does nothing to alter the remarkable improbability of the universe being in a life-permitting condition.

It is important to note that using these facts to conclude that the universe is improbable requires some background assumptions, and those assumptions may well be questioned. For example, to say that life is permitted only within a very narrow range of values for the physical constants and parameters does not *in itself* mean that life is improbable. To see why, consider an analogy involving die-rolling. If you have a standard die, the chances of rolling a three with it ten times in a row is very low—a mere 1 in 60 million. If the die has been loaded with an internal weight that makes the three-face much more likely to be rolled, however, the chances of rolling a three ten times in a row could be very high—perhaps just 1 in 2 or 1 in 3. Thus the fact that the result of ten threes coming up can only be very narrowly satisfied (compared with the total number of ways the die could theoretically be rolled in the course of ten rolls) does not *in itself* mean that getting that result is improbable. Similarly, if the universe effectively *had* to have the physical properties that ours does, or if it was strongly biased towards having those properties, it would follow that the probability of the universe being life-permitting was high even though the range of conditions under which life is physically permitted is very narrow.

---

[10] Collins (2003). What is a physical constant? It is a number that appears in the mathematics of physical laws. For example, Isaac Newton's law of universal gravitation was given as $F = G(m1.m2/r^2)$. F is the total strength of that attraction, G the gravitational constant, m1 and m2 the masses of the two things you are looking at, and r^2 the square of the distance between them. Unlike the variables m1, m2, and r, which changed depending upon what things the calculation is being done for, the value of G is fixed for everything—i.e., its value is "constant." The actual value of G is only determined empirically, meaning that it can only be found by going out into the world and measuring it in experiments designed to reveal what it is.

[11] Kross (n.d.).

Because of this, one of the key assumptions that arguments from fine-tuning need to make is that life-sensitive physical constants were not fortuitously constrained to favor life-permitting over life-inhibiting outcomes. This assumption is essentially one of a *uniform probability distribution* where each outcome for the universe's constants is assumed to be equal in probability relative to every other. In the language of the analogy before, it is assumed that every face of an uninspected die has an equal chance of being rolled (i.e. it is assumed that the die is not biased towards any particular outcome). If we didn't assume this, we couldn't say that the chance of a three being rolled (or any other number, for that matter) with a single roll is 1 in 6.

While this might be a safe thing to assume in the case of dice, is it safe to assume it about universes? After all, couldn't the assumption be wrong? It certainly could. Despite that, it still seems reasonable to assume a uniform probability distribution in many ordinary cases, including even in the case of the universe, at least until there is some specific reason to think we shouldn't. After all, assuming the opposite—that a die *is* biased just because we don't know that it isn't—seems decidedly unreasonable. If we're going to assume anything at all here, then, assuming a uniform probability distribution seems the most prudent.

But what if we simply refuse to make an assumption either way, and therein effectively treat the question as unanswerable? While some might be drawn to agnosticism about the matter, I can't see that it is normatively required as part of the obligations of rationality, and hence is something that all people must do on pain of failing to live up to those standards. It is certainly possible that the physics behind the universe could be biased so that not every arrangement of the constants and parameters is as likely as every other. Theoretically, it could even have been biased towards life-permitting outcomes over non-life-permitting ones. Still, in the absence of a reason to positively believe something like this, it doesn't strike me as unreasonable to assume a lack of physical bias *either* towards or away from the physical conditions that permit the development of life, so long as we are clear in our minds that any conclusions we draw are dependent upon the truth of that underlying assumption.

If you accept that there is something to the idea of the universe being immensely improbable in permitting life, the natural question to ask is: what does it *mean*? It depends on who you ask…

Theoretical and Epistemological Options

According to physicist Paul Davies, fine-tuning was a bit of a taboo subject to discuss in physics for a number of years. One reason for its disreputable standing had to do with its apparent violation of a longstanding cosmological principle known as the *indifference principle*. This principle tells us that our place in the universe is unremarkable and nonspecial, and hence that we shouldn't expect to discover anything indicating to the contrary. The principle serves as a very useful antidote to the human tendency (clearly evident in older cosmological traditions) to locate ourselves in special places, such as at the center of the universe, thereby forcing the universe to acknowledge us in some way. This is a problem for fine-tuning, for it seems to indicate that our position in the universe *really is* special, as the fact that we are here at all depends upon the most extraordinarily unlikely set of physical coincidences. The conflict between the expectations of the indifference principle and the implications of fine-tuning led to considerable suspicion being leveled upon the latter by physicists.[12]

A second reason came from the fact that fine-tuning could be interpreted as opening a scientific door to the existence of a divine cosmic tuner—god. Not only is this contrary to the spirit of modern science, which has done superbly well by assuming that the true explanations of physical phenomena lie in the natural rather than metaphysical domain, it would probably be fair to say that most working physicists are not exactly inclined to believe in the existence of god. Taken together, these two facts didn't win fine-tuning many physicists as friends, and as a consequence talk of it was suppressed as something that serious-minded physicists concerned with their careers and academic reputations shouldn't really engage in.[13]

This was deeply unfortunate in hindsight, but what eventually brought relief to the situation was the development of viable alternative naturalistic explanations for fine-tuning. Better yet, some of those explanations actually seemed to *reinforce* the point of the indifference principle, not put it at risk.

In considering the issue for ourselves, we will canvass five prominent options, both explanatory and epistemological.

---

[12] See Davies (2006).
[13] *Ibid.*

The God Hypothesis

One possibility already raised is that god exists and explains the universe's fine-tuning. Why is the universe so improbably life-permitting? Because a divine being created the universe with the intention that it would play host to the emergence and development of life. The universe essentially had to be suitable for life's development, then, because that was the reason for which it was divinely created.

Which god should be the subject of *the* god hypothesis, though? Many gods have been taken to exist over the course of human history, and which one of them is placed at the center of the god hypothesis will very much affect its overall epistemic character. The Christian god represents one distinct way of thinking about the god hypothesis, for example, but so too does every other conceptual variant out there.

For this reason, there is a sense in which the god hypothesis is really a *family* or *collection* of different distinct hypotheses rather than any particular version of it. Naturally enough, if we judge the question of fine-tuning by the least plausible among them, a god-based explanation will not appear very promising at all. Since there are good reasons to view religious formulations of the god hypothesis as ranking among the least plausible, we won't be interested in those, but will instead use the one sitting at the core of this book.

The Multiverse Hypothesis

A second possibility is that our universe is just one of many in a vast collection known as the *multiverse*. There are a number of ways a multiverse could theoretically exist. One way is that there could be either tremendously many or an infinite number of universes that exist entirely independently of one another. These universes might exist either as brute facts, meaning that there isn't any reason why any of them exist other than the fact that they do, or as the result of some kind of universe-generating mechanism.

A second way a multiverse could exist is if there are either very many or an infinite number of physically distinct spacetime regions within the same wider universe. You might imagine a quilt that has been sown together from many different patches as an apt analogy. Though each patch is physically distinct from its immediate neighbor, they all exist as part of the same patchwork quilt. Should this kind of multiverse exist, our universe would be just a single life-permitting region of a much larger (and possibly infinite) collection of adjoining spacetime regions.

A third type of multiverse is rather less like the other two in resemblance. If our universe were to cycle endlessly through expansion and contraction phases one after another, such that after an expansion phase there eventually came a big collapse, followed repeatedly by more expansion and collapse phases, then very many (or an infinite number of) universes could be said to exist over a very large (or infinite) expanse of time. This would result in the existence of a multiverse, but it would be spread out temporally rather than spatially.

For the multiverse hypothesis to succeed as an explanation of fine-tuning, it is necessary to postulate that the many universes exhibit variation when it comes to their life-sensitive constants and parameters. If there are a large number of physically distinct universes (or subregions, or temporal oscillations), the chances that at least one of them will randomly have the right physical characteristics to be life-permitting go up. The same logic operates when you buy more than one lotto ticket in the hope of winning a lottery: the more tickets you buy, the better your chances.

The interesting thing about multiverse hypotheses is that they make use of an *observation selection effect* while exploiting the logic of multiple tickets in a lottery. Given the sheer number of physically distinct universes, it is probable that at least one of them would support life. More than that, since we wouldn't exist if the universe wasn't right for life, we could *only ever* have observed a universe that was life-permitting. Put these two points together and you have what looks like a pretty good explanation of fine-tuning: the multiverse hypothesis explains why there is a life-permitting universe, and an observation selection effect explains why we observe our universe to be one of that kind.

Note that we accept the same line of reasoning in at least one other cosmological case. If we want to know why Earth is home to complex forms of life, we can note that had it sat very much closer to the Sun its surface would be too hot for anything to live. Very much further away and it would be too cold for liquid water, and hence too cold for life as well. [14] While the chances of Earth having been within the right "goldilocks" band of distance from the Sun may not have been great, if there are very many stars and planets it was likely that at least *some* planets

---

[14] Ignoring possibilities like chemical and geothermal energy, which could well provide for oases of simple life on planets and moons very distant to their star.

would have ended up there around their parent star. If some of those planets come with chemical compositions supportive of life, it would not be surprising if some in turn end up with life on them. And of course, we could only ever have found ourselves evolving on a planet that wasn't too hostile to the emergence of life for it to form.

One notable difference between these two cosmological cases is that while we can look out and see other stars, we cannot look out and see other universes.[15] Does that really matter, though? Epistemically it is not clear that it should. We have no right to expect that the entire contents of reality should sit within the reaches of our biological senses or technology, and hence cannot just assume that the limit of what we can see (or detect) is the limit of what there is.

While the god hypothesis and the multiverse hypothesis are explanatory rivals, it is worth noting that they are not actually mutually exclusive of one another, even if that is how they are most often treated.[16] To put that another way, accepting the truth of one of them does not strictly require denying the truth of the other. God could have created a universe-generating mechanism instead of creating the universe directly, for example, with the idea that a universe-generating mechanism would inevitably lead to a universe very much like ours (along with many others, of course). There are costs to the merits of the god hypothesis in arguing something like this, however. If the size of the mystery that surrounds a universe-generating physics is much less than the size of the mystery that surrounds our universe having life-permitting characteristics, the value of the god hypothesis in explaining the universe-generating physics will be less impressive than when it is employed to explain the life-permitting physics of the universe directly.[17] This is why the god hypothesis and the multiverse hypothesis tend to be treated as rivals when it comes to fine-tuning: although the two are not logically incompatible, the success of the multiverse hypothesis does stand to undermine the evidential support the god hypothesis might otherwise pull from the problem of fine-tuning directly.

---

[15] At least directly. According to some inflationary models it may be possible to indirectly detect the existence of other universes by looking for marks left by collisions between them on our universe's cosmic microwave background.

[16] Bostrom (2002).

[17] However, if there are no naturalistic explanations of the universe-generating mechanism, the god hypothesis would still fill an explanatory gap at that point, even if it is only less impressively so than when compared with what it stands to do in connection to the universe's fine-tuning.

Perhaps the most prominent scientific theory out there right now with multiverse implications is inflationary theory. While you don't *need* inflationary physics to have a multiverse, the physics of inflation provides a natural way of getting one, and as a research program inflation has received a tremendous amount of scientific attention in the last 30 years.

Inflation theory came about in the 1980s as an attempt to solve outstanding problems with the standard Big Bang model of the early universe. The Big Bang theory tells us that the universe began around 13.8 billion years ago in a very hot and dense initial state, and that it violently expanded from that initial state to cool and evolve into what we see today. Considerable evidence exists for the idea that the universe began with a Big Bang. For example, it was discovered by Erwin Hubble in the 1920s that almost all other galaxies that populate the universe are getting further and further away from us, and that the rate they are receding away at is proportional to their distance: the further away they are, the faster away they are traveling. If you take this present situation and reverse it back in time, it is clear that the universe must have started out as a single point, which is exactly what the Big Bang theory tells us was the case.

Four decades after this it was discovered that the universe is bathed in a sea of microwave radiation with a temperature of around 2.7 degrees Kelvin (about −270 degrees Celsius, or −455 degrees Fahrenheit). The interesting thing about this light is that it comes to us from all directions in space. It was realized that it must be a cosmic relic of the intense light that would have existed at the time when the early universe was explosively expanding. If we could rewind the tape of the universe back and watch it as it went, we would see the temperature of the cosmic light steadily grow to be many tens of billions of degrees as the universe contracted down to its tiny, ferociously hot beginning.

Though the evidence for an initial Big Bang is compelling, the standard model cosmologists used to describe it has always been encumbered by a number of problems. Prime among these is an inability to answer the following two key questions: why is the light we receive from the cosmic microwave background so homogeneous (i.e., uniform), and why is the universe so "flat"?

First, the homogeneity problem. Better known as the *horizon problem*, the mystery here relates to the fact that the light that makes up the cosmic microwave background is very nearly the same in temperature and density in all directions. What that in turn indicates is that the temperature and density of the different regions of the early universe must have also been very nearly uniform, for that is where the light came from. The question is, how did the early universe get to be like that?

To help illustrate why this is such a puzzle, think about what happens if you drop an ice cube into a glass of water. Because the water is warmer than the ice, heat is transferred from the water to the ice cube. This causes the ice to melt and the water to cool down. The situation inside the glass therefore goes from a nonuniform state where one bit is cold (the ice cube) and one bit is warm (the surrounding water) to a more uniform state where all the bits are the same temperature.

The different regions of the early universe would have interacted with one another in this same kind of way. Any regions that were initially hotter and denser than others would have interacted with those next to them that weren't to produce a situation that was more uniform overall. In this handy way, any differences that existed between different regions of space at the very earliest moments would have been smoothed out. Though this explanation of the puzzle makes sense, there is one rather unfortunate problem with it: it can't possibly have happened that way.

Why not? Well, ever since the publication of Einstein's special theory of relativity in 1905, it has been a cornerstone of our understanding of the universe that nothing can travel faster than the speed of light. This is not because light possesses some special power to tell other things how fast they can travel, but because that particular speed—300,000 kilometers per second—represents the maximum speed of *anything* physical. From the existence of this cosmic speed limit, it follows that no information can ever travel from a point A to a point B within the universe more quickly than light can travel between those two points, because nothing physical can act to transfer that information faster than 300,000 kilometers per second. The horizon problem with the Big Bang theory comes from this simple fact.

Imagine taking a very powerful telescope and looking out to the edge of the observable universe. What you would see is an image of galaxies that are so far away their light has only just now had time to reach us. If you then swung the telescope around the other way and pointed it in the opposite direction, you would see the exact same thing but on the other side of the observable universe. Now, because these galaxies lie directly opposite to one another, it follows that they cannot see each other, for we sit in the middle of them and their light is only now reaching us. But that means they can't presently be in any causal contact with one another, either, because the distance their light has traveled represents the maximum range they can affect anything within.

What about in the past, though? Could regions of the universe that are not presently interacting because they are too far away have interacted when it was younger? It turns out the answer is no. If you could rewind the tape of the universe all the way back to the beginning, what you would find is that while the matter in the universe gets increasingly compacted, the horizons of light (and hence horizons of possible interaction) that extend out from any region of space shrink at a greater rate than the rate at which those regions merge together at. This means that it wasn't any easier for regions of the universe to causally "speak" to one another in the past—it was actually harder. But this means that the incredible uniformity of temperature and density in the early universe can't have been produced *after* the Big Bang—it had to be there before it got underway.[18] This is a problem, for just chalking up the early uniformity to a brute fact about the universe explains nothing about why that was so.

The "flatness problem," as it is known, concerns the shape of the universe. As we saw earlier in the chapter, matter has the interesting

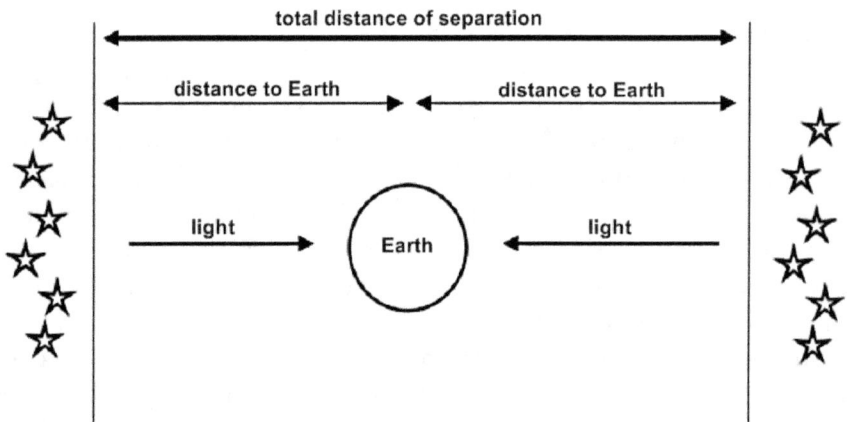

Figure 5.4: The horizon problem. Light from galaxies lying at opposite edges of the observable universe has had enough time since the Big Bang to reach Earth, but not enough time to reach each other. Each galaxy must therefore be "blind" to the existence of the other.

---

[18] Vilenkin (2006).

property of making space warp around itself. While this occurs most noticeably in the immediate vicinity of massive objects like planets and stars, all objects, from individual atoms to pens and people, affect the curvature of space. One of the major consequences of this is that the universe's overall shape is also affected by its contents.

The three most basic shapes the universe can have are open, closed, and flat. In an open universe the fabric of space is curved away from itself, just like the sides of a horse saddle. In a closed universe the fabric of space is bent into the shape of a sphere. Finally, in a flat universe the geometry of space is perfectly flat like any ordinary sheet of unwrinkled paper. What shape the universe has today is closely related to the amount of matter and energy it contains and the explosive power of the Big Bang in setting things into motion. If the mass-energy density of the universe had been slightly larger at the time of the Big Bang, it would have caused the early universe to curl up into a closed geometry and collapse almost immediately after it began expanding. If the density had been slightly less, its shape would have been open and the rate of its expansion would

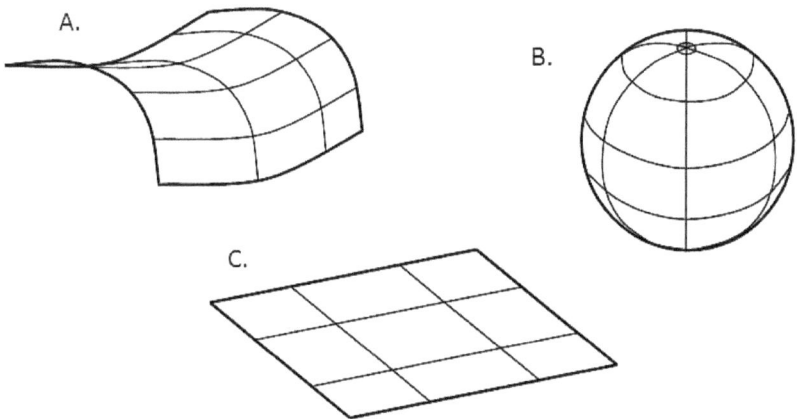

Figure 5.5: The shape of the universe. Represented here in a dimensionally-simplified way, universe A is open, B is closed, and C is flat. Astronomers have measured the shape of the universe by looking at the way light reaches us from very distant galaxies, and those measurements indicate that it is very close to being almost perfectly flat across observable distances.

have driven its contents apart much too quickly for gravity to have had a chance to gather it together and form stars and galaxies.

As far as we can tell today, our universe is flat. In order for that to be the case, the mass-energy density at the start had to be very close to what is called the "critical density." This is the point at which the values of the mass-energy density and the expansion rate are in balance and yield a flat spatial geometry.[19] Now, because flat universes sit on a very, very fine line between collapsing too early or expanding too rapidly, asking "Why is the universe flat?" amounts to asking "Why is the amount of mass-energy in the universe just right to not collapse only moments after expansion started, or fly apart too quickly for any meaningful structure to form?"[20]

The issue becomes particularly acute when you consider that the expansion of the early universe tends to drive its shape *away* from flatness. If the universe had started out with a mass-energy density parameter one percent away from flatness towards closed, for example, in less than a minute after expansion began that departure would have increased to 100 percent and in less than three minutes the universe would have collapsed.[21]

The propensity of the universe to be driven away from flatness means that, in order for it to be as flat as it is today, it needed to be *extraordinarily* flat to begin with. In fact, according to one calculation, it had to be within an astonishing 0.00000000000001 percent of the critical value at the one-second mark.[22] Only by being that close to flatness at that time could it have remained as flat as we find it today, some 13.8 billion years down the road. While it is possible to chalk this up to yet another brute fact about the Big Bang, doing so does not sit very well with the effort to find a better explanation for things than, "Well, it just happened that way."

Although the flatness and horizon problems were known to researchers as early as the 1960s, they were almost never discussed. One

---

[19] The universe cannot actually be *exactly* flat because the matter and energy in it cause local indentations in spacetime. If you average things out, however, you can get something like flatness.
[20] The correlation between what shape the universe has and what its cosmic fate is slated to be changes once you allow for a positive cosmological constant (i.e., "dark energy" that causes the expansion of the universe to accelerate rather than coast along unaffected). It wasn't known until recently that our universe actually is actually speeding up in its expansion, however.
[21] Vilenkin (2006).
[22] *Ibid.*

reason why was because nobody had the slightest clue how to solve either of them. Beyond that, though, they raised very hairy metaphysical questions about times and physical states prior to the Big Bang. Working physicists therefore largely set them aside as questions that physics was either not ready to answer yet, or that did not properly belong within physics.[23]

This all changed in the 1980s when a bright postdoctoral physicist reintroduced the problems in the course of proposing a solution to them. The physicist in question was Alan Guth, and the theory he proposed was inflation theory.

The heart of inflation theory requires a significant revision to how the universe is modeled to begin. The standard Big Bang account posits that the universe underwent an explosive expansion at all points in space 13.8 billion years ago. Thrown into motion by the power of the Big Bang, the expansion of the universe is taken as having started out fast and then having been slowed down ever since by the weak but far-reaching effect of gravity. The inflationary model changes the details of this by having the universe's expansion start out slowly, undergo an incredibly fast phase of constantly accelerating expansion, and then return to a situation where gravity works to slow everything down. It is the continuously accelerating aspect of the inflationary scenario that is important, for that is what will work to solve the flatness and horizon problems.

The mechanism that inflation theory proposes as having been behind the universe's accelerating rate of expansion is something called *false vacuum*. We'll get to why it is called *false* vacuum in just a moment, but for now just note that vacuum is what you would have left if you could subtract all matter and radiation out of any given region of space. While we usually think of empty space as nothing at all, we saw just a moment ago that that cannot be right: empty space has a shape and it can be stretched and shrunk. Not only that, modern physics takes there to be energy in the fabric of empty space. Because Einstein's famous $E=mc^2$ equation treats matter and energy as essentially different manifestations of each other, to say that empty space has energy amounts to saying that it has mass. (Indeed, one way to talk about how much energy is contained in empty space is to work out how much matter that energy would be equivalent to if it was converted.)

There are two important things to understand about vacuum energy. First, whereas things with mass and energy are usually gravitationally

[23] Brawer (1996), Vilenkin (2006).

attractive, the energy that is uniformly suffused throughout space produces a gravitationally *repulsive* effect. The reason why was given by Einstein. What the general theory of relativity tells us is that it is not *just* the mass and energy of something that determines its gravitational influence, but its *pressure* as well. If you could take Jupiter in your hands and compress it down to be just half the size it was, for example, you would increase the gravitational attraction that Jupiter exerts. True, by compressing it you would also be adding energy to it, for it would require energy from your arms to compress it down (just as it takes energy from your arms to pump up a bike tire). Yet the energy you would be adding in compressing Jupiter down would be less than what is needed to account for the total increase in its gravity. In other words, pressure (and not *just* the energy added in the process of creating pressure) independently affects the strength of the gravitational force an object exerts.

If pressure adds to the attractive gravity of something, does tension (i.e. negative pressure) take away from it? According to general relativity, it does. If you took a rubber band and stretched it out, for example, this would add a very slight repulsive gravitational force. While this is certainly strange, it is attested to by the equations of one of the most successful scientific theories of all time.

It turns out that the universe is no different, and that if the vacuum of space has a uniform positive energy, it will exist in a state of tension. If the amount of energy in the vacuum of space is great enough, the tension this generates will cause a repulsive gravitational force that *exceeds* the conventional attractive gravitational pull of that same positive energy. And should that happen, empty space will want to repel things within it more than it wants to attract them together. This gives rise to the physical reasoning that sits at the heart of inflation theory: if the vacuum energy of the early universe had been simply enormous and uniformly suffused throughout, it would have caused the universe to violently expand at an unthinkable rate.

The second important thing to note is that vacuum energy has the curious property of not diluting down in the same way that matter does. If you take a rubber band and stretch it out, its mass does not increase but redistributes over the area it is pulled. Vacuum energy is fundamentally different from this in that the total amount of energy contained in the vacuum is proportional to its volume. As space expands there will therefore be *more* total energy in the newly expanded vacuum than there was before. Since that increase in energy contributes to the overall gravitational repulsiveness of the vacuum, the inflationary expansion of space leads to a runaway process where the more vacuum there is, the more repulsive its gravitational force becomes, the faster it will therefore expand, the more vacuum there will then be, the greater its repulsive force will then become, the faster its rate of expansion will then be, and so on. This might seem as if it must violate the law of conservation of energy, but since the positive energy gained by the expansion of the vacuum is canceled out by the negative gravitational potential energy that applies to it, you don't actually get any true net increase.[24]

What makes the state of the vacuum with a large amount of energy suffused in it "false" is that it has a tendency to decay from that state into the lower energy, "true" vacuum state we see existing all around us today. The tendency of the early universe false vacuum to want to decay is very strong, and it may happen in as little as a millionth of a trillionth of a trillionth of a second. However, because of the exponential way in which space is driven to expand while in the false vacuum state, that is all the time that is needed for the universe to inflate to an unfathomable size.

So how does any of this solve the horizon and flatness problems? The horizon problem is solved in the fact that, before inflation takes hold, there is a short window of time where the different regions of the universe are able to directly communicate with one another. It is during this time that they enter a state of equilibrium and look like one another. After that phase inflation kicks in and accelerates everything away from itself, but by this stage the remarkable agreement that exists between the different regions of the universe will have already been established. It's a bit like taking a glass of water, allowing an ice cube to melt in it, and then throwing it on the kitchen floor—it's no surprise that the water is the same temperature when it's spread over the floor's surface.

As for the flatness problem, it is solved by the fact that the exponentially accelerating rate of inflationary expansion drives the universe *towards* flatness, not away from it. For reasons similar to why Earth appears to be flat to those of us standing on its surface, if the universe was inflated to an unimaginably massive size very quickly early on, we could not help but see our observable region as being spatially

---

[24] Although I should mention that it's not clear whether we can talk about the total energy of the universe. If we can't, we naturally can't say that the total amount of energy of the universe remains unchanged.

flat, for that part of it would represent just a minuscule fraction of its total volume.

As an added bonus to all of this, inflation theory even solves something called the *monopole problem*. The monopole problem isn't so much a problem for the standard Big Bang model as it is a problem for grand unified theories (GUTs). GUTs deal with physics at extremely high energies, and that is exactly the kind of physical situation that would have existed shortly after the Big Bang. All versions of GUTs predict the existence of magnetic monopoles—very massive long-lived particles that have the rather interesting property of having a single magnetic charge (either positive or negative). This is quite different from our ordinary experience with magnets of course, which always have two poles of opposite magnetic charge. The problem with GUTs and magnetic monopoles is two-fold. First, if GUTs are correct there should have been an enormous number of magnetic monopoles created shortly after the Big Bang. Yet given how massive magnetic monopoles are supposed to be—somewhere in the order of a quadrillion times the mass of a proton—this would have led to the gravitational collapse of the universe a very long time ago. Second, nobody has ever seen a magnetic monopole. If so many exist, where exactly are they all hiding?

Inflation theory gives us the answers. Since only as many magnetic monopoles are produced as there are observable regions of the universe at the time of their creation, and since when inflation gets going all of those cosmic horizons are separated from one another by the enormous expansion of space, the magnetic monopoles would have been diluted down by inflation to such an incredible extent that we are incredibly unlikely to ever find one.[25]

At this point you might be thinking, "Ok, that's great, but where is the multiverse in all of this?" The answer comes from the false vacuum and the rate of its expansion. While the false vacuum tends to decay into non-inflating bubbles of true vacuum very quickly, when exactly this happens is affected by quantum fluctuations in the value of the vacuum

---

[25] Earman and Mosterin (1999). It is hoped that no new magnetic monopoles are created when inflation energy is turned into matter and radiation with the decay of the false vacuum. Earman and Mosterin make clear that they do not regard magnetic monopoles as a problem for the Big Bang theory specifically—it is a problem for GUTs and any version of inflation that relies upon GUTs. If inflation should rely upon GUTs, the fact that it provides a solution to the monopole problem cannot be used as extra reason to believe inflation theory—it just means that inflation theory won't face an additional problem.

energy in those regions. While some regions of false vacuum will manage to decay into true vacuum within a certain period of time, others will remain momentarily stuck in the false energy state by quantum fluctuations that push their energy values higher. Since those regions will continue to inflate and produce more regions with the same false vacuum energy value, their continued expansion essentially leads to more and more regions of false vacuum being created.

The trick of it is that even though all of the newly created regions are subject to decay, overall the false vacuum is inflating so unthinkably quickly that its total volume increases much faster than the rate at which it can decay. Once it begins, then, common versions of inflation theory see inflation as never-ending, for there are always going to be regions of false vacuum that avoid decay to grow enormously and spawn more inflating false vacuum.

The picture we're left with is one of an infinite sea of false vacuum with islands of true vacuum constantly popping out of it. As soon as those bubbles form, they are carried away from one another by the constantly expanding false vacuum in-between.

In order for inflation theory to solve other problems of fine-tuning beyond the horizon and flatness problems, like the strength of gravity or the weak nuclear force, each of the bubble universes needs to be characterized by different values for their physical constants. While it is unlikely that any one universe will be compatible with the existence of life, if the size of the multiverse is exceedingly large or infinite, this becomes either entirely possible or certain.

It should be stressed that establishing the existence of a multiverse was never a motivation behind the development of inflationary cosmology. Rather, multiverses are an immediate consequence of the physical mechanism that inflation theories use to solve the horizon, flatness, and monopole problems. The multiverse aspect of inflation theory is not contrived, then, but follows directly out of its essence.

Though the idea of inflation presently dominates the field of cosmology, the theory itself is not without problems. For one thing, questions can be asked about where the false vacuum originally came from and how it obtained enough energy to start inflating. One possibility that has been considered there is that a tiny region of false vacuum just spontaneously popped into existence at some point through

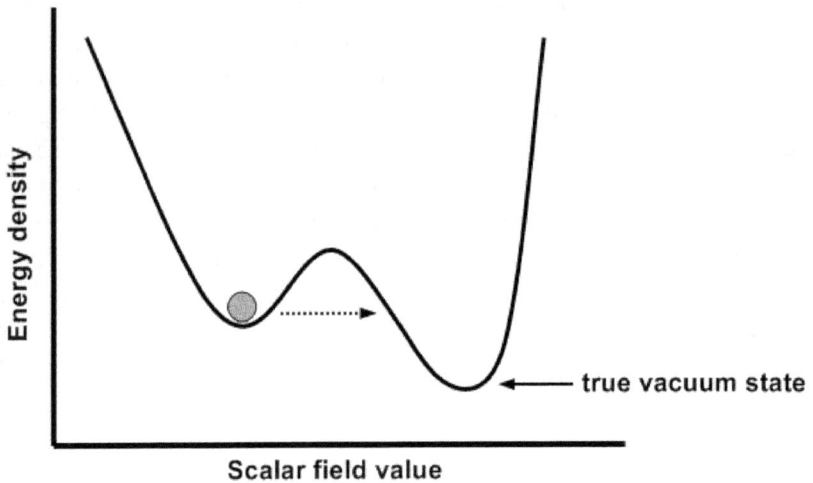

Figure 5.6: "Old" inflation.[26] The valleys in the diagram represent natural points for the value of the inflaton field to settle into. In Guth's original formulation the value of the inflaton field starts out in a "false" vacuum state that is separated from a lower energy, "true" vacuum state by an energy barrier. This setback is only temporary, for it is possible for the ball to "quantum tunnel" through the energy barrier and appear on the other side. When this happens, a bubble of true vacuum forms in the sea of surrounding inflating false vacuum and expands at a speed approaching that of light.

random quantum processes. The size of the newborn false vacuum region matters a great deal for its survival. If it is too small, the mass-energy it contains will gravitate too strongly and will cause the mini-universe to immediately collapse down to a point. However, if the size of the mini-universe is large enough there will be enough false vacuum in it to overcome that gravitational attraction and expand exponentially fast.[27]

---

[26] Vilenkin (2006).

[27] See Vilenkin (2006). While the spontaneous formation of a universe with the sufficiently large size is much less likely than a universe that is too small, it is theoretically possible for a universe that is initially too small to spontaneously quantum tunnel through to a size that is large enough to inflate. Through a double quirk of quantum mechanics, then, it is thought to be possible that a universe could pop into existence, jump to a larger size, and end up inflating.

It is not just the fact that a region of false vacuum existed at some point or that it had enough energy to begin inflating that needs an explanation, however. The energy that drives inflation is contained in a quantum field called the *inflaton field* (the "i" from inflation is intentionally dropped).[28] While inflation requires the existence of a field to confer space with the energy needed for exponentially fast expansion, the theory doesn't tell us why the inflaton field has a potential energy curve that is consistent with successful inflation. The problem is, many curves are possible, and not all of them are consistent with successful inflation. The issue is one of some importance, and can be better explored by imagining how a ball would roll down a hilly landscape.

In Alan Guth's original formulation of inflation theory, the potential energy curve of the inflaton field looks like what is depicted in figure 5.6. The height of the ball on the landscape represents the amount of energy contained in the inflaton field in a particular region of space, while its distance along represents the value of the field in that region. What the shape of the potential energy curve does is set the relationship between those two values as the field undergoes decay. We can see in this example that the ball has settled into a valley that is separated from a second valley by an energy barrier. Because the energy density of the inflaton field is higher in that valley than in the second, this represents the false vacuum energy condition. If the value of the inflaton field remained there, the universe would be permanently stuck in a false vacuum condition and there would be no stars or galaxies to speak of.

Thanks to one of the many peculiarities of quantum mechanics, however, something interesting can happen: the ball can "tunnel" through the barrier and spontaneously appear on the other side.[29] When

---

[28] A field is an entity which exists with a value at every point in space. More familiar examples of fields include the magnetic field, the gravitational field, and the electric field. In some models the inflaton field is identified with an existing field, such as the Higgs field, but in others a new field is postulated in order to facilitate the inflationary mechanism.

[29] Quantum tunneling sounds like magic, and in a way it kind of is. In ordinary life we just don't see balls spontaneously tunneling through walls—let alone through whole hillsides—to appear on the other side of them. What has to be remembered, though, is that the quantum mechanical world of atoms and particles is a very different place to the world at our level of experience, and that quantum tunneling is a very real and empirically well-confirmed phenomenon that plays a role in a variety of different quantum-scale processes, including things like radioactive decay and the nuclear fusion of elements within stars.

this happens the false vacuum decays into true vacuum and expands very quickly in the sea of false vacuum surrounding it.

In Guth's original model, matter and radiation are formed when the walls of the bubbles of true vacuum collide and release the energy that is stored within them. Unfortunately, it was discovered not long after Guth went public with his ideas in seminars that this gave rise to a rather catastrophic prediction. If the rate of false vacuum decay is very rapid, the rate of true vacuum bubble formation will be high. While that in itself would be good, a rapid rate of vacuum decay would not leave enough time for flattening and smoothing of those regions to occur, and hence would not result in flat and uniform universes. On the other hand, if the rate of bubble formation is much slower, then because the bubbles of true vacuum all sit in a sea of exponentially expanding false vacuum, the mathematics of the situation makes it exceedingly unlikely that true vacuum bubbles would meet and collide in the right sort of way to produce matter-filled universes. It's a "damned if they do, damned if they don't" kind of situation.

When Guth finally got around to publishing a paper on inflation, he added a comment towards its end explaining that he had pressed ahead with publication despite the problems in the hope that others might be able to solve them.[30]

This they were able to do, but it required making a rather substantial change to the way that false vacuum was theorized to decay into true vacuum. Instead of relying on quantum tunneling through an energy barrier, "new" inflation posits that the value of the inflaton field rolls down a smooth gradient, as illustrated in figure 5.7.

The reconfigured shape of the potential energy curve allows the ball to smoothly transition from a high energy, false vacuum state to a low energy, true vacuum state without any interruption by an energy barrier. So long as the ball sits high up on the hill, the false vacuum will inflate at an exponentially rapid rate. When it decays smoothly down to the bottom, however, inflationary expansion ends and the ball oscillates back and forth at the minimum of the valley. As it does this, the energy that was contained in the inflaton field erupts into the universe as a shower of matter and light.

While quantum tunneling is not needed in new inflation, the evolution of the inflaton field still depends in a critical way upon quantum effects. Most significantly, the inflaton field's energy value in a

[30] See Guth (1981).

particular region of space is subject to random quantum fluctuations that can drive the ball jerkily back up or further down the energy hill. Since these fluctuations act upon the ball in a completely random way in different regions, one region of false vacuum can decay while another region, having just had its ball kicked further back up the hill, does not. Just as in the case of old inflation, then, new inflation results in bubbles of true vacuum universes popping out in an inflating sea of false vacuum. Because matter generation does not depend on the collision of true vacuum bubbles, however, the problem that vexed old inflation is avoided.

There is a new issue brought about, though, and that is that in order for new inflation to work the shape of the potential energy curve of the inflaton field has to be just right. If the curve is too steep, the ball will run down the hill too fast and inflation will end before there has been

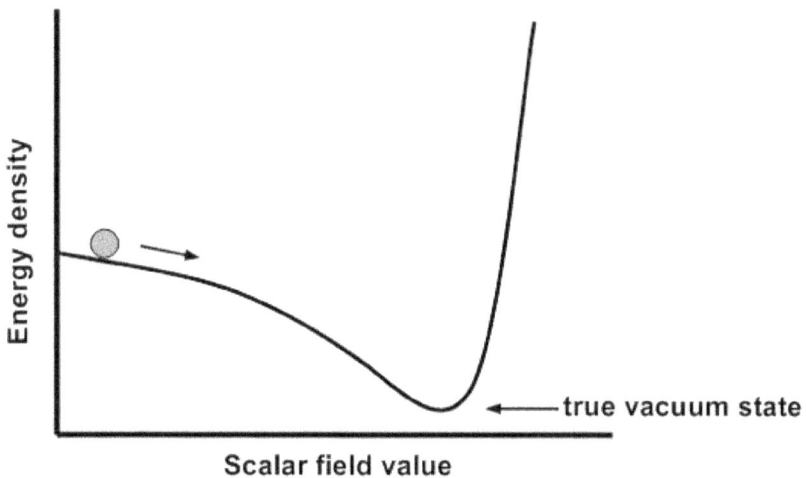

Scalar field value

Figure 5.7: **"New" inflation.**[31] Models of inflation since Guth's have re-envisioned the shape of the potential energy curve that controls the evolution of the field driving inflation. In this example the energy value of the field starts high up on a potential energy curve and then rolls steadily down a smooth gradient to reach the bottom. When it gets to the bottom, the value of the field oscillates back and forth in the minimum of the valley. This oscillation causes the energy that is contained in the field to be dumped into the universe as matter and light and allows the field to settle into a true vacuum state.

[31] Vilenkin (2006).

enough flattening of the universe. In essence, the energy potential curve needs to be fine-tuned so that inflation can successfully explain other cases of fine-tuning.[32]

Explanatorily speaking there is no great problem in that so long as the amount of fine-tuning that is required to construct a workable potential energy curve is less than what is required to explain other elements of the universe's fine-tuning via the inflationary mechanism. Still, when the ideal goal would be to discover a theory that requires either very little or no fine-tuning in order to explain fine-tuning, the fact that inflation requires some of its own may be a source of frustration.

A somewhat related criticism has been made of the patchwork-like theoretical picture that inflation theory contributes to of the universe. The standard cosmological model presently consists of the union of three things: the Big Bang theory, inflation theory, and dark energy. The last of these items was added after it was discovered in 1998 that the rate of the universe's expansion is actually speeding up, not slowing down (as you would expect under the attractive pull of gravity). The most natural explanation for this invokes the existence of an otherwise unseen ("dark") amount of energy contained in the vacuum of space. While this makes use of essentially the same physical concept that inflation theory relies on to get the exponential expansion of the early universe, the repulsive force of the dark energy is many, many orders of magnitude smaller than what would have been needed for inflation. In the minds of some, this leaves us with a less than completely natural collection of ideas tacked together as our accepted cosmological picture. Insofar as the naturalness or cohesiveness of ideas can be taken as a guide to truth, the fact that this has been needed can be taken as some grounds for thinking the overall theoretical picture is not right.[33]

Nevertheless, as things stand inflation is the accepted explanation of the Big Bang in the field of cosmology, and enormous amounts of time, energy, and money have been invested carrying out scientific research into it. What is relevant for us here is the fact that if inflation theory is true, the multiverse hypothesis is very probably true as well.

---

[32] Steinhardt and Turok (2008).
[33] *Ibid.*

The Deeper Physics Hypothesis

A third option involves claiming that the life-sensitive physical constants and parameters of the universe were determined to have the values they have by a deeper level of physics than we are currently aware of. What therefore seems to us to be a series of highly unlikely finely-tuned coincidences is really nothing of the sort, and if we could only uncover that deeper physics we would see why that is.

An analogy by Steven Weinberg helps to illustrate the essence of this idea.[34] Imagine a world that is perpetually shrouded in thick cloud, such that direct sunlight never reaches the people who live on its surface. Looking around, they might well wonder why the clouds shine brightly enough for life to exist. After all, much more light and the surface of their world would be too hot for anything to live, while much less light and the surface would be too cold. What a remarkable thing, then, that their world should receive enough light for life to survive and flourish.

What they do not know, of course, is that the universe is much larger than the cloudy horizons of their world. If they knew that they would know that the intensity of light through the clouds is determined by the brightness of the star their planet sits in orbit around, their planet's distance to that star, and the physical properties of the atmosphere. What accordingly appears to them to be just another basic fact about the physics of their world—that the clouds shine with that level of brightness—is actually the result of a deeper set of physical facts concerning where they sit in relation to the wider cosmos.

We can easily imagine in an analogous kind of way that the various constants that set the strength of things like the electromagnetic and the weak nuclear forces are determined to be what they are by other physical truths, and in just such a way that they effectively *had* to have their actual life-permitting values. If so, no multiverse or divine being would be needed to explain why our universe is life-permitting—it is life-permitting because somewhere in the physics of things those values are forced to be just as we see them.

Of course, we might still want to know *why* our universe ended up with a deep physics that constrains its higher level physical properties to fall within a life-permitting range.

---

[34] Weinberg (1993).

There are two possibilities there, each aligning with a weak and strong version of the deeper physics hypothesis.[35] In the strong version, there is taken as being just one self-consistent set of physical laws that any universe must have if it is to exist, and that leads (for reasons of mathematical necessity) to a universe with life-permitting properties identical to ours. In this version, any universe had to be exactly as ours is, for no other set of physical laws was possible.

On the weaker version, there are many possible self-consistent sets of physical laws, and hence not every universe needs to look exactly as ours does. However, it is still maintained that our universe came with a set of underlying physical laws that for reasons of mathematical necessity led to its higher level life-permitting physical character. Once those laws were in place, we simply couldn't have seen any other result: the universe *had* to be life-permitting, given its deeper physical makeup.

The Chance Hypothesis

A fourth possibility is to put the entire matter of life and fine-tuning down to chance. We know that the universe had to be in *some* way or another just to exist at all, and we know that extremely improbable events happen all the time. People win lotteries, hit holes-in-one, and get struck by lightning multiple times even though the chances of these things happening is low. Who is to say, then, that it could not have been by blind luck that the universe came out in a life-permitting way? According to the chance hypothesis, we are the beneficiaries of the equivalent of a cosmic lottery win, and there is no deeper explanation for fine-tuning than that.

Metaphysical Agnosticism

The fifth and final possibility we will consider is metaphysical agnosticism. Unlike the other options, agnosticism is not an attempt to explain (or explain away) fine-tuning. There are two main claims an agnostic might make. The first is that we simply cannot know (at least for now, but also possibly at any point in the future) what the true explanation of the improbability of the universe is, given that it is

---

[35] Davies (2006).

improbable. Since this is exactly what we will be interested in looking at, this much about agnosticism can be set aside and answered as we go. If you find that any of the explanations brought up in the discussion are convincing, you will be implicitly disagreeing with the agnostic who thinks that no hypothesis can be reasonably favored over any other.

A second and more interesting agnostic claim is that there is no justification for saying that the universe is improbable. Of course, if we can't say that the universe is improbable, we can't say that it is fine-tuned. And if there's no justification for claiming the universe is fine-tuned, there is no reason to seek an explanation of it.

It is to this agnostic claim that we will turn in the next section. I should say in advance that while the philosophical discussion of it does get a bit tricky, it is still worth persevering with, for the whole debate depends on the validity of fine-tuning as something that applies to the universe. While I have done my best to present the issue in a clear and accessible way, readers who find themselves getting frustrated may feel free to skip ahead to the next section.

Battling with Infinity

One of the most challenging critiques given to arguments based on fine-tuning in recent years was put forward by three philosophers, Mark Colyvan, Jay Garfield, and Graham Priest.[36] Among other criticisms, the authors argued that the way that notions of probability are used in relation to claims about fine-tuning is entirely questionable and that the wisest position to take about the whole matter is one of unknowing. Their argument takes no particular side between the different metaphysical camps; if they're right, atheists who use the multiverse or a deeper physics or chance to explain the fine-tuning of the universe are just as wrongheaded as those who explain it via the existence of a divine intelligence.

So what exactly is the issue? Suppose that there is a physical constant k that governs one of the physical features of the universe, and whose value must fall somewhere within the upper and the lower values of the interval [x, y] if the universe is to permit life. Think of the gravitational constant as an example. Its value could be a bit higher or a bit lower than

---

[36] Colyvan, Garfield, and Priest (2005). See also McGrew, McGrew, and Vestrup (2001).

what it actually is with no ill effect to life. However, there is a certain point both above and below its actual value where, if the value were to lie outside of that range, the universe would have turned out lifelessly. Those extremes form a two-sided limit that the gravitational constant needs to fall within if the universe is to be life-permitting.

Here is the question: what is the *total* range of possible values for k such that we can then say how improbable it is that the value of k would fall within the life-permitting range [x, y]? In other words, how many different values outside the life-permitting range can the constant k logically take? Since there is nothing logically restricting k from having any value whatsoever, it seems as though we should say k could have an infinite number of different values. The problem with this is that it causes major headaches for anyone who wants to say that it is improbable that k should fall within [x, y].

To see why, let's look at a more familiar problem of probability. Suppose we have a deck of cards and want to know what the chances of drawing out the three of clubs in a single random draw are. Since we know there are 52 cards in a standard deck, and since we know there is only 1 of each card in a standard deck, the chances are easy to calculate: it is 1 in 52. What if the deck was magical, though, and had an infinite number of cards of infinite variety in it? Even though there's still only one of each type of card, the chances of pulling out the three of clubs would be 1 over infinity. But 1 over infinity is equal to it being a zero (or an undefined) probability.

You can see why k being logically capable of taking on any value would be such a great problem, then. If the different possibilities for k's value are infinite, the probability of k having a value that falls within the range [x, y] is zero (or undefined). And it doesn't matter how wide or narrow the life-permitting range [x, y] happens to finitely be, for the result is always going to be the same when measured against infinity.

It follows from this line of argument that we cannot call the universe fine-tuned, for the values of the universe's physical constants are subject to this problem.

The issue here fundamentally comes from the way that infinite numbers interact with finite numbers. Indeed, from the point of view of minds like ours, infinity has some very strange properties. For example, infinities can be either bound or unbound, where bound means being limited in some respect. The set of all positive numbers (1, 2, 3, 4...) is both infinite and bound, because while the set of all positive numbers is infinite, it excludes all negative numbers (-1, -2, -3, -4...). Infinities can also be nested or unnested, where being nested means there are infinities sitting inside infinities. You might think of a room of mirrors where each mirror contains the infinite reflection of itself in another, or if not that, of a magical map that is so detailed that it even includes itself in its depiction of the world from above. Given that the map shows itself, it also shows itself showing itself, and thus itself showing itself showing itself, and so on, resulting in an infinite recursion of maps within maps within maps. Strangely enough, infinities can even come in different sizes, meaning that some infinities can be larger or smaller than others in size.

The paradoxical nature of infinity has the ability to wreak serious havoc on ordinary intuitions of probability. An easy example involves a lottery with an infinite number of tickets for sale. Strange as it might seem, it would make no difference how many tickets a person bought if they only bought a finite amount, for they could not win. The reason why is exactly the same as it was before with fine-tuning: whether they owned one ticket or one hundred million, the range of tickets in the draw is infinite (and hence the chances of winning in both cases is zero or undefined).

Likewise, suppose that in some imaginary metaphysical space you found an apple and decided to cut it up with a knife infinitely many times. By doing this it seems you would have an infinite number of parts of the apple in front of you. And, if you were to then piece the parts of the apple back together, you would have the original apple once more. But, would you? After all, how can the sum of an infinite number of things add together to be a finite thing? Since you had an infinite number of apple parts, shouldn't the apple now be infinitely big, for an infinite number of things aggregated together is infinite? Well, perhaps, but then again perhaps not. The parts of an infinitely divided apple could each be regarded as being infinitely small, since they were all divided an infinite number of times over. If so, though, how can the reconstituted apple come to anything at all (whether finite or infinite)? After all, if an infinity of zero is zero, the sum of infinitely many infinitely small slices should add up to nothing, shouldn't it? Strangely, then, it seems that the sum of an infinitely divided apple should be both finite, infinite, and nothing all at once.

It is not just within the domain of imaginary spaces that infinity causes problems. If our universe is infinite, it seems unavoidable that somewhere out there in the deepest reaches of space is another "you" on a planet that looks identical to Earth. Unsettling as that thought might be, since it is both logically and physically possible for there to be another world out there identical to our own with another "you," the infinite expanse of the universe would ensure that it is actually the case.[37] Worse than that, if the universe really is truly infinite there won't just be one other "you" somewhere out there—there will be an infinite number. And while an infinite number of these doppelgangers will have just read the exact same sentence as you did reading this book, an infinite number of them will also be doing completely different things. For example, somewhere out there "you" will have just won $50 million, saved that world from the plotting of a criminal mastermind, and been visited by aliens. And for every incredible event that might just have happened, there will also be an infinite number of "you" who have just experienced something that was either really bad or entirely mundane and trivial (clearly the latter segment in the collection of "you" must be doing something other than reading this book!). As hard as this might be to believe, we are required to accept it if the universe really is infinite in the appropriate sense.

When it comes to problems with infinity and fine-tuning, the obvious solution would be to try and restrict the range of values that physical constants can take. The problem there is, how can we justifiably do that? While there could be natural limits to the values of physical constants, knowing where to draw them is a mystery. Moreover, simply drawing an arbitrary limit on those values will beg the question, for we will want to know why we should draw the limit there and not elsewhere.

How to respond, then? We can start by noting that this argument against fine-tuning risks proving too much, for surely it should be possible (at least in principle) for there to be some empirical evidence of the existence of a designer or of a multiverse? Suppose we were to find "made by god" written on rocks and pebbles everywhere throughout the universe. This would count as rather startling and tangible evidence for the existence of god, would it not? If the same line of reasoning undertaken before is taken to hold, the answer is no. Why? Because finding "made by god" written throughout the universe would represent just one among an infinite number of different logical possibilities for how the universe could be, and from a purely logical standpoint the prior probability of any such formation would be 1 over infinity.[38] Such is the

---

[37] Assuming that exhaustive randomness applies, as it does with quantum mechanics.
[38] A fact which might suggest that it (along with every other conceivable state of the universe) is impossible—something our experience stands in direct conflict with.

conundrum of infinity that it stands to render even the most direct and obvious indications of god's existence nothing of the sort.

The same point holds true in evidential reverse. For example, the level of natural evil in the world could not be counted as evidence *against* the existence of god, either, for a world with just that level of natural evil would represent only one among an infinite number of logical possibilities for it (and so on). The actual content of the universe-wide conclusion doesn't matter, for the problem here is not one for the existence of god but for inductive reasoning. And since induction sits at the heart of scientific reasoning, this problem undermines many ordinary scientific inferences, too. For example, the essence of the problem can be given a temporal twist so that if we know there are an infinite number of different universes that exist and take them as our guide, we can't have inductively favored expectations for how the future of our own universe will unfold, for all possible ways it could turn out will be represented infinitely many times over in the set of actual universes. Since we don't know which universe ours actually is among that infinite set, all outcomes for it must be said to be equally likely.

To give a concrete illustration, it is logically possible that gravity will suddenly cease tomorrow and everything that is unattached to the surface of Earth will float off into space. If there are an infinite number of universes exhaustively representing all logical possibilities, there will be an infinite number of universes identical to our own in every respect except that, for an infinite number of them, gravity will fail tomorrow, and for an infinite number of others, gravity will not fail tomorrow. Our universe's past would not provide any indication as to which set of universes it belongs to, for there are an infinite number of universes with exactly the same history as ours but that lose their gravity tomorrow, and an infinite number that do not. Which universe will ours turn out to be, then? Going by the numbers, there does not appear to be a way to tell.

Colyvan, Garfield, and Priest are aware of this problem, and their response is to say that because they are not the ones advocating a line of reasoning that relies upon logical probability, they are not the ones tasked with the burden of having to solve it.[39] In other words, yes, it is an issue for standard probability theory that it falls apart when infinity gets involved, but it is not up to them to know the answer. They are just arguing that in the absence of a solution, agnosticism about fine-tuning is the most rational position to adopt. Given the scope of their

---

[39] Colyvan, Garfield, and Priest (2005).

argument's application, however, it seems that agnosticism would be required about more than *just* fine-tuning.

This leads us into a second counterargument, and that is to point to the paradoxical nature of infinity as a reason to not let it weigh too heavily on the matter. Consider one of the Greek philosopher Zeno's most famous paradoxes. So the story goes, Achilles and an unusually accommodating tortoise were matched against one another in a running race. The match-up was arranged so that the tortoise would start halfway down the track. Zeno noted that by the time Achilles got to the tortoise's starting point, the tortoise would have moved closer to the finish line. When Achilles reached that new point, however, the tortoise would have moved on once again. Extending this line of reasoning out, it seems as if Achilles can never ever win the race, for he will always be catching up to where the tortoise just was before having moved on. Starting ahead, the tortoise must win.

"Absurd!" we say, but where exactly is the error? Even knowing directly from our own experience that faster-moving things can overtake slower-moving things, it wasn't easy for anyone back in Ancient Greece to say where Zeno's mistake was.

There are, I suppose, two different kinds of people. On one hand, there are those who, having committed themselves to the rigors of logical demonstration, would have elected to agree with Zeno and believe against the force of their own experience that Achilles could not have won the race. On the other, there are those who would have held firm to the convictions of their own experience and rejected the conclusion of the argument, even though they could not point to anything wrong with it beyond the fact that, by the light of experience, it *had* to be wrong.

Personally, I can't imagine myself having sided with Zeno; experience speaks much too loudly in favor of Achilles's victory over the tortoise, and it strikes me as being barely any better to be agnostic about the winner. If this attitude is not irrational, it must be rationally permissible—at least in some cases—to refuse to believe an apparently faultless argument if it blatantly conflicts with experience. If so, it is possible to extend this to the problem caused for fine-tuning arguments by infinity, given that the line of reasoning involved with them also undermines inductive inferences about the universe which we have compelling reason from experience to think are legitimate.

A third response is to be very clear that the intended sense of probability underlying fine-tuning arguments is not logical or statistical but epistemic.

Logical probability, as the name suggests, is the probability of something as determined by purely logical criteria. If the number of horses running in a race is seven, and you know nothing at all about them to advantage one over the others, one might say that the logical probability of any one of them winning is one in seven. In the context of fine-tuning, since it logically seems as though the value of a physical constant could be any real number whatsoever, the logical probability for it to fall within any finite range within the infinite set of real numbers ends up being zero or undefined (as we saw).

Statistical probability, in contrast, seeks the probability of something by looking at its relative frequency within an appropriately chosen reference class. Suppose you want to know what the chances of a three coming up on a certain die is. Rather than note that the die has six sides and assume that each side has an equal probability of being rolled, you might have a machine roll the die ten thousand times and record how often the different sides come up within that sample of rolls. This would have the added benefit of potentially revealing any hidden biases in the die itself. It would be fantastic if we could do something like this with the universe, for that would really help us understand not only the size of the range of possible values its constants can take but also their distribution within that range. Sadly, this is completely out of the question, for we cannot reroll the physics of our universe from the beginning or peer into other universes to see how they nomologically turned out.

Epistemic probability is different from logical and statistical probability in that it is a measure of the degree of confidence we should rationally have in the truth of a proposition, given what else we know. Because of this, epistemic probability is necessarily conditional to the information we have available and what we are assuming in interpreting that information. In the case of fine-tuning, what we are interested in is what has been called the *epistemically illuminated range*: the range of values over which we can make some reasonable inference as to what the effect on life would be, given what we currently know.[40] This, of course, is heavily dependent upon our present scientific knowledge of the universe.

---

[40] Collins (2003b).

Those values will still need to be limited in their possible range if epistemic probability is to function, though, so how can we do that reasonably? One suggestion that has been put forward is to look to the minimum and maximum observed values for physical constants in our universe and allow those to serve as the minimum and maximum possible values for any physical constant.[41] This is arguably not arbitrary, since it is informed by empirical observations of the range of values that physical constants actually take in our universe.[42] With the total range for those values then finite rather than infinite, the problem of infinity and fine-tuning can be avoided.[43]

Still, one has to admit that these are all less than perfectly satisfying responses to a difficult logical problem. While we should carry a sense of caution away from that fact, I don't think it needs to lead to the conclusion that the universe cannot be said to be improbable. All it needs to do is remind us of the ever-present possibility of our error, and the need to frame any conclusions we draw about the universe's origins based on fine-tuning as conditional to the legitimacy of the fine-tuning claims underpinning them.

---

[41] *Ibid.*

[42] Another possibility worth mentioning is to invoke Solomonoff induction and assign each universe in the infinite range of those that are logically possible a prior probability in accordance with the formula $1/2^L$, where L is the length of a program written in a binary universal programming language describing it. Though the prior probabilities this method will generate will no doubt all be *very, very, very* low, they will also have the feature of being exponentially improbable as the length of the program increases, and that mercifully means that those prior probabilities will all sum to 1 (in just the same way that if you were to add the converging series $1/2 + 1/4 + 1/8 + 1/16 + 1/32 + 1/64...$ together, it would all sum to 1.) That is what we need, for even if there are an infinite number of possible universes in that case, this method allows them to each have a non-zero probability, thereby avoiding the problem. This method will only work if no two universes have descriptions that run the same program length L.

[43] But what if the true range of physically possible values extends well outside of that range? That surely is a very real possibility. However, this will only cause significant strife for any arguments based upon fine-tuning if the true but finite range of values that encompasses the empirically defined range leads to a higher frequency of universes with life than values selected within the empirically defined range. If it does not, limiting the values to the empirically defined range will actually make the problem of fine-tuning appear less severe than it actually is.

Goals and Values: Axiology in Science

If agnosticism hasn't persuaded you, the natural next question to ask is how we can rationally decide between the different candidate hypotheses before us. Help in making a choice can come by looking at how theory-choice decisions are made in the sciences. Scientists, after all, are accustomed to making difficult choices between competing theories, and as a form of inquiry, science has been spectacularly successful.

So how does theory choice work in science? One of the fundamental goals of science, of course, is truth, and decisions about which theory to believe are made with that in mind. Unfortunately, it is impossible to tell whether a scientific theory is true simply by looking at it. What happens in practical terms, then, is that theories are assessed in light of a range of epistemic values. Epistemic values pick out traits or qualities in a theory that can be taken as connected with the truth.

We will take a closer look at eight such criteria for determining the truth of a theory: predictive accuracy, consistency, scope, simplicity, fruitfulness, explanation, symmetry, and aesthetics.[44] Keep in mind that if any of these values are not reliably connected with the truth, judging the merits of theories by them will potentially lead us astray of it. Which of them actually are connected with the truth, then, and to what extent, is a question of paramount importance.

Predictive Accuracy

Perhaps no other criterion is as important in the evaluation of scientific theories as predictive accuracy. In conjunction with background knowledge and other information about the world, theories in science are expected to give rise to testable predictions that, in the process of being tested, either confirm or disconfirm the theory. Indeed, the failure of a theory to give rise to any testable predictions may lead to that theory being labeled non-scientific.

---

[44] Though they are presented as distinct from one another, many of the values overlap in some way. For example, what makes a theory explanatorily strong or aesthetically beautiful may have much to do with the simplicity of that theory. The other thing to note is that there are pragmatic (rather than epistemic) reasons supporting the use of some of these values. For example, simpler theories may be easier to perform calculations on and conceptually work with, but that may be a point of fact entirely aside from their truth.

A good illustration of the power of prediction involves a historical dispute between Newtonians and Cartesians over the nature of gravity. Because of their views on gravity, the Newtonian and Cartesian theories of gravity offered conflicting expectations for the shape of Earth. If the Newtonian theory was right, Earth should have been slightly bulged around the equator. The reason had to do with the centrifugal effect of Earth's rotation around its own axis, which should have been greatest at the equator and nonexistent at the poles. The Cartesian theory of gravity suggested that the very opposite should have been true. Indeed, because Cartesian theory viewed gravity as the result of a vortex of invisible matter pressing down upon the surface of Earth, and because the movement of that vortex was taken to coincide with the rotation of Earth, Earth should have been thinner around its equator than at its poles (where the effect was understood to be the least).

In the eighteenth-century the Academy of Sciences in Paris sent out a scientific expedition to settle the dispute. Careful measurements were made at various places around the globe, and from this it was unequivocally concluded that Earth is indeed wider at the equator than at the poles. In a stunning example of the scientific method at work, Newton's theory was vindicated while Descartes's theory was falsified.[45]

While making predictions is important, making precise predictions is better than making vague predictions. Indeed, the more precise the predictions that a theory offers, the better that theory can be regarded as being (even before any testing is done).[46] One astronomical theory might tell us that there will be a lunar eclipse on the night of January 27 over North America, for example, while a second such theory might tell us both this and the time of its occurrence, down to the hour and the minute, and the location it is most visible from. If an eclipse is indeed observed on that night within the time frames that both theories specified, it stands out as being more in favor of the second theory that it was more precise with the time the eclipse occurred at. This doesn't mean the prediction of the other theory was wrong, of course—just that it wasn't as exact as that of the second.[47]

---

[45] Laudan (1990).

[46] Note that this is a purely methodological preference showing through. An exact but as yet unconfirmed prediction lends nothing to the truth of that theory, but it can still cause the theory to be thought of more positively by scientists who see the exactness of its (presently untested) predictions as a virtue.

[47] Salmon (1990).

Consistency

The consistency of a theory comes in two different measures. The demand for internal consistency refers to the unexciting requirement that a theory not be self-contradicting. If a theory assumes that the effect of pumping greenhouse gasses into the atmosphere is to both increase Earth's mean surface temperature *and* decrease Earth's mean surface temperature at the same time, it is quite clearly self-contradictory. According to the wisdom of logic, contradictory theories cannot possibly be true.

The more interesting side to consistency is external consistency, which stipulates that a theory should be consistent with what else is scientifically accepted as true. Charles Darwin's theory of evolution by natural selection faced a major external consistency problem when first proposed. While it was understood that the evolution of life from simple to more complex forms needed great lengths of time to occur, calculations based upon known processes of the age of Earth by the esteemed nineteenth-century physicist William Thomson (otherwise known as Lord Kelvin) showed that it could not have been more than about 400 million years old (this figure was later revised down to not more than 40 million years). This was not nearly enough time for Darwin's theory to have been right, and so left it with a rather great problem to account for.

Ernest Rutherford's model of the atom also suffered from an external consistency problem. On the basis of experiments involving firing helium nuclei at a thin sheet of gold and observing the angles they were deflected off at, Rutherford proposed that atoms must consist of negatively charged electrons orbiting around a very small and dense positively charged nucleus. The existing atomic model at the time held that atoms were an even mix of their positive and negative components (an arrangement that Rutherford recognized was incapable of explaining the pattern of deflections). Though Rutherford's model made good sense of what he had experimentally observed, it was also inconsistent with the classical theory of electrodynamics, which said that any charged particle that undergoes acceleration (i.e., experiences a change in either speed or direction) should radiate. Since on Rutherford's account electrons would be constantly changing direction as they orbited around the positively charged central nucleus, they should have radiated. But in radiating the electrons would have had to lose energy, and if they did that they would quickly fall into the nucleus and be annihilated. This clearly isn't the case, for we know that matter is not almost instantly self-annihilating (we wouldn't be here if it was). Rutherford's atomic model was therefore inconsistent with a well-accepted scientific theory, and insofar as consistency with that theory was a positive virtue, that was a bad thing for Rutherford.

Happily for the two theories in question, these problems were eventually all ironed out. In Darwin's case it was found that Lord Kelvin's calculation had relied upon faulty assumptions concerning what kinds of physical processes occur inside Earth's core, and hence had vastly underestimated its true age. In Rutherford's case it took the Danish physicist Niels Bohr to fix the problem by making major modifications to Rutherford's essential idea. In order to do it, Bohr proposed that electrons exist in fixed orbital shells where their tendency is to occupy the lowest energy shell they possibly can, where only a certain number of electrons can occupy any one shell, where radiating movement occurs only when an electron jumps between shells of different energy levels, and where electrons in the lowest energy shell are stipulated *ad hoc* to be unable to collapse down any further towards the nucleus. Bohr's atomic model asked a lot, but it also allowed precise calculations to be made that, it turned out, sat in remarkably good agreement with experimental measurements (though this was only true in the case of the very simplest atomic element, hydrogen).

The take-home point of this is that even though things worked out well for both Darwin and Rutherford, the inconsistency of their theories with what else was regarded as being known at the time was still a serious problem for them. This gives us the general rule in science, which is that the more inconsistent a theory is with accepted background theory, and the more established that background scientific theory is, the worse the new theory may be regarded as being, all other things being equal.

Scope

The scope of a theory concerns the range of phenomena it extends over in explanation and prediction. It is often considered that the wider the scope of a theory, the better that theory is.

Consider the work of Johannes Kepler, who, on the basis of many days and nights spent pouring over astronomical data, first asserted in the seventeenth-century that the planets move in slightly elliptical (i.e. slightly squashed-circular) orbits. Prior to this, the prevailing idea had been that the planets moved in circles, but circular orbits could not make exact sense of observations of where they appear in the night sky.[48] Kepler noted that elliptical orbits *would*, however, and was eventually able to formulate three different laws to describe their motion around the Sun. Significantly, though, Kepler's laws were limited in application to *planetary* motion only.[49]

It was Isaac Newton who did the remarkable and kicked off the scientific revolution in earnest by connecting the orbits of planets with things as small and terrestrial as falling apples. As discussed earlier, Newton's theory of universal gravitation maintains that all objects with mass are attracted to one another, irrespective of where and what they are, by a force that is proportional to the product of their masses and inversely proportional to the square of their separating distance. Using this idea and his three laws of motion, Newton was able to explain the elliptical orbits of the planets, the path of comets in and out of the solar system, the fall of objects towards Earth, the wobble of Earth's axial tilt, and even the daily rising and falling of the tides. It was perhaps the single greatest scientific achievement of all time.

For all its merits, there was something that Newton's theory could not explain, and that was a peculiarity to do with the orbit of Mercury. Because the orbits of the planets are elliptical rather than circular, every planet has a point in its orbit where it is closest to the Sun. This point is called the *perihelion*, and the perihelion is said to precess when it moves around the Sun. The curious thing about Mercury's perihelion was that it drifts around at a rate that Newtonian theory was unable to explain. When Einstein came up with his general theory of relativity, however, it could explain that rate, and did so along with every other fact previously explained by Newtonian theory. This meant that Einstein's theory had a wider scope than Newton's theory, explaining all that Newton's theory did plus at least one thing it didn't.

To take scope as a scientific value is to say that all other things being equal, the broader the scope of a theory, the "better" that theory is. Were we to measure them purely in terms of scope and nothing else, we should

---

[48] Saying "prior to this" is actually slightly misleading, for Kepler's idea of elliptical orbits did not take hold with everyone instantly. Indeed, Galileo, who perhaps did more than anyone to advance the case for the heliocentric model, clung to the idea of circular planetary orbits for the reason that they were simpler than elliptical orbits were, and also (to him) more beautiful.

[49] Or, almost. The moons of planets were found to obey Kepler's laws as well.

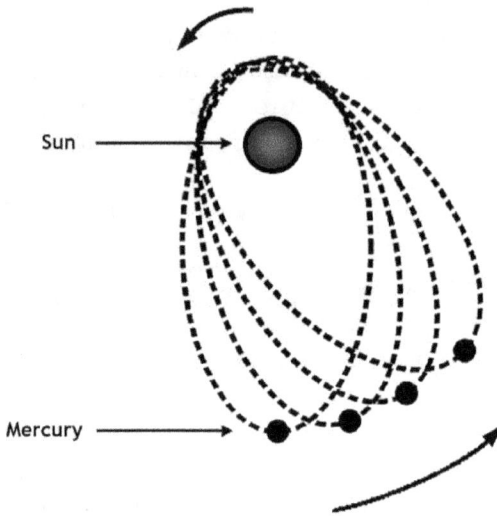

Figure 5.1: the precession of the perihelion of Mercury. As Mercury completes an orbit, the point of its closest approach to the Sun drifts. While Newtonian physics was unable to explain the full rate at which the perihelion was observed to precess, Einstein's general theory of relativity could. Note that the depiction of Mercury's orbit here is exaggerated.

prefer Einstein's theory to Newton's, Newton's theory to Kepler's, and Kepler's theory to nothing at all. Moreover, if scope is regarded as an *epistemic* value, then theories with wider scope are more likely to be true than their more narrowly scoped competitors, all other things being equal.

Simplicity

The value of simplicity in theories was famously captured by a fourteenth-century principle known as *Occam's razor*. What this principle tells us is to avoid multiplying entities beyond what is necessary. If you can explain all of the facts of a crime scene by positing that there was just one criminal rather than three, for example, you should not arbitrarily say there were three, for doing so goes beyond what is most minimally required for an explanation.

One way to assess the comparative simplicity of a theory is to look at the number and, more importantly, the "size" of the assumptions needed. If two theories stand to explain some phenomenon A, and one does so using twice the number of assumptions as the other, we may say that it is less simple as compared with the second if all the assumptions are roughly the same size in terms of plausibility. It gets more complicated if the assumptions are not equivalent in plausibility. If the second theory's assumptions are deeply implausible, for example, it may not matter at all that it has relatively fewer of them.

The pursuit of simplicity has left an indelible mark upon the history of scientific thought. It was known in the nineteenth-century that the orbit of Uranus was different from what one would expect for it, given only the laws of Newtonian physics, the Sun, and the planets known to exist back then. In an effort to explain its orbital deviation, the French mathematician and astronomer Urbain Jean Joseph Le Verrier postulated the existence of an as yet unseen planet out beyond the orbit of Uranus. If such a planet existed, he reasoned, its gravitational influence on Uranus's orbit could account for why it was not orbiting in the expected way. While this proposal added to the complexity of our picture of the solar system, it was a relatively smaller postulation to make than to assume that Newton's law of gravitation operated differently on the most far-lying planets in the solar system. And happily for Le Verrier, he was right: discovered in 1846 on the basis of calculations of where an unseen planet needed to be if Uranus's orbit was to be explained by it, Neptune became the eighth known planet in the solar system.

Another way of assessing the simplicity of a theory concerns conceptual simplicity. To prefer conceptually simpler theories is to prefer those that are more cognitively accessible or graspable. If conceptual simplicity is treated as an epistemic value, we should prefer those theories that avail themselves more easily to us in comprehensibility relative to some other as more likely to be true.

Fruitfulness

There are two very different ways of thinking about the fruitfulness of a particular theory. The most standard method treats fruitfulness as a measure of a theory's success in predicting previously unknown phenomena. A good example comes from historical theories of the nature of light.

At the beginning of the nineteenth-century, there were two competing views about the nature of light. According to the corpuscular theory, light was made up of atom-like "corpuscles" of matter. According to the wave theory of light, light was a wave that moved in some kind of medium, just as waves in the ocean move within the physical medium of water.

While the nineteenth-century French mathematician S. D. Poisson did not himself believe in the wave theory of light, he was able to mathematically demonstrate that if light really were a wave then a suitably illuminated circular disk should manifest a bright spot at the center of its shadow. Poisson actually took this as a reason *not* to believe in the wave theory, for he saw it as ridiculous that a bright spot would exist at the center of the shadow of a circular disk. Yet when someone actually bothered to do the experiment to see if Poisson's bright spot was there, the rather astonishing result was that it did. Quite unexpectedly, then, the wave theory of light led to the successful prediction and subsequent discovery of a wholly new phenomenon, and this was taken as powerful evidence in favor of its truth.

A second way of talking about fruitfulness relates to the opening that a theory leaves to scientists to work on it and develop it. Few scientific theories are born into the world entirely free of problems. While some might find this fact surprising, historians of science have noted that the history of science can often be presented in an artificially idealized and smoothed-out manner. While great scientific accomplishments are highlighted as important, comparatively little may be said about any problems those theories faced or what modifications had to be made to them along the way. Sometimes it can appear as though all of the best theories in science sprang whole and complete from the minds of geniuses in an ever-progressing and complementary fashion.

The truth is much more interesting and messy. The fact is that even the very best scientific theories routinely require significant effort to get them into a more complete and satisfactory state than they first started out in. That this is so is not necessarily a bad thing for individual scientists, though, for it gives them something creative and productive to do with their time. Indeed, one may say that the more work an impressive but problem-troubled theory leaves for scientists, the more positive attention and effort it may receive from them (for entirely pragmatic, career-orientated reasons).

Interestingly, there is a way of looking at this second sense of fruitfulness that gives it an explicitly epistemic reading. A theory that has overcome many of the problems that were facing it in a convincing fashion could begin to look as though it will continue to do that in the future with further development. Conversely, a theory that appears to be accumulating more and more problems without much success in solving them may not strike scientists contemplating where to invest their energy in a very attractive light, because it could be taken to suggest that the framework of the theory is what is at fault. Either way, the track record of a theory in dealing with problems can be taken as indicating something about the essential truth or falsehood of the theory itself, and therein set expectations for how the theory will finally end up.

Explanatory Power

Why do peacocks grow such bright and colorful tails when that makes them easier for predators to see? Why do some mountain ranges have fossilized seashells in them? Why do some people experience crippling shyness in the presence of others? Why do migrating birds fly in flocks? Why does ice float in water? Why is the sky blue? Why is the birth ratio of males to females almost exactly 1:1? One of the primary goals of science is to *explain* the phenomena we see around us. Although it isn't easy to say exactly what scientific explanation involves, examples of explanatory success in science reveal its importance as a scientific and epistemic value.

Consider the following puzzle: why are Mercury and Venus only ever seen within a short distance of where the Sun either last appeared or is about to appear in the sky? While all the other planets are unrestricted in where they can be, Mercury and Venus are never found beyond a certain point.

On the wisdom of the Ptolemaic, Earth-centered model of universe, the reason was thought to do with an invisible line that connected Mercury and Venus to the Sun so that they travel around Earth as a triplet. Being joined to one another in this way, it was to be expected that Mercury and Venus would never appear beyond a certain distance away. On the Copernican model, which treats Earth as orbiting the Sun rather than the other way around, the answer is rather different. Since Earth was modeled as being outside the orbits of both Mercury and Venus, it *had to be* that those planets would only ever be seen inside a fixed maximum distance from the Sun, and simply because of the perspective we take on them as we orbit. Moreover, this arrangement explained why the other planets in the solar system are unrestricted in the distance that they can have to the Sun in the sky, for they all orbit farther out than Earth.

What we can see here is that while the Ptolemaic model could only muster a rather forced and artificial solution to the problem of restricted elongation, the explanation that followed out of the Copernican model was entirely sense-making and uncontrived, and this spoke independently for its truth.

All other things being equal, to see explanation as an epistemic value is to regard theories that offer high quality explanations of phenomena as being more likely to be true than those (like the Ptolemaic model) that don't.

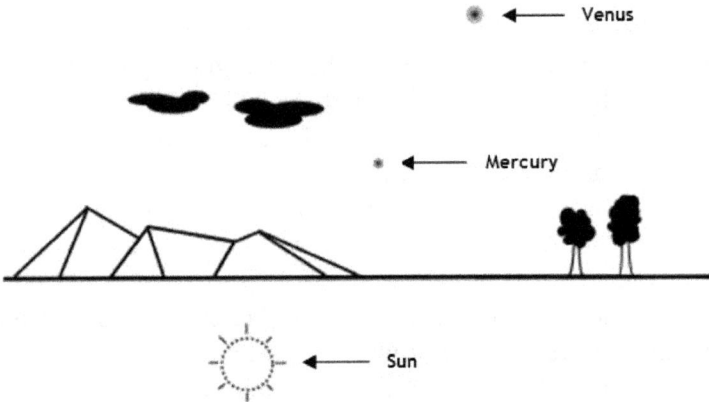

Figure 5.2: the restricted elongation of Mercury and Venus. The Sun has set below the horizon to reveal the presence of Mercury and Venus nearby. Unlike the other planets, there is a maximum limit to the distance that Mercury and Venus can appear to have from the Sun in the sky.

Symmetry

Whatever justification may exist for believing that nature exhibits symmetries, the search for symmetry has historically led to some remarkable discoveries. Louis de Broglie's hypothesis concerning the dual particle-wave nature of matter offers a good example.[50] It was long known to physicists in the early twentieth-century that light behaves as if it is both a particle and a wave, sometimes being more like a wave and other times being more like a particle (depending on how you arrange the experimental setup). Knowing that particles and waves both possess linear momentum, de Broglie suggested in 1924 that particles might also exhibit wave-like characteristics (such as wavelength and frequency). De Broglie's highly unorthodox prediction was right, and his hypothesis received its first empirical confirmation not long afterwards with the discovery by physicists Clinton Davisson and Lester Germer that electrons do in fact behave like waves under experimental conditions.

Symmetry also played an interesting role in the discovery of antimatter. It appeared before the attention of the English physicist Paul Dirac while studying an equation for the electron he had formulated that it could be solved in two different ways. While one of the solutions gave a description of the electron, the other led to a description of a particle that had all the same properties except one: it was positively rather than negatively charged. Using this solution to predict the existence of a new particle with those same properties in 1928, when the antimatter form of the electron (the positron) was discovered four years later by Carl D. Anderson in 1932, Dirac famously quipped that the equation had been smarter than he was.

Aesthetics

On first sight aesthetics looks like it would be the kind of thing that would be thoroughly irrelevant to the question of a theory's truth. After all, whatever could it be about a theory being beautiful that makes it more likely to be true? And in any case, isn't beauty in the eye of the beholder? Couldn't one person's idea of a beautiful theory be different from another's?

---

[50] Salmon (1990).

The subjectivity of aesthetic appreciation aside, aesthetic considerations are influential in science, most notably in the area of physics. As Steven Weinberg has pointed out, it is possible to get the sense while listening to a piece of music that all of the notes needed to be just where they are, and that there is not a single one of them you would change if you had the power to, so perfectly well do they hang together. He notes that something analogous can be true with how theories in physics (like quantum mechanics) theoretically tie in with themselves to leave no room for modification. When this feature is present, it generates a sense of beauty about the inevitability of that theory's structure or form.[51]

Similarly, part of what entices many physicists and mathematicians to conduct research on string theory is that they find its mathematics very elegant and beautiful. Not every way of measuring beauty will be truth-related of course, if indeed any are, and there is no *a priori* reason for thinking that the laws of nature should be composed in ways that mathematically gifted humans find aesthetically wonderful. Still, if the most beautiful mathematical descriptions of reality have historically tended to be true, that would give us at least some empirical warrant for favoring mathematically beautiful theories over mathematically unremarkable or ugly ones.[52]

Pragmatism in Reason: Interests, Standards, and Evidential Plasticity

These values give a set of possible criteria to judge the truth of competing theories by. If we think of them as epistemic values, then the more predictively accurate, explanatory, simple, broadly scope,

---

[51] Steven Weinberg (1993).

[52] This line of reasoning is not unproblematic, however, for there is always going to be an alternative explanation for why truth and mathematical beauty have tended to historically coincide: we have tended to select mathematically beautiful theories out from the total pool of theories and then called them "true." If that is so, it should hardly be any surprise to us if the surviving "true" theories are found to be aesthetically beautiful in some way. You might think a way around it would be to try and justify aesthetics by making reference to the empirical warrant of another value. For example, perhaps beautiful theories also tend to be simple theories, and perhaps simpler theories have historically tended to be true. Unfortunately, this inevitably raises the very same problem, but this time in relation to the truth-connectedness of simplicity.

symmetrical, beautiful, fruitful, and consistent a theory is, the more confident we can rationally be that it is correct.

There are a couple of things to note about this, however. First, not every value in the list just covered needs to be thought of as epistemic or ranked equal to one another in terms of significance. You might see explanatory power as being very important in the determination of truth, for example, while another person might see it as relatively less important compared with predictive accuracy or simplicity. Second, even where all the same values are agreed upon by different people, and all according to roughly the same system of weighting, challenges exist in the fact that there can be ambiguity involved in how they are applied in particular cases.[53]

Being rational, though, there are at the end of the day three things that we should want as belief-holders: to have true beliefs, to have many beliefs, and to have precise beliefs.[54] That is, we want our beliefs to reliably reflect reality, we want to have as many reality-reflecting beliefs as we can, and we want those beliefs to be detailed in what they tell us about it. Unfortunately, these goals sit in a logical relationship with one another such that seeking to extend or advance one of them can undermine one or both of the others. One way of attempting to secure true beliefs over false beliefs, for example, is to be very strict about the level of evidence we require before committing ourselves to something in belief. The downside of this is that it will reduce the overall number of beliefs we are then able to have, for not every belief we hold or consider will meet that higher evidential standard. Moreover, it will tend to rule out having precise beliefs over more general ones, for the more precise our beliefs are, the more likely they are to be wrong.[55]

---

[53] A point made most forcefully by Kuhn (1996).

[54] Note that this does not exhaust all possible goals we might hold for ourselves in relation to our beliefs. Research in psychology shows time and time again that one widely shared goal of belief is to believe nice things—things which make us happy, or which resonate with us, and so on. It is easy to see how this goal might sit in tension with the goal of believing truly, where the truth is directly counter to something pleasantly or happily believed.

[55] For example, the proposition "zebra's exist" is logically weaker than the proposition that "zebra's exist in Africa," and is accordingly less risky in terms of the likelihood of its being true than the logically stronger comparison. By narrowing down the location of zebra's to Africa we need only check all of Africa to know if the second proposition is false, whereas we need to check the whole world (or the universe) to know if the first proposition is false. Though it is more likely to be true, the first proposition is less detailed than the second proposition is—we learn less about the world by knowing that "zebra's exist" than we do by knowing that "zebra's exist in Africa."

So how do we balance these jointly conflicted goals of belief? The answer seems to be that it is decided by practical judgments concerning the relative costs and benefits of pursuing one goal more heavily than another. One person might really want to avoid having any false beliefs, for example, and thus choose to adopt a higher evidential standard in relation to what they believe. While this would mean they are less likely to hold false beliefs, it would also mean limiting themselves in the total number of beliefs they are likely to have, for the number of beliefs likely to meet that higher evidential standard is smaller. A second person might not be so concerned about being maximally right, yet be very concerned to know as much about reality as they possibly can. They might therefore choose to adopt a lower evidential standard than the first person. While this would maximize the overall number of beliefs they are then potentially open to, it would also likely mean believing more false things. They might still end up with a greater absolute number of true beliefs than the first person, however.

How so? Suppose that a person A believes 1000 things, but because their evidential requirements are not terribly strict, only 60 percent of those beliefs are true (not that they know this themselves, of course). Person B, being much more concerned to avoid false beliefs, adopts a higher evidential standard than person A. Because fewer beliefs meet that higher evidential standard, they might only believe 100 things.[56] However, because their evidential standards are higher, 90 percent of the things they believe might be true. In that case, while person A has a lower ratio of truth to falsehood in the set of their beliefs (person A's 60 percent versus person B's 90 percent), overall they still have more true beliefs (person A has 600 true beliefs while person B has 90).

Which is the better way of believing? It all comes down to what you want. Person B might justify their more limited sphere of belief as an acceptable cost of being so much more right than wrong, especially given how false beliefs can lead to personal and moral harm. Person A might justify their higher ratio of false to true beliefs as an acceptable cost of knowing more in absolute terms.

Either way, we can't simultaneously have all that we might ideally want for ourselves in relation to our beliefs. Somewhat reminiscently of Heisenberg's uncertainty principle, a trade-off occurs between belief-

---

[56] These are absurdly low numbers of beliefs for anyone to have, but we can use them simply for purposes of illustration.

goals, such that to seek to increase the realization of one goal can be to end up threatening the realization of another.[57]

Happily, we are not completely powerless to help ourselves. Indeed, one way we can achieve a better fit between conflicted aims of belief is to allow for *variability* in evidential standards. Where the consequences of falsely believing a certain proposition appear to us to be undesirably high, we can demand more for ourselves in terms of evidence before we will believe it.[58]

Descriptively, at least, it does seem that we do something like this. Suppose you want to take the bus to the museum and are unsure what time it is due. Asking the person sitting next to you to see if they know, it doesn't matter terribly much if the time they give you is inaccurate. You are in no particular hurry to get there and nothing bad will happen if you get there much earlier or later than whenever you imagined. You might therefore be willing to accept whatever time they tell you and leave it at that.

Now change the situation so that instead of going to the museum, you need to get to the airport to tell someone you love them in person before they leave forever. Suddenly it has become all important to know exactly when the bus will come. If you're late because the bus didn't come when you thought it would, you could miss the opportunity to tell them before they enter through the security area. Raising your evidential standards about this question of timing, a stranger's word may now no longer be enough, especially if the person seems vague or unsure in giving it. What then might you do? One option is to ask a second person. After all, if two people independently give the same answer as each other, the likelihood of their answer being right goes up. Alternatively, you

---

[57] According to Heisenberg's uncertainty principle, there are sets of paired properties in relation to particles such that the more accurately you know about one property in the pair, the less accurately you know about the other. For example, position and momentum are linked to one another in uncertainty; the more accurately you know a particle's position at any given moment, the less accurately you will then know how fast it is going and where it is heading from that point on (and vice versa). Because of this, you have to make a choice about what you would like to know more accurately.

[58] To see pragmatic interests like this involved in our beliefs should not come as a surprise. After all, the value of truth itself is largely instrumental. We want to know the truth not because we must (who says we must?), or because it is good in itself to know the truth (though some truths might have this status, there are an indefinite number of entirely uninteresting truths that it would be quite worthless to know), but because our lives stand to go better when truths are cognitively represented within us (exceptions aside).

might just jump in a taxi, being unwilling to risk being late on what other people say.

The only difference between these two cases—heading to the museum or heading to the airport—is that the level of evidence we would feel satisfied with changes in relation to the significance of the personal consequences of being wrong about the arrival time. The same sensitivity to the consequences of being wrong shows through in scientific practice as well. Scientists who want to determine the level at which a particular substance in a water supply becomes toxic might require a very high standard of evidence before making a public statement on it, for example, for the consequences of advising people that the water is safe to drink when it is not could be profound.

Both of these examples have involved bringing higher evidential standards to bear on questions of a proposition which, if both false and believed, would result in negative consequences. This is not the only way that evidential standards might conceivably shift in relation to human interests. For example, we might choose to bring lower evidential standards to bear on questions of a proposition which, if *not* believed and *true*, would generate significant negative consequences. An example would be the nearly universal belief that people have in the existence of other people's minds.

We are all intimately familiar with the fact that we each have a conscious mind—there is "something that it is like" to consciously be us. For all the certainty of that belief, though, there is no way to know for sure that anyone else has a mind. I mean, how do we really know that other people subjectively experience anything? We can't scan their heads to see if they do, for minds are not the kind of thing that can be detected with scanners and instruments. What justifies our belief in the existence of minds other than our own, then?

Short of it just being an assumption that we are all irresistibly drawn to make, one possible argument goes as follows: there are certain behaviors we perform that we introspectively know in our own case are associated with distinct inner subjective experiences. When we feel happy we smile, when we feel sad we cry, when we feel confused we lower our brows, and so on. We also know that other people display all of these same kinds of behaviors too. If we tell a joke (and it is a good one...) they laugh and smile, if we insult them they frown and react angrily, and so on. It can be argued that the best explanation for why they perform these kinds of behaviors is that *they too* have the same kinds of inner qualitative experiences as we do.[59] Alternatively, it can be argued that because we know there is a conjunction in our own case between subjectively experiencing something (e.g., feeling happiness) and doing something (e.g., smiling), that when we see others doing these kinds of things there is most likely a conjunction there too.[60]

Notice that in both cases the justification for believing that other people have minds is not exactly overwhelming; we are in essence taking a single case—ourselves—and using it as a basis for making inferences about everyone else. Of course, we also know that other people have brains more or less physiologically the same as ours, and that unless there is some special difference between them, we should probably expect that the same kinds of qualitative experiences that attach to our brain states attach to theirs as well. But at the end of the day, this is still all quite a bit less than evidence beyond any reasonable doubt that other minds do exist.

Now consider the consequences of believing that other people don't have conscious experiences. If there is nothing that it is like to be them, what possible reason could we have for treating them well? We don't feel bad about kicking rocks, for there is nothing that it is like to be a rock kicked. If other people are as lacking in experience as rocks are, why should we treat them morally? It stands to reason that there is no need to. If we're wrong in believing they lack minds, though, we may end up doing them a tremendous amount of moral harm. This is where variability in evidential standards comes in, for the danger of that possibility can be used to drive down the standard of evidence necessary to justify our belief in other minds, and up to the point, I think, that inductive arguments like those outlined can satisfy them.

The same point should hold with questions about animal consciousness. That is, precisely because the moral consequences of treating animals with a high level of cognitive development as though they don't have conscious experiences are so negative, the level of evidence we should need should be lowered, and once again up to the extent that it is reasonable to believe that many animals are bearers of consciousness.

---

[59] This argument won't work if one takes minds to be essentially non-causal, such as on an epiphenomenal view of consciousness.

[60] These two arguments might look the same, but they rely on two different kinds of inductive reasoning. The first argument relies upon an inference to the best explanation, while the second argument relies on analogical induction.

This account of variability in evidential standards is intended to be both normative and descriptive. That is, it is intended to set out not just what we do actually do, but what we *ought to do* as part of being rational. If it's correct, we ought to be evidentially more demanding of propositions that risk negative consequences in being believed when false, and evidentially less demanding of propositions that risk negative consequences in not being believed when true.

This idea of evidential variability is not without its problems. Imagine the existence a button that needs to be pushed every hour or it will result in everyone on Earth suffering horribly. With consequences like this, the moral importance of someone acting to push the button seems incontrovertible—there might perhaps be nothing that is more important for someone to do than to push the button at least once an hour. Suppose someone was to claim that they actually had such a button in their possession. Following the principles set out before, the level of evidence we should need before believing them should be lower thanks to the acutely negative consequences of the button existing and someone failing to push it. But how much lower? Even though it seems incredibly implausible that such a button could exist, with the consequences of being wrong so high, it seems possible that all we might need is the solemn testimony of a single person to believe that it really does exist.

But this would give someone an effective way of ruining the lives of other people. All they would need to do is to go around telling people that a certain button they hand them has this property, give them a plausible explanation for why they themselves can't push it, and flee the scene. If evidential standards really do bend to negative consequences, their word alone might be enough to lock people into a life of pushing the button out of fear of the consequences of someone's not.

You may have noticed already, but this is exactly how religion proceeds: it exploits the sensitivity of our evidential standards to negative consequences by promising people the most devastating consequences imaginable if they do not believe in it. And it is not just religion that hijacks this feature of human rationality; more orthodox examples of superstitions do as well. Whether it is avoiding opening up umbrellas inside, touching wood to cancel jinxing yourself, walking around ladders rather than underneath them, or wearing lucky underwear to fend off bad luck while playing professional sports, the cost-benefit analysis relating to each of these behaviors is skewered by the imbalance of the consequences imagined in not doing them (e.g. years of bad luck, a cursed marriage, or playing very poorly) relative to the low costs of complying with them (e.g. simply walking around a ladder rather than underneath it, waiting until you're outside to open an umbrella, or wearing the same underwear every game). While bad luck from opening an umbrella isn't on the same level as an infinite amount of torture in hell for not believing in god, the principle it depends upon is the same.

Is this issue with evidential plasticity resolvable? I think so. Returning to the button case, one option is to ensure that the negative consequences of believing that the button has its purported power when it doesn't *increases* the applicable standards of evidence required to believe that about it. After all, wasting your life on a needless superstition is far from a good thing. The problem here, however, is that the consequences of the button really having that power and not believing it vastly outweigh the consequences of it not having that power and believing it does.

A second possibility is to treat considerations of consequences as subject to diminishing returns. That is, as the negative consequences of having a particular belief or lacking it grow ever greater, the effect of that on either increasing or decreasing our evidential demands drops off. Yet if the consequences were to be infinite, as is true in the case of hell, then presumably the effect of that in lowering evidential standards would still be absolute, no matter how steep the curve of diminishment.

Given this, a third possibility is to set a fixed upper and lower limit to our evidential standards for any question of belief, such that we cannot then be overwhelmed by considerations of consequences into adopting beliefs and behaviors of the kind just outlined.

Finally, a fourth possibility is to simply ignore the negative consequences of a belief if the probability of that belief being true is lower than a certain minimum threshold, or to treat those consequences in a reduced-significance kind of way. Combined together, these four possibilities offer a workable solution to possibility of variable evidential standards being hijacked by extreme consequences.

You might wonder what any of this has to do with belief in god. It matters for at least the following reason: if people see the idea of god as being morally helpful or necessary, they are likely to be less evidentially demanding of it as an idea.[61] Equally, if they see the idea of god as being

---

[61] My thoughts about the moral importance of the idea of god are covered in the next chapter, but to give away the conclusion of that discussion now: god is by no means necessary in order for morality to make sense and be important. As such, being less demanding of the idea of god because you think it is needed in order for morality to make sense or for there to be moral seriousness is a mistake.

morally or socially harmful, they are likely to require more of it from an evidential point of view before they will be willing to accept it. Even if those in the latter group think that some versions of it (like the one I have advocated, hopefully) sit on the harmless end of the moral spectrum, they may still worry that by acknowledging any rational legitimacy to the idea of god at all, they could be taken by others as giving legitimacy to religious formulations of it too. And given the rolling philosophical and moral disaster that religion has been for the world, this is something to want to avoid.

All I can do in response is reiterate that those who religiously believe do not merely believe in the existence of god—they believe in the existence of a *very particular* kind of god. In the case of Christianity, belief is maintained (or at least is expected to be maintained) in a god who is three-in-one, who came to Earth in human form two thousand years ago, who, after first judging them, either punishes or rewards people according to their spiritual performance, and whose death in physical form made it possible for everyone to be forgiven for their sins. Not a single one of these ideas is natural to the idea of god, and all have had to be theologically tacked onto it.

This means that there is a sizeable logical gap between religious formulations of the god hypothesis and conceptually more minimal god hypotheses. To infer the truth of Christianity from the mere fact of god's existence—if indeed a convincing case for that could be made—would be dramatically unjustified. It would be a bit like someone learning that a crime had taken place in New York and concluding *from that and only that* piece of information that the perpetrator was Bill, a forty-five year old car mechanic from New York who plays bass guitar and loves sushi. While it could have been Bill, it could also have been any one of many millions of other people who live there. Indeed, I would think that Bill would have every right to feel indignant about being accused of the crime. Much more is needed than just the possibility that Bill could have done it to show that he did, just as much more is needed to show the truth of any one religion than just evidence suggesting the existence of a divine being. And as I hope to have convincingly shown there, there are excellent reasons to doubt the truth of religious hypotheses concerning god and reality.

General Objections to the God Hypothesis

Though my goal is to defend just one specific version of the god hypothesis, general objections exist that apply to a broad range of different formulations of it. The problem of evil raised in the first chapter is a good example, for it argues in a highly general way against the existence of any divinely capable, knowing, and good being. If any of these arguments are successful, there will be reason in that to doubt the truth of the one this book presents.

What we will do next, then, is look at five such objections. Though there are certainly more out there than that, these are the ones that seem to me to come up most regularly in the list of objections people have to the idea of god.

Objection 1: *The god hypothesis is objectionably metaphysical. It tells us that the universe was created by a divine being that can neither be observed, measured, or otherwise interacted with (except perhaps in a handful of very special cases). Ideas like this are next to useless. How can we know if any being like this actually exists? The invisible and the nonexistent look suspiciously similar.*

Is the metaphysical character of the god hypothesis a mark against it? Metaphysics itself has certainly come in for criticism in the history of philosophy. Leading the charge against it was the eighteenth-century Scottish philosopher David Hume. One of the primary targets of Hume's philosophical crusade was an idea that most of us would find rather familiar: causation.[62]

As Hume asked, where in our experience of the world does the idea of causality come from? It isn't in our experiences themselves, for we don't ever see, touch, or smell the causes of events. When we see a twig break and an apple fall from a tree, for example, we don't actually see the twig's breaking *cause* the apple to fall—what we see is one thing happen (the twig breaks) and then another thing happens (the apple begins to fall). We *say* that the twig's breaking caused the apple to fall, but this is something we add to the basic description of what we saw. The most it seems we ever find in our experiences are just two things happening in conjunction with one another.

---

[62] See Hume (1748).

We tend to think of causality as being something more than just uniform coincidence, though. For most of us, the idea of causation serves as a kind of abstract glue that nonarbitrarily joins events together with one another. When one such event happens, it *brings about* the other. Hume was adamant that thinking like this puts us into dangerous philosophical territory, for it goes beyond what is most strictly found in our experience. He therefore chose to speak of causation as involving nothing more than the uniform coincidence of events. Breaking twigs "cause" apples to fall, but only in the sense that we always observe twigs breaking just before apples fall—not because the first event ever *brings about* the second. To think of causality as being something more than constant conjunction is to turn it into a metaphysical idea, and given that Hume took metaphysics as nothing more than a wasteland of useless and empty ideas, he argued against doing so.

Are we required to follow Hume and reject the metaphysical yet intuitive notion of causality? We aren't. What Hume succeeded in showing was that causation isn't something found in our immediate experience of the world. On this point he was right: when you see a twig break and an apple fall, you don't literally see one event causing the other. What he didn't show, however, was that causation, as a metaphysical idea, was a silly, bad, or unjustified concept. He didn't show this because he never established that metaphysics is nothing but a wasteland of useless and unjustified ideas—he simply asserted it and proceeded from there. [63] This is a bit like someone saying that all multinational corporations are inherently bad and evil, and then arguing that because corporation X is a multinational corporation, that corporation X is inherently bad and evil. That may or may not be so, but they would need to say more to support the claim that all multinational corporations are inherently bad and evil before the argument will work. Likewise for Hume: if you didn't already agree with him that metaphysics is a complete waste of time, his argument to the effect that the idea of causality is empty isn't going to persuade you.

So what can be said on behalf of causality in its intuitive, non-Humean form? Well, for one, it is very useful for making sense of the world. The idea of causation serves as a kind of framework for our experiences, and applies to them so that we can then make thorough-going sense of things. For reasons of confidence, Hume wanted to tie what can be known as tightly as he could to the bare inputs of our

---

[63] Ross (2010).

experience—sense data, like what we see, smell, hear, and so on. Since causation isn't found in sense data, it had to go. Appreciable though Hume's intention was, abandoning causality required paying a price, and that was denying himself the possibility of finding any deeper connection between events than simply continuous (and miraculously unlikely) happenstance. That strikes me as an excessively heavy price to pay.

Being useful is not the same as being necessary or true, of course, and Hume (for one) seems to have been willing to think of the ordering of certain events as just long chains of inexplicable coincidences. What might be said to those who, like Hume, tell us that they can get by just fine without the metaphysical idea of causation? Probably not much. That doesn't mean we are forced to follow suit with them, however. Nor does it mean that there aren't other metaphysical ideas that *are* necessary if we are to hold a view of the world anything like what most people would be willing to accept.

The fact is that even the most diehard of Empiricists (spelled with a capital *E*, an Empiricist is someone who thinks that knowledge only comes from experience) must make use of metaphysical ideas *somewhere* in their thinking if they are to avoid being an idealist. Idealism is a philosophical stance that says that objects only exist in the mind, and hence that there isn't anything "out there" in some objectively existing world beyond our experiences. An apple only exists in the sense that you have experiences of an apple-like thing, for example, not in the sense that there is an apple somewhere independently of you that brings about apple-like experiences. Most people are realists rather than idealists. That is, we tend to think that the world really exists and that our experiences routinely reflect something about it.

In order to look at the world through realist eyes, we need to have some way of telling which of our experiences reliably reflect its objectively existing reality, and which are just illusions or hallucinations. What we're going to need, in other words, is an error theory. Therein lies a serious problem, however, for whatever theory we use to do that cannot *itself* be wholly derived from our experiences of the world. Why not? Because we're going to need that error theory prior to our experiences before we can even begin to make experiential sense of what is going on. If we're going to believe that the world is illuminated to us through our experiences, then, the theory that is going to help us do that needs to be at least partly metaphysical in nature.[64]

It looks from this like metaphysics is not only useful but necessary (at least if we're to avoid being idealists). However, just knowing that metaphysical ideas can sometimes be useful or necessary does not tell us that *just any* metaphysical idea is worthwhile, or that the idea of god is one of the worthwhile ones. Yet equally it can't just be because something is metaphysical that it is bad, for we've just seen two cases where not everything that is metaphysical is bad.

One reason someone might give for why god is a bad metaphysical idea is that if god cannot be observed, measured, or otherwise interacted with (by *our* initiation, at least), then god's existence looks suspiciously similar to his nonexistence. And if that is so, what possible difference could it make to say that he exists? If god does not causally interact with the universe in any detectable or predictable way, won't the idea of him be useless?

No, for the fact is that observable predictions are not the only thing of any value that we get out of theories. With historical roots going all the way back to Ancient Greece, the atomic theory of matter was for most of its history a paradigmatic example of a metaphysical thesis. It proposed that everything we see around us is composed of units of matter called "atoms" that are far too small to ever be directly seen, but which combine in various sorts of dynamic ways to form the things we can see. As a thesis about the ontology of reality, it yielded no testable or observable predictions, yet that did not mean it didn't have considerable explanatory value. It was able to explain why objects exist in such great variety and why they can be divided into parts over and over again to the limits of what our senses are able to detect. Moreover, by proposing that atoms could interact and link together with one another, it explained why solid objects cohered as wholes rather than just fell apart. It wasn't until the nineteenth-century that the first solid empirical support for the atomic theory of matter came in and it began to lose its metaphysical character. That didn't mean it lacked any value up until that point, however.

Even if the god hypothesis doesn't offer any observable predictions about the universe, then, I take it that it can still be valuable in exactly

---

[64] Chakravarrty (2007). Note that this doesn't mean the error theory *comes to us* metaphysically—such as by being handed down by god—just that it is metaphysical in virtue of its necessary priority to our experience.

that same kind of way: by helping us to make *explanatory* sense of the universe.

Objection 2: *The god hypothesis is not falsifiable, and as such it must be rejected.*

The champion of the idea of falsifiability was the Austrian philosopher Karl Popper. According to Popper, scientific theories are distinct from pseudoscientific theories in the fact that, while scientific theories are open to being shown false by observation and experiment, pseudoscientific theories are not. Indeed, the defining difference between science and pseudoscience for Popper just was falsifiability: if it is possible to show that a particular theory is false, it can be regarded as scientific; if it is not possible to show that a theory is false, yet it purports to be (or is widely regarded as being) scientific, then that theory should be regarded as pseudoscientific.[65]

Popper took astrology as a good example of a pseudoscience. While astrology can be used to predict all manner of things about personality types and the events in a person's life based on the position of the planets and the Sun at various times, these predictions have a tendency to be so vague, imprecise, or widely applicable that they never really seem to be falsifiable. Astrological predictions like those you might find at the back of a magazine at the supermarket checkout, such as "money will be an issue for you this week," are sufficiently imprecise that they are able to be confirmed by a wide range of different things. Because of that, they are unlikely to ever be decisively established as false.[66]

If astrology is a pseudoscience, what does a genuine scientific theory look like? Popper saw Einstein's general theory of relativity as exemplary in this regard. First published in 1916, general relativity made the radical suggestion that gravity is really a curvature in the fabric of spacetime caused by matter and energy. One of the predictions that emerged from this idea was that light passing by a massive object should have its path

---

[65] Popper (1963).
[66] Contrary to the views of Popper and many others, key astrological claims regarding the influence of celestial bodies on human personality types *do* in fact appear to be testable and falsifiable when they are considered over populations of people. For example, if it is true that those born under the sign of Mars are more likely to be soldiers and athletes than people born under other signs, this is something that can be statistically tested and falsified by examining census data. By Popper's own criterion, then, astrology would *not* qualify as a pseudoscience (at least in respect to that set of predictions).

deflected, for the space it is traveling through should be warped by the mass of that object.

To test this prediction, all that was needed was to look very closely at the most massive object in our local vicinity—the Sun—and observe whether any of the stars nearest to it in the sky change positions compared with when the Sun is not sitting right next to them. That sounds straightforward, but the Sun is ordinarily too bright to see any stars. Luckily, rare opportunities do present themselves. By nothing more than good luck, the Moon happens to be the right size and distance from Earth to cover the disk of the Sun as it passes in front of it. When this happens, stars that are normally obscured from view by its intense light are revealed. An eclipse that took place in 1919 allowed astronomers to put Einstein's theory to the test, and photographs they took showed that the stars really are moved from where they would have normally appeared to be. Better than that, they were displaced by the same extent indicated by general relativity's equations.

One of the most impressive things about this episode in the history of science was that Einstein never formulated general relativity with the intention of explaining the deflection of light by massive objects. In fact, as a phenomenon light bending was only realized to be an implication of

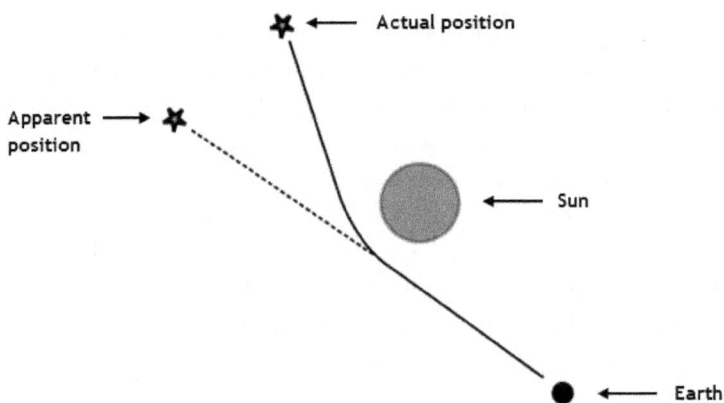

Figure 5.3: the deflection of starlight under the influence of gravity. The mass of the Sun curves space in its immediate area, which in turn causes the path of light traveling from a star to be deflected. As a result, the position of the star appears to observers on Earth to change.

the theory *after* it had already been published. A bold prediction by anyone's standards, Popper believed that if light had not been seen to bend, or if it had not been seen to bend to the extent predicted by the mathematics of general relativity, it would have been decisively refuted.

What made general relativity an exemplary example of a scientific theory in Popper's eyes, then, was that it was remarkably open to the possibility of being discovered as false. It did not hide questions about its truth behind vague predictions or ambiguity, or (we're to imagine) cover over its error with an endless series of *ad hoc* excuses. Rather, it set forth in a very precise way an expectation for how the physical world should be found to be, and left itself vulnerable to being discovered as wrong in light of that.

Though the idea of falsifiability is appealing in its simplicity, it has not been looked upon favorably by most philosophers of science as a way of differentiating science from pseudoscience.[67] Interestingly, though— and unusually for the influence of any philosopher—the idea has been proven to be something of a hit among scientists. All we are interested in here, however, is whether the god hypothesis really is unfalsifiable, and if it is, whether that should count as a reason to reject it.

To answer this, let's consider three different senses in which a hypothesis might be said to be falsifiable and examine whether they apply to the god hypothesis.

Logical falsifiability: concerns the ability to show on logical grounds that a statement or a collection of statements is false. Suppose I made the following prediction: "either it will rain tomorrow, or it won't." Hardly earth-shattering stuff, but if we assume for the sake of argument that there is no middle ground between raining and not raining, it is clear that this statement really can't be wrong. Come rain or shine, what I have said will be proven right for no other reason than the fact that it covers all logical options for what might happen. Tautologies are logically unfalsifiable, too, for they are statements that are true simply in virtue of the meanings of the words involved. For example, the

---

[67] The reason is that it is encumbered with a number of significant problems, prime among which are that the story of scientific practice as an attempt to falsify one's own theory is inconsistent with actual scientific practice, that it is far from clear that we should actually want scientists to abandon their theories on first sight of an apparent falsification, and that theories are not falsifiable in the decisive way that Popper needs them to be.

statement "as overall job losses increase the level of unemployment will rise" cannot be shown false, for net job losses and unemployment amount to the same thing. If you have one of them increasing, you necessarily have the other increasing.

Empirical falsifiability: concerns the ability to show by empirical means that a statement or a collection of statements is false. Because we are all finite beings, not every statement allows for this kind of falsification *in practice*. Consider the existential claim "at least one advanced alien species in the universe exists." To know that this claim is true would only take the discovery of a single advanced alien species. To know that it is false seems impossible, however, for the universe is too big to check everywhere within it and find that it is false. By allowing a multitude of different interpretations (and hence for many conceivably satisfying conditions), vague statements can also approach empirical unfalsifiability.

Methodological falsifiability: concerns the willingness of proponents to let a theory stand refuted in the face of problems. If defenders of a theory commit themselves to endlessly modifying the base theory with amendments in order to meet its difficulties and challenges, we may regard that theory as methodologically unfalsifiable. To regard a theory as such is to judge that no foreseeable test will be counted by those who assert its essential truth to warrant its abandonment.

In which (if any) of these three different senses of falsifiability is the god hypothesis unfalsifiable? Unless god is a logically necessary being, there doesn't seem to be anything logically prohibiting us from denying his existence. Moreover, if it did turn out that god is a logically necessary being—and I don't know of any good reason to think that—it is difficult to see why his existence being unfalsifiable would matter in that case.

Whether the god hypothesis is empirically falsifiable depends on what empirical implications it holds, and that tends to be dependent upon the specifics of the hypothesis in question. The traditional version of the Christian god hypothesis tells us that the world was created between six thousand and ten thousand years ago in six days, that life did not evolve but was created, that a series of catastrophic events like the Noarchic flood have historically taken place, and so on. These claims are all testable. For example, we can look for any evidence of a great historical deluge in the geology of Earth, we can examine the fossil record for any evidence of life coming into being at a single point rather than gradually over millions of years from simpler to more complex forms, and we can use scientific dating techniques to estimate the age of the world. The traditional Christian god hypothesis is entirely open to being empirically falsified, then. In fact, not only is the hypothesis open to empirical falsification, it has been empirically *falsified*, for all of the evidence we have suggests the falsehood of those empirical claims.

What about more general formulations of the god hypothesis, though? Even they tend to lead to at least limited expectations for how the world should appear if god exists. The problem of evil is widely accepted as a considerable problem for the existence of any divinely-propertied being. If so, many god-based hypotheses will be subject to at least some degree of empirical disconfirmation. Of course, proponents of the idea of god don't just leave the problem there, but make significant efforts to explain why there is widespread pain and suffering in the world.

And that takes us into what is probably an equally significant gripe with the god hypothesis—its methodological falsifiability. As it might be pointed out, no matter what counterarguments are produced or what empirical evidence is presented against either the existence of god generally or against specific versions of the god hypothesis, believers can be so committed to the truth of it that they will go to just about any length to explain it away. The result can be what seems like just one endless explanation or *ad hoc* modification after another in order to retain belief in god.

But is this really any fault of the god hypothesis itself? Methodological falsifiability looks much more like it is a criticism of *persons* than it is of *hypotheses*. The criticism here might be more properly laid at the doorstep of the god hypothesis as a research program rather than a set of theoretical claims, for the idea of a research program incorporates the idea of a community of inquirers under its conceptual umbrella.

There is at least one good reason why we should think less of, and at a point reject, theories that are continually defended against their problems to the bitter end, but it has nothing to do with the failure of people to abandon them. The reason is simply that the more we amend a hypothesis with *ad hoc* alterations designed to meet its problems, the more its likelihood of being true will diminish. Why? Because the conjunction of two independent statements can have a probability no higher than the probability of either conjunct, and modifying hypotheses by way of *ad hoc* additions often involves tacking new theoretical statements on to existing ones.

Suppose I hypothesize that there are unicorns at the bottom of your garden in order to explain why the flowers there have been chewed to pieces. Noticing that there aren't any unicorns when I come over, it would be possible to explain their absence by saying something like "Oh, unicorns must only come out at night." My initial unicorn hypothesis has now been amended to take the form "There are unicorns at the bottom of your garden, and they are nocturnal." Waiting until it is dark and then peering out in nervous trepidation, I may once again see nothing out of the ordinary. At this point I could turn the hypothesis into "There are unicorns at the bottom of your garden, they are nocturnal, and they only allow themselves to be seen by people they trust." Note that each addition to the original reduces its likelihood of being true, since the number of truth conditions that now need to be satisfied by the modified unicorn hypothesis has gone incrementally upward.[68]

This alone is a good enough reason to look less favorably upon methodologically unfalsifiable theories: though continually saved from refutation by negative observational results, they are not saved from looking all the worse for wear for it.

Even if the god hypothesis is regarded as empirically or methodologically unfalsifiable, does that mean it should automatically be rejected as untrue? Popper was unequivocal that the correct answer is no. From a Popperian point of view, all that a theory's being unfalsifiable means is that it is not scientific, not that it is false or that it must be rejected because it is nonscientific. Unfalsifiable theories can be true, after all; there is nothing implied by the notion of being unable to show that something is wrong that means it cannot be right.

We don't have to be strict Popperians about falsifiability, of course, and someone might want to reject unfalsifiable theories simply because they are unfalsifiable. If so, it is entirely their choice, but that epistemic policy will need to be justified if it is to be recommended to others as normatively correct.

---

[68] Note that while the second amendment is testable in this particular case, the third amendment doesn't appear to be. After all, how are we to know in advance who the unicorns might trust to see them? We could send a whole bunch of people one by one into the garden at night and have them report back whether they saw any unicorns, but if they didn't, that might just be because none of them were unicorn-trusted.

Objection 3: *God is said to be a "non-physical" being that exists "outside of space and time" and has created the universe "ex nihilo" (i.e., from nothing), yet none of what any of that consists of or involves has been explained. Without some kind of explanation of what these things come to, the god hypothesis is unacceptably flawed.*

Let's accept for the sake of argument that no good account exists of what it would be for god to exist "outside" space and time, to be a "nonphysical" being, or for the universe to have been created "from nothing." What does this imply for the acceptability of the god hypothesis? Must it be regarded as unacceptably flawed, as the objection suggests?

Not if other cases are anything to go by. Consider once again Isaac Newton and his law of universal gravitation. According to Newton, all objects with mass are gravitationally attracted to one another in a way described by a mathematical law he came up with. Newton could not say *why* that was the case. His theory provided only the form of gravity's law, not its cause, and his silence over what caused gravity was something his Cartesian opponents felt particularly strongly about. As they saw it, the fact that Newton could only plead ignorance about such an important issue as gravity's cause was a major problem, especially given that Descartes's theory *had* provided an explanation. What was it? According to Descartes, gravity is the result of swirling vortices of tiny corpuscles of invisible matter pressing down upon the world and holding the planets in place around the Sun. Where Newton had not been able to explain the cause of gravity, then, Cartesian gravitational theory purportedly could.

It was actually worse than that for Newton, though, for in taking objects to mutually attract one another instantaneously and over great distances, he seemed to be proposing something that was for many people at the time an absurd notion. It could be understood well enough what it was for two objects to interact with one another via *contact action* (essentially, by banging into one another), but to say that objects instantaneously *attracted* one another, in the absence of any medium, and at great distances, bordered on the occult.

Many hold essentially the same objection when it comes to the idea of god being non-spatiotemporally located or having created the universe from nothing. Not only are these things unexplained, they appear to involve some kind of absurdity. Surely only nothing can come from nothing? Surely it is in the very idea of a nonabstract object that it must exist within space and time?

Faced with criticism, should Newton have caved to the demand that any successful theory of gravity needed to identify what caused it? We can be quite happy that he didn't. While he confessed his ignorance, Newton appealed to the precision with which his law of gravity and three laws of motion were able to account for the observed celestial facts. In Newton's mind at least, and within a century virtually everyone else's mind as well, the question of gravity's cause was simply not significant enough to warrant the rejection of the Newtonian framework.

The problems facing Alfred Wegener's theory of continental drift were at least as bad. Set forward in 1912, Wegener's theory attempted to explain a wealth of geological facts by proposing that the continents move very gradually over the course of many millions of years. Wegener argued that if this was true, a whole host of apparently disconnected facts could be neatly tied together under one explanatory account. It could be explained, for example, why the shorelines and the continental shelves of different continents appear to fit together like pieces in a jigsaw puzzle, why certain geographical features (like mountain ranges) appear to be continuations of one another on different continents, why some parts of the world once had climatic conditions very different to what one would expect for them if they had always been where they are, and why there are remarkable similarities in the fossil records of geographic regions separated by thousands of kilometers of ocean.

Wegener's theory faced what many at the time considered to be a very serious problem, however, and that was that he was unable to say what caused the continents to move. That in itself was certainly something, but the problem ran deeper in the fact that *whatever* physical mechanism he might have proposed for it, it appeared to require a physical impossibility: that whole continents—massive structures of earth and rock—could plough through thousands of kilometers of solid granite in Earth's crust to end up where they are today. Not only was there an explanatory gap in his theory, then, but whatever he might have found to fix it would have only propped up an absurdity.

While many geologists rejected Wegener's theory for precisely these sorts of reasons, not all of them did, and it seems unfair to condemn that support as irrational when one takes into account the explanatory virtues of the theory in bringing together such a diverse range of geological facts so neatly.

The story eventually ended happily for Wegener's idea. By the 1960s further evidence that continents move had been found, and a physical mechanism behind their movement was discovered in the form of convection currents beneath tectonic plates. Wegener himself didn't live long enough to see it become widely accepted, but the idea that Earth's continents drift over great periods of time is now the established geological view.[69]

As a final example, consider the fact that while Niels Bohr's model of the atom improved upon Ernest Rutherford's earlier atomic model, it offered no explanation of the decay of electrons from higher energy states into lower energy states within the structure of an atom, or how decaying electrons emitted radiation from formerly radiationless situations, or why only a limited number of electrons could occupy any given electron shell, or why they couldn't decay any further down towards the nucleus than the first shell. Requiring all of these things to be true, his theory simply treated electrons as behaving in that sort of way within atoms.[70] Despite that, Bohr's theory still achieved remarkable success in predicting the previously known emission spectra of hydrogen atoms, and in virtue of doing so, it constituted a notable scientific advance.[71]

While these are just three examples, many more from the history of science could be placed alongside them. What they go towards showing is that incompleteness is a common feature of even our best efforts to understand reality, and that it doesn't necessarily need to be seen as defeating to theories. Depending on the size of what is left unexplained, it should be entirely possible, at least in principle, to regard the god hypothesis as theoretically incomplete without also thinking that its incompleteness renders the hypothesis rationally untenable. This at least is the view I hold in relation to the ideas of the nonphysicality of god, creation *ex nihilo*, and the fact that god does not sit within the spatiotemporal frame of reference we do.

Objection 4: *It is not a genuine explanation of the universe to say that god caused it. This is no more of an explanation than it was an explanation of the Sun and its*

---

[69] See Parsons (2006), McMullin (1982).
[70] Sachs (1988).
[71] Explanations were eventually found for some but not all of what Bohr's theory left unaccounted for. Within the more mature quantum mechanical view of the atom, for example, the decay of electrons from higher to lower energy states was treated as essentially lacking in cause, thereby leaving this feature of electron behavior as fundamental to the physics of the universe as Bohr's model did.

movement across the sky to say that it was the Sun god Apollo's chariot. And at any rate, if god explains the universe, what explains god?

There are probably three main objections that can be reconstructed out of this objection as criticisms of the explanatory value of the god hypothesis. They are:

1. The god hypothesis is explanatorily incomplete because it relies upon something that is itself unexplained—god. It is therefore unacceptable.
2. The god hypothesis is unacceptable because the thing it uses to do the explaining—god—is a larger mystery than the thing that it purports to explain—the universe.
3. The god hypothesis is unacceptable because it uses an unacceptable mode of explanation.

Putting aside everything we've just covered in relation to theoretical incompleteness, the first of these criticisms can be faulted as based upon a mistaken understanding of the logic of explanation. It has never been a strict requirement for a good explanation that the thing doing the explaining (called the *explanans*) is itself explained. The reason why is simple: if circular explanations (A explains B and B explains A) and self-explanation (A explains A) will not do, the demand for explanatory completeness would lead to an infinite regress. Supposing that B stands to explain A, an explanation of B would be needed before B can actually do that. But if one goes ahead and explains B by appealing to some fact C, C will now need an explanation before it can explain B, and hence before B can explain A. This problem goes on *ad infinitum*, and risks meaning that we could never truly explain anything if everything that explains must itself be explained, for we can never complete the infinite series to achieve explanatory closure. For reasons of logical necessity, then, all explanations must *somewhere* rely upon something that is just accepted.

Probably the best-known proponent of the second criticism is evolutionary biologist Richard Dawkins. In his bestselling book *The God Delusion*, Dawkins argues that as the universe's creator, god must be more complex and improbable than the universe itself. As he puts it, a "God capable of continuously monitoring and controlling the individual status of every particle in the universe cannot be simple. His existence is going to need a mammoth explanation in its own right."[72] If so, how can it help to posit the existence of something that is more mysterious than the thing you are attempting to explain? That is a bit like taking two steps forward and four steps back—you just don't get to the place you want to go by doing it. The name of the game with explanation is mystery reduction, not mystery maximization. Dawkins's argument depends on his claim that designing things are necessarily more complex (and hence more improbable) than the things they design. If that claim is right, our ignorance about the particulars of the ontology of god doesn't matter— we can know that *however* he is composed, he is more complex than the universe itself.

So, is it necessarily the case that designers are more complex than what they design? I don't see that it is. If we wanted to, we could create a physical structure somewhere out in the depths of space that was composed of extremely intricate and ordered parts (for artistic purposes perhaps, or just so we could say that we did), and then continually add to it until the level of its complexity exceeded our own according to some appropriate measure of that.[73] It might take a ridiculous amount of time and money to do it, but in principle it could be done. Creators needn't always be more complex than the things they create, then.

Let's suppose that Dawkins is right, though, and that in virtue of having created the universe and knowing everything about it, god *must* be more complex than the universe is. This will only harm the explanatory merits of the god hypothesis in the case that god himself cannot be given a satisfactory explanation in terms of his complex state of divinely being. By analogy, imagine that astronauts in the far future come across what looks like the ruins of an ancient city on a distant planet. Marveling at the wonders of the scene before them, they would surely seek to explain it by appealing to the (prior) existence of an intelligent alien species over unknown natural processes. This explanation would involve appealing to the existence of something that is, by the aforementioned principle, more complex than the thing they are explaining. So long as the aliens themselves can be simply explained,

---

[72] Dawkins (2006).
[73] The choice of measure is important. Mandelbrot sets, for example, can produce fantastically elaborate and complicated patterns despite being generated from (and hence being mathematically describable by) comparatively simple mathematical formulas. Depending on how you wish to describe them (either mathematically or as a pixelated image), those images can be regarded as either very simple or very non-simple.

however, this does not matter. And the obvious explanation to give the aliens, of course, would be evolution by natural selection.

This shows that there nothing wrongheaded about using more complex things to explain less complex things so long as the more complex things are explainable in such a way that the *chain of explanation* reduces rather than increases the overall mystery. This in turn leaves the way open to god to serve as an effective explanation of the universe, even if he himself is more complex than the universe is, so long as his complex state of being can be explained simply.

So can it? On account of the theory of life's meaning developed in this book, it can: god's divine state of being can be explained as the result of a long, self-guided process of spiritual evolution involving the broadening and deepening of his understanding, and the choices he made in respect to himself, given all of that. His spiritual development could not be said to have been helped along its way by a created universe, but it was never suggested that spiritual progress and development can *only* occur by way of experiences in the world. The universe was postulated as something that assists with our spiritual evolution, not as something that is necessary for it. If so, there is no need for us to suppose that god has timelessly existed in a divine (and so by prior contention, non-simple) form.

Of course, the notion that god could have once been less than divine is likely to strike some as an unsettling idea. You need only to look at how the idea of god is religiously treated to get a sense of how important god's permanence and unchangingness is to people in their way of thinking about him. Speaking for myself, though, I find no difficulty in imagining god having evolved into his divine state of being. By my lights, it has a rather attractive simplicity and elegance to it, and serves to unify humanity with divinity by fundamentally the same process of spiritual change.

Since this is only an explanation of god's *divinity*, it is not an explanation of everything about god. For example, it does not explain the very existence of conscious agency or the alleged fact that the structure of being allows for a state of divinity as a metaphysical possibility. As was mentioned, though, there are always going to be unexplained elements (in the form of brute facts) within any explanation that avoids both circularity and appeal to self-explanation, and I can't see why taking either of these two things as brute facts means that the god hypothesis cannot be successful.

The third criticism faults the god hypothesis for using an unacceptable mode of explanation in explaining the universe—namely, *intentionality*. Intentional explanations, it can be argued, are inferior to non-intentional explanations when it comes to physical phenomena, and as such should be avoided whenever possible.

We use intentional explanations all the time, of course, and could not get by without them. They are probably the most successful kind of explanation we have, in fact, for they constitute the majority of the explanations we come up with and accept from others. When we examine phenomena beyond the social world, though, things become different. The history of science shows that the most successful kinds of explanations in that domain have always tended to be non-intentional in character.

Take the illustrative case of Isaac Newton once again. In the course of theorizing about the universe, Newton invoked god to explain why the Sun is the only luminescent body in the solar system, why the only luminescent body in the solar system is at its center, why all the planets lie on a single plane of orbit around the Sun (rather than at all angles to it, as was noted in the case of comets), and why the planets travel on that orbital plane in the same direction. Most famously of all, though, Newton invoked god to solve a tricky problem to do with the orbits of the planets.

The problem was this: according to Newtonian theory, all bodies with mass gravitationally attract one another across empty space. What this means is that it is not just the planets that are attracted to the Sun (and the Sun conversely to them), but also the planets to one another (and their moons too, and so on and so on). This raised the rather unpleasant possibility that the planets might destabilize one another's orbits as they tug and pull on each other and either slide towards a fiery death or hurtle off into the frozen depths of space. The risk appeared greatest in the case of Jupiter and Saturn, for they both have relatively large masses and sit next to one another in the ordering of the solar system. A devout believer, Newton's solution was to say that god's hand enters periodically into creation and prevents it from all going wrong.

Looking back, it is hard to see how he thought this was a good explanation. After all, it hardly seems like a beautiful or divinely-minded system of physics for god to have to constantly miracle amendments to the solar system's configuration to keep it in good working order. Surely he could have found some better way?

The world would need to wait about a century for the brilliant French mathematician and astronomer Pierre-Simon Laplace to find a non-supernatural solution to the puzzle of planetary stability. Despite all concerns held to the contrary, Laplace showed on mathematical grounds that the orbits of the two planets are actually stable over long periods of time, and hence that there is no real danger of them destabilizing one another any time soon.

An even more impressive example comes from the replacement of god as the explanation of the biological diversity found in the world with Darwin's theory of evolution by natural selection. What explains the incredible number of organisms on Earth and their amazing fit with so many different environmental niches? Not the creativity of god, said Darwin, but the elegance and simplicity of an evolutionary process acting over hundreds of millions of years.

Taken as general pattern of development, the tendency of god-based explanations to be replaced with purely physical, non-intentional explanations in science could make it appear to some as if god acts as nothing more than a placeholder for the truth when we don't know what it is. But if that is the case, should we even bother with god-based explanation of physical phenomena in the first place? And in the case of fine-tuning, what are the chances that the god hypothesis will succeed there when it has failed as an explanation of so many other physical phenomena, including natural disasters, disease, biological diversity, and planetary stability?

There is a flaw in this so-called "god of the gaps" argument against the explanatory value of god, though, and it has to do with the contingency of history. Suppose that, historically speaking, twice as many scientists had been twice as enthusiastic in their religiosity, and that this had inclined them to appeal to god as an explanation of many more things than history records. This would have presumably led to many more explanatory failures on the part of the god hypothesis, and therein provided (by the logic of the 'god of the gaps' objection) ever more reason today to think that god-based explanations of fine-tuning are unlikely to succeed. But surely our assessments of the likelihood of a theory's truth should not depend so heavily upon contingent social and historical facts, like the religiosity of scientists over history and the number of attempts they made to inject god into science?

The real issue raised here is deciding which reference class it would be wisest to judge the merits of the god hypothesis by when it comes to the problem of fine-tuning. Suppose you wanted to know what your chances of living to at least eighty years old are. Since you're a human being rather than a turtle or a dog, one way you might try and do this is by looking up the average human life expectancy. This choice of comparison would then constitute your choice of reference class. Yet taking the category of all things human is not the only reference class you might try and assess the probability of living beyond eighty by, and it may not be the best one. For example, while you are indeed a human being, you also very likely fall into one of two further biological subcategories—male or female. Since females tend to live slightly longer than males, you'd get a different answer if you assessed the probability by choosing the more limited reference class of "human males" or "human females." But all sorts of other things affect life expectancy, too. For example, people who live in first-world countries, exercise daily, and eat healthy food typically live longer than people who drink lots of alcohol, live in polluted and/or third-world countries, or who live below the poverty line. Reference class choice clearly matters a great deal, then, and if we choose reference classes badly we can get misleading answers.

Suppose we want to treat the god hypothesis as just another intention-based explanation and judge it by the success or failure of intention-based explanations generally. If so, it won't come out too badly, for in the social world of human beings intention-based explanations are very successful. Yet if we choose to see it as an intentional explanation and judge it by the success of intentional explanations in the natural sciences, it will not come out anywhere so well.

Neither of these reference classes strikes me as a sensible choice, however. For one thing, while god-based explanations are examples of intention-based explanations, intention-based explanations aren't necessarily god-based explanations. This means that treating the god hypothesis as just another intentional explanation will inappropriately advantage it with the success of intention-based explanations in social domains. On the other hand, we should see that when it comes to fine-tuning, what we are really trying to explain is not some physical fact *within* the universe (like the orbital stability of our solar system or the biological diversity of life), but something about the physical characteristics of the universe as a whole. As such, the historical failure of the god hypothesis when applied to phenomena within the universe really isn't all that relevant. Moreover, by the lights of the thesis suggested in this book concerning god and his spiritual function, the god hypothesis really isn't something that should have been ventured towards those phenomena in explanation in the first place.

In short, then, while the god hypothesis may or may not be successful as a metaphysical explanation of the universe as a whole, it is far from clear that weighing it down with the full history of its applications to scientific facts within the universe is a sensible thing to do.

Objection 5: *The tendency of people towards belief in god can be largely explained as a result of the architecture of our evolved brains, and in particular about that, to our hyperactive agency detection devices. For evolutionary reasons we have been disposed to "see" intention behind all sorts of things when the reality is that there isn't any there. The sometimes irresistible tendency to ascribe intention to things inclines us to the idea of a god (or gods) as an explanation of the universe. Yet because we know we have brains driven towards seeing the world in intentional terms, we should ignore (or at least look very suspiciously upon) the intuitive appeal of god-based explanations of the universe.*

Imagine the scene two hundred thousand years ago as one of our early human ancestors sets off in search of food one stifling hot day. As they pass by a dense thicket of bushes, a rustling noise is heard to come from within. A spike of adrenaline surges through their system as they wonder alarmed: *what caused that?!!* If it was a lion, leopard, or something similarly large and predatory, the noise represents an overwhelming need for action on their part. If it was just an unexpected gust of wind on an otherwise calm day, however, there is no need to panic.

Whatever the cause, there are two major behavioral options open to them: our protagonist could either flee the moment they hear the noise, or they could continue on as normal. Combining these behavioral pathways with hypotheses concerning the cause of the rustling, we get a combination of four different causal interpretations and actions. If they assume it was a large predator, run, and it was a large predator, they will increase their chances of survival, for they have a better chance of escaping if they do. If they assume it was a large predator, run, and it was just the wind, it will only cost them some lost energy and perhaps a little embarrassment. If they think it was just the wind, do not run, and it was something large and predatory, they have a good chance of ending up as something's lunch. Finally, if they think it was just the wind, do not run, and it was just the wind, no harm is done and nothing is lost.

If we run a cost-benefit analysis on these different possibilities, it seems that evolution would have selected for ancestors who were pre-programmed to run by default, for those who did would have tended to live longer than those who didn't. One of the easiest ways to get our ancestors spontaneously running, of course, was to predispose them to interpret phenomena like rustling bushes as caused by something possessing intentionality and awareness. In predator-rich environments like those in which our ancestors evolved, that policy would have resulted in longer lasting hominids. It is better to be safe than sorry, after all.

The evolutionary conclusion of this is that as human beings we have inherited minds over-primed by evolution to infer the causes of things as intentional rather than non-intentional. In the harsh and often short-lived environments of our evolutionary past, thinking like this served our ancestor's survival needs better than other approaches. Needless to say, any early philosophers who reflectively paused to contemplate whether they were justified in regarding the cause of a sound as coming from something with intentionality would have been deliciously selected against.

If that is so, we're at risk of being drawn into belief in god simply because we're biased towards explanations that validate the intuitive feeling we have that the world was intended. Why? Because seeing events has having intentional causes is intellectually satisfying; it's what our brains want to do by default. What we fail to realize, however, is that the feeling of intention behind the universe is an indirect consequence of a long-running and rather basic evolutionary goal of not ending up as something's lunch.

The idea that our thinking might have been affected in such ways seems plausible and is relevant to the god hypothesis insofar as our initial estimates of its probability could be pushed higher by the intuitive appeal of the idea that the universe was born in purpose. It is worth noting, however, that the fact that we might be naturally predisposed towards accepting intentional explanations doesn't mean that the true explanation of the universe *can't* be intentional. I can be biased towards believing that I am a morally good person, for example, and still genuinely be a morally good person. In and of itself, being biased does not preclude us from having true beliefs in the same direction as our biases point us. In addition, there are probably other more powerful sources of bias operating in favor of the god hypothesis than hyperactive agency detection—like the fact that it stands to alleviate a great deal of the anxiety that people feel about death. And, of course, inasmuch as one can be biased *towards* the god hypothesis, one can be biased *against* it as well. Because of this, it is necessary to keep one's eyes open for bias no matter which side of the question one happens to fall.

The other thing to note is that this objection against the god hypothesis risks entering us into somewhat dangerous argumentative territory. To see why, imagine that I was a Marxist and wanted to convince everyone that Marxism is fantastic. To achieve this, I prepare a long presentation on the virtues of Marxism that includes a wealth of different arguments, tables of economic data, and detailed analyses of history. Also imagine that after presenting all of this information to you, you casually lean over to the person next to you and whisper, "Don't worry, he only believes all of that wish-wash because he wasn't hugged enough as a child."

On one hand, it could be entirely true that my advocacy of Marxism causally hinges upon my not having felt loved enough as a child. Perhaps feelings of abandonment or not being loved led me to develop a certain set of psychological and emotional characteristics that, had they been absent, would not have resulted in my present Marxist outlook. Even so, it would be wholly inappropriate for someone to raise that as though it somehow defeats the arguments I presented. Whether good or bad, the merits of my arguments on behalf of Marxism are independent of my psychological particulars. What this means is that stories about the causal trajectory of my thinking cannot be used as a substitute for addressing the reasoning I defend my Marxist beliefs with.

It is similarly the case with god. The plausibility of the outlined evolutionary scenario points us to a need to approach the intuitive appeal of intention-based explanations of the universe with added scrutiny, for their appeal could be (indeed, is likely to be) at least partly due to a general bias in human thinking favoring intentional explanations (though exactly how strong that effect may be is unclear). What it does not do, however, is show that belief in god is irrational or misplaced, that the god hypothesis cannot be true because we are biased towards it, or that the arguments given in defense of belief in god are erroneous.

Weighing Up God's Theoretical Adequacy

Assessing the merits of the god hypothesis as an explanation of the universe is a largely comparative enterprise. That is, we form a judgment about the god hypothesis's adequacy in explaining the universe by looking at how well it compares to its rivals in doing just that. Aside from agnosticism, three major competing theories to god were introduced on this front: the multiverse hypothesis, the deeper physics hypothesis, and the chance hypothesis. By looking at how these theoretical possibilities do in relation to the criteria of evaluation set out before, we put ourselves in a position to determine which one of them offers the strongest overall explanation. We'll start with the chance hypothesis.

The Chance Hypothesis

That there could be no deeper reason for the fine-tuning of the universe than dumb luck is, by anyone's admission, a clear possibility. If we imagine the values of the constants and parameters being set by little dials somewhere, we know that the dials had to be set to *some* value or another, and that if they were spun around randomly, they could conceivably fall upon a combination of values that results in life-permitting conditions. Even if the chances of that occurring are extremely improbable, improbable isn't the same as impossible. And just think: highly improbable events happen all the time. Every one of us is testimony to the truth of that, in fact, because of all the many millions of sperm that *could* have fertilized the egg we developed from, only one of them actually did. And naturally enough, if the universe had not turned out in possession of a life-permitting physical character, not a single one of us would be here to notice that about it.

Still, while chance certainly could have been the reason why the universe is finely-tuned, to give it as the answer is to effectively capitulate on explanation as a theoretical virtue. Chance is capable of *accounting* for why the universe is life-permitting, but it cannot truly *explain* it.

More than that, there doesn't seem to be anything that can't be explained—or perhaps more accurately, explained away—by appealing to chance. One explanation of how Mozart was able to write such astonishingly beautiful music is that every time he picked up a quill he just scribbled randomly, not knowing the slightest thing about what he was doing, and by nothing more than pure luck managed to compose serenely beautiful music. We can even imagine that he couldn't really play the piano, either; whenever he sat down in front of one he would just start tapping away at the keys, and wouldn't you know it, by nothing more than chance he got enormously lucky every time.

Yet just because we can explain away Mozart's musical ability with chance doesn't mean we should. Compare the chance hypothesis with the prodigy hypothesis. According to the latter, Mozart was extraordinarily gifted and pursued music with a voracious appetite throughout almost his entire life. From that baseline of outlying talent and knowledge came his music. If the value of explanation means anything, surely the latter hypothesis is the better of the two.

And so it goes with fine-tuning. Insofar as explanation is treated as an epistemic value, chance comes up very poorly as a theoretical solution to the problem.

The Deeper Physics Hypothesis

If anticipations of a deeper physics are well-placed, the constants and parameters that make our universe life-permitting, and that presently seem to us to be unconstrained, were determined to have their life-permitting values by a more ultimate set of physical laws than we are presently aware of.

The example used to illustrate was of a world that is permanently encased by a thick layer of cloud. Because the cloud obscures the sky, observers there never see the star that is their sun, and so come to believe that it is just a basic feature of physical existence that light of a certain intensity shines down from the cloud. This could be viewed as a remarkable coincidence. After all, much more light and the surface would be too hot for life to survive, while much less and it would be too cold. What people there fail to realize is that the level of light is determined by deeper facts about their planet's atmosphere, the star it is in orbit around, and the distance of their planet from that star. If they could only see beyond the clouds, they would know that the light's intensity is not an unconstrained constant of physics, but something determined by an unseen aspect of reality.

Something much like this might be true of the constants and parameters that life in our universe depends on. If it is, all this talk about the problem of fine-tuning could well have been misplaced, for it could all be an artifact of our own ignorance—an illusion stemming from our incomplete understanding—and not something that needs metaphysical entities like god or a multiverse invoked over.

Two major considerations lend themselves in support of this view. First, in the minds of many physicists, it would be ugly or inelegant for the universe to have so many free numbers floating about within the laws that give it its physical definition. If nature is maximally elegant or simple at the fundamental level of description, then we can expect that the laws we presently have for it are not the most ultimate laws of the universe.

Second, the history of physics evidences a certain pattern of reduction whereby collections of higher level phenomena have been reduced to simpler sets of unifying physical laws. The unification of electricity with magnetism by James Clerk Maxwell in the nineteenth-century and of electromagnetism and the weak nuclear force by Salam, Glashow, and Weinberg in the twenty-first are two of the clearest examples. If we take this pattern of increasing unification and simplicity as telling us something about what the deepest laws of the universe would be like, assuming they exist, there are grounds in that to hope that one day we will discover a simple and elegant set of physical laws that is responsible for everything we see.

One scientist who believed very strongly in the idea of an all-encompassing set of physical laws neatly and concisely describing the universe was Albert Einstein. As he said at one point, "What I'm really interested in is whether God could have made the world in a different way; that is, whether the necessity of logical simplicity leaves any freedom at all."[74] By "God" Einstein didn't mean a divine being; for whatever reason it was, Einstein annexed the three lettered word to mean *nature*, or the totality of everything that is naturally a part of the universe. While this was confusing, what he was really asking was whether the universe could have come out in any other way, or whether there was some deeper, internal reason why the universe had to be as ours is. Einstein expressed his answer to that puzzlement in the following way:

There are two kinds of constants: apparent and real ones. The apparent ones are simply the outcome of the introduction of arbitrary units, but are eliminable. The real ones are genuine numbers which God had to choose arbitrarily, when He deigned to create this world. My opinion now is—stated briefly—that constants of the second type do not exist and that their apparent existence is

---

[74] Barrow (2003).

caused by the fact that we have not penetrated deeply enough. I therefore believe that such numbers can only be of a basic type, as for instance π or e.[75]

Earlier we saw that there are weak and strong versions of the deeper physics hypothesis. The strong version maintains that there is just one self-consistent set of physical laws that the universe could have ultimately had, and for reasons of mathematical necessity those laws lead to a physical outcome that permits life. The weaker version is not as constraining as this, for it allows for the existence of many different self-consistent sets of physical laws. However, there is said to be at least one set of ultimate laws that, for reasons of mathematical necessity, leads to our universe having life-permitting characteristics.[76]

While the strong version would provide a compelling answer to major questions about why the universe ended up as it is, the weaker version would not do so quite as effectively. To see why, suppose that the values of the parameters and constants are fixed by a deeper set of physical laws P_1. One of two things is possible for P_1: either P_1 holds for all possible universes, or it holds for only a subset of them.[77] This corresponds to the strong and weak versions of the deeper physics hypothesis. If it is the former, the conclusion we are forced to accept is that no universe aside from our own was possible. If it is the latter, however, the question of why our universe happens to be one governed by P_1 instead of some other set of physical laws P_n would remain. While the mystery of that puzzlement might certainly be less than the one that surrounds the question of full-blown fine-tuning, there is still something to be answered there, and it cannot be answered by the deeper physics hypothesis.

Assessing it for simplicity, the great advantage of the deeper physics hypothesis is to avoid relying upon any metaphysical entities like god or the multiverse to explain why our universe allows for life. And as we've seen, it sits consistently with a certain pattern of reduction found in the

---

[75] Quoted in Barrow (2003) from a letter sent to Ilse Rosenthal-Schneider. The symbols π and e are mathematical constants, and take on the particular values that they do for reasons of mathematical necessity.

[76] Davies (2006).

[77] Exactly how many of the values of the constants are explained by a deeper physics matters quite a lot here. If it is possible to explain the values of only most of those constants in this way, things get rather more complicated. For simplicity's sake I'll treat the deeper physics hypothesis as relating to the case in which all of the life-sensitive constant's values are explained by a deeper set of physical laws.

history of science where various phenomena have been unified and reduced to simpler underlying laws. On top of that, it is appealing at least insofar as it eliminates constants as brute facts from our picture of nature.

At present, however, there isn't any theory identifying the constant-determining physical laws the deeper physics hypothesis needs to explain why the values of the constants are exactly as they are. Because of this, the deeper physics hypothesis is more of a statement about what sort of explanation we will have in our hands in the future, and hence can suspect as being the case right now (despite our ignorance about the details). It could conceivably be true that while there *is* a constant-determining deeper physics to the universe, that it is too complicated for human beings to ever understand, of course. Should that be the case, while the deeper physics hypothesis would be right, it would never come to be known as such.

It could also be true that there just isn't any deeper system of physics waiting out there in nature to be discovered. After all, there is no *need* for the universe to have the most elegant and simple set of physical laws possible governing its existence. Physicists might long for that to be the case, but it isn't required. And as we'll see with the multiverse hypothesis in the next section, there are theories in physics that treat the values of many constants as coming about entirely randomly through quantum fluctuations when universes are born. If so, there isn't any deeper reason for the values of these constants than the inherent chanciness of quantum mechanics.[78]

Still, if the universe obeys a deeper set of physical laws, and if those laws are humanly comprehensible, they are something we can hope to discover at some point. Only time will tell how that goes.

The Multiverse Hypothesis

The Ancient Greeks believed that the stars existed in a giant crystalline sphere that rotated around the contents of the solar system. Sitting outside the sphere was nothing—not void, not matter, just nothing at

---

[78] Equally, if the hopeful theory of quantum gravity that is string theory is right, the dream of a constant-determining deeper physics to the universe is just that, for string theory allows for the existence of unfathomably many physically distinct universes across the string landscape (the number is usually quoted at 10^{500}).

all.[79] The limits of the solar system and the limits of the universe were therefore one and the same.

Helped along by the invention of the telescope, it dawned on European astronomers in the seventeenth-century that the universe was considerably larger than had been previously thought, and that the stars in the night sky are in fact actually other "suns" much like our own in an enormous galactic collection.

By the late eighteenth-century the idea that our galaxy might be just one of an untold number had arisen, but it wouldn't be until the 1920s that compelling astronomical evidence was found for this proposition.

That such a massive expansion in our vision of reality could have taken place so recently—less than one hundred years ago—is at once both remarkable and unsettling. Over the course of centuries we have gone from seeing reality as composed of a single solar system to one made of a single galaxy, and then from that have accepted the existence of billions upon billions of galaxies. How much more might there be, beyond even this? If the multiverse hypothesis is right, the answer is simple: there is one step left to go.

As we've seen, the basic premise of the multiverse hypothesis is that what we take to be our universe is really just one of either vastly or infinitely many. Just like the god hypothesis, the multiverse hypothesis should be viewed as a collection of multiverse-themed hypotheses rather than any one hypothesis in particular, because there are many different ways in which to get a multiverse. Unfortunately, this raises problems for us in assessing its merits. After all, which one should we look at when trying to focus in on a concrete example? Inflation theory strikes me as the best choice, for not only is it part of the presently accepted cosmological model of reality, we have seen that it gives rise to a multiverse in a very natural kind of way.

Interestingly enough, though, with as many as fifty different versions of inflation in the literature as far back as 1997,[80] and with many more having been thought up since, inflation theory is itself really more of a research program or a family of different hypotheses than any single theory. While many of these variations have since been ruled out by very fine observations of the pattern of light found in the cosmic microwave background, the fact that there have been so many formulations is an indication of both the adaptability of the basic inflationary idea and the

---

[79] Kuhn (1957).
[80] Earman and Mosterin (1999).

fact that there has yet to be any complete and widely agreed upon understanding of it.

It is true that inflation does not require the existence of any brand new ontological class of things to get off the ground, but it still requires the existence of a quantum field capable of driving inflation, and in some versions a new field is specifically invented for that purpose. Moreover, the shape of the inflation field's potential energy curve must be right if it is to lead to life-permitting inflationary expansion, and this raises questions over how much fine-tuning the inflation field needs to do that.

Though the discovery of the universe's accelerating expansion can be seen as lending support to the idea that the universe could have been compelled to expand by a massive amount of energy contained in empty space, it is worth noting that the existence of dark energy was not predicted by inflation theory, plays no role within inflation theory, and the two forces that are associated with these expansions—dark energy on the one hand and inflation energy on the other—are many, many orders of magnitude different from one another in terms of their strength.[81]

If we draw away from inflation theory to look at more general considerations concerning multiverses, there are a number of things to be said. For one thing, if the size of the multiverse is infinite, the scope of physical reality is expanded upon infinitely.[82] This could mean different things for the simplicity of the multiverse hypothesis. Depending upon the particulars of the multiverse hypothesis in question, it could either mean that an infinite number of universes of a certain limited type or range exist, or that an infinite number of universes of all possible types exist. In the latter case we might say that while the multiverse is conceptually simple (since it does not require us to draw a boundary between universes that exist and universes that don't exist), it is about as ontologically complex (at least according to one measure of that) as any hypothesis can be. This particular measure of ontological simplicity may not be anywhere as important as others are when it comes to determining theoretical truth, however.[83]

---

[81] Steinhardt and Turok (2008).
[82] One might believe that the universe is already infinitely large, and hence say that the multiverse would not really infinitely expand the size of reality. Even if that is true, an infinite multiverse would still unbound the infinite scope of reality in the direction of other universes.
[83] For example, the measure that looks at *types* of things rather than their number strikes me as far more relevant to the question of a scientific hypothesis's truth. For the record,

If there does happen to be an infinite number of distinct universes, two somewhat unwelcome consequences must be faced. First, and as we've already seen, there must be an infinite number of "you" somewhere out there within the framework of reality. These doppelgangers can be subdivided into two broad groups. On one hand are the infinite number of "you" in other universes who experience everything exactly the same as you do. On the other are the infinite number of "you" who have histories exactly the same as yours up until some arbitrary time t_1, but who experience something divergent from that point on. Since the number of universes is being taken as infinite, every possible experience for "you" would be realized an infinite number of times over, no matter how absurd or unlikely it might be (like spontaneously turning into a chicken and clucking around in the drape of one's former clothes, to give just one example). While it might be tempting to put thoughts of implications like this aside when thinking about the reality of an infinite multiverse, they follow as an absolutely certain consequence of it, and cannot be legitimately ignored. Even those who find themselves most skeptical about the idea of god must surely wonder which of the two would do more violence to our sense of reality: the existence of a divine being, or the existence of an infinite number of people who are more or less identical to us.[84]

The second unwelcome consequence is that an infinite number of universes would cause us problems for what we could then predictively say about our own universe from a statistical point of view. For example, in the scheme of all possible universes there will be an infinite number that are identical to our own up until now, but where a horse is elected as the next president of the United States. There will also be an infinite number where a human is elected as the next president of the United States. If we take the set of all existing universes as a statistical guide to how our universe will proceed, it seems as though we should be at a

---

I take the standard version of an infinite multiverse to be randomly exhaustive and non-exclusive. That is, it covers every logically possible outcome without restriction, and manifests each of those logical possibilities an infinite number of times over. Note that neither of these two assumptions are necessary properties of an infinite multiverse. One could have it such that only one of every logically distinct universe is represented, for example, or where the set of universes is restricted somehow concerning the full spread of what is logically possible for them, but where the universes are still infinite in number.

[84] It could be argued, however—and entirely reasonably as a response, in my opinion—that all that the difficulty of accepting the latter represents is the erroneous limitations of human intuition and cognition.

complete loss to say which of those two outcomes is more likely, for both of them are equally well represented in the set of existing universes. But surely it is absurd to think that the next US president could really be a horse, let alone think that the odds of that happening are 50/50.[85] While a merely finitely-populated multiverse would avoid both of those problems, we would then need to know where the line should be drawn in order to compose the finite limit on which universes exist.

Explanatorily speaking the multiverse hypothesis does do very well to explain the fine-tuned features of the universe. The sheer abundance of universes and the fact that they vary in physical characteristics makes it entirely unsurprising that at least one universe would exist with life. If we add in the fact that evolved observers like us will only ever encounter universes where the physics is consistent with the evolutionary development of life, we have a good explanation of why our universe is life-permitting: it is just one of enormously many, and some of those universes were bound to be life-permitting just by chance. Indeed, if the number of universes in the multiverse is infinite, it was certain that an infinite number would be life-permitting.

Unfortunately, the explanatory method used by the multiverse hypothesis does raise a certain problem, it relates to the possibility of "Boltzmann Brains" (named in honor of the nineteenth-century Austrian physicist, Ludwig Boltzmann). The essential idea is quite simple. In much the same way that quantum physics permits individual particles to spontaneously pop into existence from the vacuum of space, it should be possible for much larger collections of highly organized particles—like a *brain*—to pop into existence from the vacuum as well.[86]

While the chances of something as large and complex as a brain forming are absurdly low, the critical point is that probability of it happening within any finite region of space with a positive energy density is *nonzero*. Because of this, if there should happen to be very, very, very

---

[85] Pointing out that there are more possibilities than just a human or a horse being elected won't help the mathematics of the situation. You might argue that because the laws of the United States prevent animals from being presidents, that it is impossible for a horse to be the next president—a horse could only ever be a pseudo-president, for by definition of both law and commonsense, only human beings can be presidents. I don't disagree, but at any rate it doesn't really matter. If you don't like this particular example, you need only replace it with something that is equally possible and equally absurd; the details here are not what is important for the point being made.

[86] Boltzmann Brains may form either through quantum mechanical fluctuations or as thermodynamic fluctuations of pre-existing matter (which is what Boltzmann himself was concerned with).

many universes out there with positive energy density spacetimes, Boltzmann Brains really will exist. Moreover, the universes don't need to be fine-tuned to the extent ours is for it to happen. In fact, if there are enough universes out there with enough volume, Boltzmann Brains will form in such numbers across the entire expanse of those universes that they will vastly outweigh the total number of evolved observers in finely-tuned universes.[87] This sounds completely crazy, I know, but many physicists—including many very eminent ones—take the possibility of Boltzmann Brains entirely seriously.

As you would expect, functioning brains won't survive for more than a fleeting instant in the cold void of space. Extended survival isn't required for Boltzmann Brains to be an issue, however, for an observer for a moment is still an observer, and that's where the problem comes in.

And what is the problem, precisely? Because Boltzmann Brains exist in such numbers, if you were to pick an observer at random from within multiverse, chances are that they would be a Boltzmann Brain rather than an evolved observer like you or me. But that makes *us* rather unusual; why are we so fortunate to find ourselves in a universe that permits us to exist in a meaningful sort of way? The mere existence of a multiverse alone does not explain it, for there is no observation selection effect associated with it.

It might be replied that because we can't actually know for sure that we ourselves aren't Boltzmann Brains, there's no reason to think we got lucky in having meaningful existences. After all, you might only have the memories you do because you are a Boltzmann Brain that has formed somewhere in the void with just the right neurological configuration for it to *seem* as though you have lived a meaningful life. As for the perceptual experiences you are having right now, that could all just be a fortuitously coherent illusion generated by the electrical activity of your vacuum-born neurons.

While this is a (scary) possibility, I think there is good justification for believing that we are not Boltzmann Brains. The reason comes from the fact that the chances of any memories and perceptions experienced by Boltzmann Brains being coherent and orderly should be very low given the way that disorder would be favored in the neurological setups by quantum and thermodynamic processes. After all, once the condition of

---

[87] Except if the multiverse is infinite, in which case the number of evolved observers and Boltzmann Brains will both be infinite. For an exploration of the philosophical relevance of Boltzmann Brains to the multiverse hypothesis, see Collins (2008b).

being an "observer" is physically satisfied, everything else to a Boltzmann Brain is entirely superfluous. There's no strict need for a Boltzmann Brain to have a highly coherent set of past memories, for example, or to have perceptual experiences that are highly structured. Dividing through the total population of Boltzmann Brains within the multiverse, then, it seems as if the vast majority will not experience or remember anywhere as coherently or orderly as we do. This in turn strongly suggests that we ourselves are not Boltzmann Brains (though it cannot be ruled out with complete certainty).[88]

Still, while we can be pretty confident about that, we can also worry that if a multiverse does exist, most observers within it still are Boltzmann Brains. This appears to suggest that our particular universe is not just fine-tuned for the existence of life, but for the existence of evolved observers who can have lasting, meaningful, and mutually-interactive shared experiences. After all, if the multiverse hypothesis is right and the Boltzmann Brain problem is real, most observers will not experience anything remotely like this—they will exist instead in a rather solipsistic way for a largely incoherent and fleeting slice of time. Why do we find ourselves exactly where we do, then—in a universe that has the shape of one well-suited to a plausibly-imagined spiritual purpose? Simply making up the rest of the explanatory distance by answering "luck" is not exactly unsatisfying. (Note that while the possibility of Boltzmann Brains is a direct problem for the multiverse hypothesis, it is also a problem for the god hypothesis insofar as god could be held to have created the universe indirectly via a many-universe generating mechanism. After all, what could the spiritual point of all those momentary and fragmented conscious experiences be?)

In terms of causes, if the inflationary mechanism is not accepted as the reason behind the multiverse, one must either try to find some other mechanism for it, or simply stipulate that they all independently exist as brute metaphysical facts. Naturally enough, questions can be asked of any mechanism that is identified. For example, where did it come from? What caused it to exist? To what extent does it itself need fine-tuning? So long as the explanatory gap is less for those questions than it is for the universe as a whole, however, an explanatory advance is possible. On the other hand, if the universes are all taken as just brute facts, we can

---

[88] You might say "but doesn't the fact that I just lived long enough to read that sentence prove I'm not a Boltzmann Brain?" It doesn't, because you have no way of knowing with absolute certainty whether you actually just read that sentence, or whether you just formed in the void with the vivid impression of having immediately done so.

justifiably wonder why things should have been that way. Why should it have been that so many different universes just exist as a part of reality? While a multiverse of this type would work to solve the problem of fine-tuning, it would only do so by super-inflating the number of things that completely inexplicably exist.

The predictive virtues of the multiverse hypothesis really depend on which particular version being assessed. For example, there are a number of concrete predictions that inflationary models make that can be tested, including the almost exactly flat shape of the observable universe and the details of the pattern embedded in the light of the cosmic microwave background. While not every model of inflation has survived analysis of the data collected on the microwave background by recent experiments, some models have proven to be remarkably consistent with it. On the other hand, if the many different universes of the multiverse all just exist as brute facts, it is unclear what predictive consequences the idea might hold, if any.

The existence of a multiverse would fit nicely with the way our understanding of the scope of reality has continually expanded over time, and its mode of explanation is consistent with the kinds of explanations that have proven to be successful in the physical sciences.

While there are clearly both advantages and disadvantages to the multiverse hypothesis as an explanation of fine-tuning, overall I think that there is a lot to appreciate about it, and I wouldn't be surprised if some version of it did turn out to be true. While that would not spell the end of the god hypothesis *per se*, it would certainly prevent the god hypothesis from drawing direct evidential support from the problem of fine-tuning.

The God Hypothesis

What the god hypothesis really represents, deep down, is a way of ordering consciousness in relation to the universe. One can have it in one of either two ways: either consciousness precedes the existence of the physical universe, or the physical universe precedes the existence of consciousness. The god hypothesis tells us that the first of those two possibilities is the correct one.

In terms of predictions, the god hypothesis tells us that the universe will have a physical character that is consistent with the existence of not just life, but intelligent life. While this is not a prediction whose truth we could have failed to observe upon being here, that doesn't matter unless we refuse to extract ourselves from the situation and look at things as though our own existence is not already part of what is known.

If some kind of external spiritual influence operates over our lives, then depending on what that consists of, there would seem to be at least the bare possibility of intersubjectively establishing that. Exactly what to expect on that front, though, and hence what to look for in trying to separate it from the background noise of life, is difficult to know in advance.

Another prediction set forward by the god hypothesis is that consciousness is not annihilated by physical death. Since the truth or falsehood of this prediction is not something that we can discover firsthand without dying, this unfortunately makes it rather unhelpful from the point of view of evaluating the god hypothesis's truth. Beyond that, it is not clear what else the god hypothesis might predictively offer.

In terms of simplicity, the god hypothesis benefits from being conceptually simple and easy to understand in its basic premise. What is rather less simple about the god hypothesis is the fact that it requires us to hold in our ontological scheme the immateriality of the conscious self and the existence of some kind of metaphysical framework for reality. While it is never desirable from the point of view of simplicity to accept an expanded ontology, this is something we must always be open to doing. Indeed, if we look back at the history of science, we can find a constantly evolving and highly adaptable ontological landscape. Sometimes the changes that have taken place there have involved the addition of new entities or properties into nature, like electric charge, neutrinos, antimatter, dark matter, and the Higgs field. Other times they have involved the elimination of previously accepted entities or properties, like phlogiston, the caloric fluid, and the electromagnetic ether. The adaptable character of what is ontologically accepted at any given point in science continues right up to today; there is nothing permanent or final about what science *presently* accepts as being part of the scheme of nature. Quantum field theory, for example, abandons the traditional view of elementary particles as fundamental to nature's inventory and treats them instead as bundles or peaks of energy in associated quantum fields. In much the same way that waves in the ocean are nothing more than energetic manifestations of the ocean itself, rather than things all by themselves that you could break off and carry around in your pocket, electrons and neutrinos are treated as just energetic ripples in associated quantum fields and do not have any truly independent existence. And if string theory (which treats the most basic constituents of reality as incredibly small, string-like rips in the fabric of spacetime that, by vibrating in different patterns, produce the great abundance of different particles that physicists have discovered) should ever come to be scientifically accepted, our understanding of what lies most deeply within the inventory of nature will experience deep change once again. The fact is that there has not been any one, wholly stable and complete view of what exists, and our best scientific answer to that question is constantly up for revision.

That said, the kind of ontological expansion that the god hypothesis requires may be a hefty one. If a physicist proposes to explain something by invoking the existence a new kind of particle with familiar properties, that is not the largest possible addition to the scheme of nature they could make, for there is already a class of things called particles and they are just adding one more thing to the recognized list. The god hypothesis is different in that it suggests postulating the existence of things that fall into a whole new class—namely, consciousness as a physically independent thing. Simple as the god hypothesis might conceptually be, then, from an ontological perspective it is more demanding. Still, the size of that ontological increase won't be the same for everyone. In particular, if your ontological scheme of what exists already holds consciousness as something that is independent of physical entities and properties, then the step required to accommodate the existence of god may not be as bad.

Where the god hypothesis does better is with its explanatory power. Most significantly there, the god hypothesis directly and effectively explains why the universe exists with a physical character that permits the existence not just of life—for a universe filled with nothing but bacteria would be enough to satisfy that condition—but complex, conscious, intelligent, feeling, social, investigative and morally apprehending forms of life like you and me. As for why that would be a divine goal in the first place, this can be explained by looking to the importance of the values embedded in the theory of life's spiritual meaning outlined in the first chapter (e.g. understanding, independence, self-creation, growth, and so on). Finally, god's divine state of being, and hence his ability to create a universe that is life-permitting, can be explained as the result of a long process of spiritual development which is not radically dissimilar from the one each of us is said to be currently engaged in (which is itself an appreciable little symmetry).

True enough, the mode of explanation used by the god hypothesis is different from what one finds in the physical sciences. While some might take that as a reason for doubt, it is far from clear that the history of the failure of the god hypothesis to explain various phenomena within the universe (like the orbits of particular planets or the biological diversity of life) provides any indication that it will not be successful when it comes to questions about the universe as a whole.

Aesthetically speaking, the beauty of the god hypothesis comes largely from the ideas themselves—from the idea of a divine being, for example, and from our lives as spiritually predicated upon values like understanding, independence, and self-improvement. Beauty of this kind has no obvious connection with truth, however, and so cannot be used as a reason to think that the god hypothesis is any more likely to be true.[89]

As far as logical coherence goes, I am not aware of any logical issue that convincingly applies either to general formulations of the god hypothesis or to this one in particular. That is not to say that allegations of logical incoherence do not exist.[90] One objection along these lines is that the idea of god existing outside of time is incoherent. After all, what meaning can the idea of god having acted *outside* of time to create the universe possibly have? To act involves bringing about a change, and for a change to occur there needs to be a time before the act when the state of affairs was one thing, and a time after the act when the state of affairs was another. If that is not the case then things would remain constant, and that makes nonsense of the idea that any action took place. If god is transcendent of time, how could he conduct any action?

I find the argument unpersuasive, for just because god exists outside of the universe does not mean he would exist outside of any spatiotemporal framework whatsoever. It is not as if our universe has unique possession of space and time, after all. We tacitly admit as much when we say that other universes could exist that are wholly independent

---

[89] As a relevant aside, we saw earlier that the deeper physics hypothesis is partly motivated by a belief that it would be inelegant for so many free variables to be included within the laws of physics, and by the fact that the history of science points tantalizingly towards the possibility of an underlying elegance or beauty deep within nature. If that is so, there is reason to think that god does *not* explain the fine-tuning of the universe— not because god doesn't exist or didn't create the universe, but because there is simply no such thing as fine-tuning within nature to be explained (i.e., it would be inelegant for god to create a universe that needed to be fine-tuned, so he didn't). This too is surely a possibility, and one that is necessary to be aware of.
[90] See Drange (1998a) for an overview.

of our own. While each universe would have its own spatiotemporal framework, it certainly wouldn't be identical with ours.

More than this, it is easy to imagine sophisticated computer programs running simulations of the world far off in the future. These simulations can be imagined as being so detailed that they even simulate people right down to the individual neurons firing in their brains. While scientists running them on the outside can pause, fast forward, and rewind the simulation at will, from the inside things would no doubt appear to proceed in a seamless and uninterrupted way. After all, the only temporal reference inside the simulation would be what is going on with it, and that is programmed to be perfectly coherent and orderly. While time on the outside would be a complete mystery to anyone who found themselves on the inside of such a simulation—they would have no access to it at all—it would not be any less real or existent because of that.

The external consistency of the god hypothesis has also come up for considerable criticism. For example, it has been objected that the creation of the universe from nothing would represent a violation of the law of conservation of energy. While energy can change from one form to another in a closed system, the law requires that the total amount of energy contained in the system can neither increase nor decrease. From this it is argued that for god to create the universe from nothing would be for him to cause the situation to go from one where there is no energy to one where there is more than zero.

This objection doesn't strike me as being persuasive either. After all, how can you violate the physical laws of a universe that doesn't actually exist yet? At any rate, the problem is a nonstarter, for there is no issue with the universe being created out of nothing if the (negative) potential energy of the gravitational field of the universe exactly cancels the (positive) energy contained in its mass-energy. If that should happen, the total amount of energy will sum to zero and no laws of energy conservation will be threatened.[91]

The possibility that our lives might be subject to some kind of external metaphysical influence is less easy to do away with as a problem for energy conservation. A natural assumption to make about any such interaction is that it would require some kind of energy transfer between

---

[91] Cf. Collins (2008a), who argues that because the total energy in the universe is undefined within the framework of general relativity, one can never actually know if the negative energy of gravity balances out the positive energy contributions made by matter.

whatever is metaphysically doing the interacting and the universe itself. The same issue arises if god is aware of what is going on inside the universe, for that too might be presumed to require some kind of transfer of energy.

By way of response, it is worth noting that it must surely be possible for god to know what is going on inside the universe and for our lives to be subject to metaphysical influences in ways that don't modify the total energy content of the universe. This might be because the energy exchange involved in the interaction is balanced out somehow, or because the interaction itself just doesn't involve any transfer of energy. While the former possibility has a notably *ad hoc* feel to it, the latter possibility has a precedent in quantum mechanics.[92] The fact is that if you have two quantum mechanically entangled particles separated from one another by a distance, what happens to one of the particles under measurement can instantaneously affect the quantum state of the other particle. Because this interaction happens instantly, and because in quantum mechanics energy is quantized and cannot exceed the speed of light, by definition this interaction cannot involve an exchange of energy.[93] But if it is possible for *some* physical-physical interactions to occur without energy exchange, it stands to reason that it should be possible for metaphysical-physical interactions to occur without energy exchange too.

Whether or not these points serve as adequate responses to the problems described, the god hypothesis being advanced has wider challenges confronting it than just these. As we saw in the first chapter, there is a difficulty in accounting for all the suffering found in the world by appealing to the value of things like understanding, independence, and self-authorship. While the issue was complex, the gap between how much pain and suffering exists in the world and how much we can easily accept a divine being having allowed for represents probably the single greatest challenge facing the theory.

A second major issue concerns the place of nonhuman animals within the spiritual theory of life outlined. While human beings are obviously cognitively advanced creatures, we are also massively outnumbered in the world by other animals, and most of them are not anywhere near as cognitively advanced as we are. If we accept that many animals are also

---

[92] *Ibid.*
[93] Quantum entanglement cannot be exploited to send information from one person to another faster than the speed of light. Though that is the case, it is also of no relevance to the fact that energyless interactions do exist in quantum physics.

the bearers of consciousness, it is something of a puzzle to say what the spiritual meaning of *their* lives might be. For us it was said to be a way of apprehending firsthand important truths of being. Could the spiritual goal of conscious animal life be essentially the same? But if it is, what kinds of truths are involved with that? Most animals are not in a cognitive position to think out the same kinds of complex thoughts as we can, after all. Is the spiritual meaning of animal life the same as it is for human life, then, or is it something altogether different?

A third problem relates to the possibility that our lives might be subject to some kind of spiritual influence or direction. The problem with that has to do with the balance and scope of our freedom in the world. In short, any metaphysical involvement would appear to compromise the spiritual value of the universe as an independent recasting of being, and perhaps our freedom and autonomy along with it, too. Since these values were identified as key to understanding the spiritual purpose of life, the theory looks like it is subject to an internal consistency problem. Though it should hardly come as a surprise if certain spiritually important values (like the value of independently seeing how things are) are not *absolute* in their importance, there is still a natural tension involved there that should not be overlooked. If our lives do tend to move us in certain directions over others for spiritual reasons, how does that come about, what is involved, and perhaps most crucially of all, how does that fit with the values the theory depends upon for its plausibility?

Sitting in the philosophical background to all those questions is the rather tricky issue of free will itself. Though others may find themselves more able to, I have great difficulty seeing how the spiritual meaning of life set out makes much sense unless we posit that humans possess some genuine form of free will. Unfortunately, the idea of fully-fledged free will is tremendously difficult to make philosophical sense of.[94]

A fifth problem is not really an issue for the truth of the god hypothesis *per se*, but its application to the problem of fine-tuning, and it has to do with the prediction that god would seek to create a life-

---

[94] There seem to be three broad possibilities: either the choices we make are fully determined by prior causes, randomly determined, or some mixture of random and determined. The problem is that none of these possibilities helps to validate the sense we have of ourselves as making genuinely free choices. If it is the former, for example, then our choices would seem to simply play out through us rather than come from us. The same goes if our choices are random somehow. And if they are some mixture of random and physically determined, they face both problems at once.

permitting universe. There are obviously different ways in which he could have achieved that. While god could have created a single universe that was finely-tuned towards life's existence, for example, it's possible that he could have also set up a universe with a very elegant underlying set of physical laws that didn't require fine-tuning to begin with. Alternatively, he could have created some kind of universe-generating mechanism that would have produced a vast amount of distinct universes, at least one of which would have been likely to be life-permitting. While the truth of the god hypothesis is compatible with all three of these possibilities, it is not indifferent to the level of support it receives from each of them as an explanation. In particular, the existence of god is evidentially better supported by the universe being directly fine-tuned to enable life's existence than it is by a deeper physics or a multiverse-generating mechanism.

Therein lies a problem, for we cannot be entirely sure god would not have used something like a universe-generating mechanism to get a life-permitting universe. After all, it would give the universe an even greater natural standing as a setting for life, and the naturalness of the universe was highlighted as something of considerable spiritual importance. Moreover, it seems clear enough looking back that Newton's use of god to explain the stability of the orbits of the planets was woefully mistaken. Any god worthy of divinity would surely have created a universe with a system of physics that needed less intervention than *that*. Should we expect something similar when it comes to the universe as a whole? It seems to me as though we should. Even granting the existence of god, then, it is not completely clear that explaining the universe directly by appealing to his actions doesn't commit the Newtonian mistake all over again.

The same issue holds for the god hypothesis and the possibility of a deeper physics. If the universe required that all the correct constants and parameters had to be plugged into it before it would be life-permitting, this was arguably not the most beautiful physics that could ever have been conceived for it. One way of getting around that, other than having a wide spectrum of all possible universes independently generated, would be to devise a system of physics that restricts things at the deepest level to inevitably lead to what we see.

These problems are certainly meaningful and I don't think it does any good to ignore them. To seek some perspective on them, though, it is worth noting that the existence of problems for theories is far from unusual, especially as they stand in their first approximations. In fact, problems are essentially par for the course for any intellectual attempt to understand the world. We've already encountered a number of examples of this from the history of science. Newton could not say what the cause of gravity was, Darwin's theory of evolution required Earth to be much older than it was calculated to be, Wegener could not give a cause for the continents' drifting apart or together, and Rutherford's early model of the atom was inconsistent with classical electrodynamics.

If additional examples are needed, we can note that Copernicus was unable to explain the unchanging size of the planets and stars as Earth orbited the Sun, Galileo was unable to explain the absence of observed stellar parallax (except in a very *ad hoc* way), the corpuscular theory of light was inconsistent with the fact that light travels faster in air than it does in water, the wave theory of light was inconsistent with the fact that a medium was needed for waves to propagate through what was apparently completely empty space, Hooke was unable to specify the physical mechanism behind fossilization, the pre-Big Bang idea of an eternally-existing universe was inconsistent with the second law of thermodynamics, Becquerel's discovery of radioactivity appeared to violate the law of conservation of energy, the Steady State model of the universe was inconsistent with observed differences between near and distant galaxies, Hubble's observation of an expanding universe gave an estimate for its age that was younger than Earth itself was known to be, Einstein's theory of special relativity was found to be inconsistent with Kaufman's beta-ray experiments in the very same year it was published, Maxwell's kinetic theory of gases was inconsistent with measurements of the specific heats of gases, and quantum mechanics was (indeed, is) famously inconsistent with relativity theory.

Examples like these point us to two things. First, even our very best attempts to understand reality have tended to have problems, and further development of them was routinely needed in order to overcome those problems. Second, having problems doesn't *necessarily* mean that an idea is wrong (a point that goes just as much for the other hypotheses covered as it does for the god hypothesis specifically).

Sometimes the problems facing a theory are so severe and numerous that we just find it more reasonable to give up on it as standing a realistic chance of being true. Other times, though, we may see just enough in a particular idea that the time and effort spent trying to find answers to its problems is not seen as misspent. I know clearly enough what our approach towards religion should be, for the problems facing it are too significant to hold out any rational expectation that it is true. The deeper question is, into which category should the idea of god when *non-religiously* formulated most appropriately fall?

Rationality and the Burdens of Judgment

Our task would be a whole lot easier if there was a simple formula or set of rules we could follow that would tell us exactly which hypothesis to regard as the most probable in light of all the points of evidence considered. Unfortunately, no such formula exists. Not only do we not know exactly which values are the best criteria to judge the theoretical profile of the different hypotheses by, or how those values should be weighed relative to one another, the values themselves tend to be conceptually hazy and ill-defined, and hence difficult to apply, and the evidence complex and conflicted.

The situation is only made worse by the fact that we are all naturally disposed towards making a comfortable home for ourselves inside the space of our own beliefs, and that can make dispassionately assessing questions like those posed in this book a very difficult thing to do. Beyond all the other ways in which one might do it, it is conceivable that someone might consciously or unconsciously arrange their epistemic values in order to advantage a certain outcome of belief over others. To do this would not be being honest with ourselves, though; when truth is the goal, our judgments are supposed to reflect our very best efforts at fairly and honestly assessing the plausibility of different hypotheses in light of the evidence and their epistemic characteristics. By intentionally arranging our values to achieve desired outcomes of belief, all we end up achieving is engaging in a very elaborate form of self-deception.

Because the question of fine-tuning and its best explanation is difficult, I expect that reasonable differences of opinion between people should be entirely possible, even given access to all of the same information and evidence. If someone holds a different judgment to me about the adequacy of the god hypothesis as an explanation, for example, and has come to their view from a space of epistemic values that appears to me to be close to my own, I needn't see their position as irrational or unreasonable simply because they don't agree with me.

As for what my own views happen to be, though, I would say that the god hypothesis is not an insensible explanation of the universe's life-bearing properties by any means. Though it can certainly be reasonably denied as true, it possesses a number of epistemic virtues in relation to the problem of fine-tuning, and that at the very least makes it a worthy explanatory option to have on the table.

That said, I also think that the more natural level of explanation for the god hypothesis to operate over isn't directly in relation to the problem of fine-tuning, but indirectly in relation to the existence of either a multiverse or a deeper-lying physics, should either of those two things be objectively the case. Whether or not the god hypothesis is superior to those other options as a direct explanation, the fact is that it is also consistent with them—it explanatorily ties in with them, in the sense that god not only could have used one or the other as a means of obtaining a life-filled universe, there is at least one reason for thinking that he would have (they provide for a more natural standing of the universe, which is taken as important within the context of the spiritual thesis outlined in this book, and they have a greater beauty or elegance about them as a method for creating the universe than simply plugging in the correct physical characteristics needed for life to emerge).

The god hypothesis covers multiple explanatory bases, then: it can either be used to directly explain fine-tuning, or it can be used to indirectly explain fine-tuning by explaining why there is a multiverse or a simple underlying physics that constrains the universe to permit life.

It's true that from an ontological perspective the god hypothesis is not the simplest of the four non-agnostic options examined, and it does come with a number of problems that need answering. However, it also does its explanatory job well, whether directly or indirectly, for it explains not simply why our universe permits the existence of life, but why we find ourselves in a universe that allows for rich developments in consciousness in moral and epistemic terms (something that is by no means necessary about it).

In light of this, I can't agree that views of the god hypothesis as either very highly probable *or* very highly improbable are justifiable in this particular evidential context. Naturally enough, there is a wide area of probability that falls within that, and how the god hypothesis ends up in our evaluations depends on many things, including its epistemic character, the nature of its problems, the character of its explanatory rivals and their problems, one's own background beliefs (especially, for example, one's existing views of the ontological status of consciousness), and the explanatory role accepted for the god hypothesis (either direct or indirect).

In general, though, there are two claims of different strength that I would make. The stronger one is that given a fairly standard set of epistemic values and value-weightings, it is not irrational of someone to see plausibility in—and even tentatively believe—the god hypothesis for its merits in explaining fine-tuning.

Even if it inadvertently overestimates the reasonableness of belief in god to say that tentative acceptance of the god hypothesis can be justified on these evidential grounds, I still hope to have shown the truth of a weaker claim, and that is that there is least *one* way of understanding the meaning of life spiritually that is philosophically interesting, morally unthreatening, and worthy of further investigation and consideration.

Insofar as difficulties and puzzles remain for that account, it would be best to think of it as a stepping stone or a foundation for a less problematic, more coherent, and more plausible future version. As for its merits in the form it currently has, however, I leave that to readers to judge.[95]

---

[95] Nothing in the foregoing analysis takes into account any subjectively-closed reasons people might have for believing in the god hypothesis, and that is something that might certainly affect individual estimations of its probability. This exclusion was quite necessary however, for our goal was to look at reasons for belief in god that are principally open to all people as a basis for human spirituality. Whatever epistemic reasons people might privately have to believe in god, they are unlikely to transfer over to anyone else. Nor does it consider any intersubjectively open reasons that are non-fine-tuning related—primarily because I am not aware of any that are convincing.

Chapter 5
Atheism and the Search for Meaning

Why, then, did the fool say in his heart: "God is not," since it is so obvious to the rational mind that you exist supremely above all things? Why, because he is a dim-witted fool.
—St. Anselm (1033–1109)

Of Atheism and Its Varieties

Ridiculed, hated, and even vilified over the course of human history, atheism continues today to suffer from an undeservedly poor reputation. The opinions like those of St. Anselm notwithstanding, with so much pain and suffering in the world it surely just is perfectly reasonable for someone to question whether god exists or not. Atheists may or may not be objectively right in the way they answer that question, just as those who believe in god may or may not be themselves, but to accuse atheists of irrationality or immorality on account of their atheism is, I think, an enormously unfair and conceited libel to make against them.

Convention recognizes the existence of two kinds of atheism. The first is known as "weak" atheism and consists of nothing more than a lack of belief in any god. "Strong" atheism, by contrast, involves positive disbelief in the existence of any god. The difference is that whereas a weak atheist knows of no reason to believe in a god, and so fails to on those grounds, a strong atheist sees good reason to positively *dis*believe in the existence of any god.

Weak atheism philosophically represents the correct default position to take, for it is always going to be the epistemically stronger of two positions to assert the existence of something than to hold no positive belief in that regard. The truth of this can be more easily seen if we simply change the topic from god to something else, such as the existence of unicorns. If we're wondering whether any unicorns graze optimistically at the bottom of our gardens, the most rational path to take is to fail to believe that any do until there is some reason known to us to justify our believing otherwise. The situation with the existence of god is principally no different. Until we have good reason to think that god exists, we should not believe that he does.

While the distinction between weak and strong forms of atheism is philosophically entrenched, it is problematic that hardly anyone will truly fall into the weak atheist category. After all, how many people are aware of themselves as atheists and yet lack any reason at all to disbelieve in the existence of the most generic and relevant kinds of gods? The problem of evil is widely recognized as a significant problem for the existence of a divinely knowing, capable, and good being, for example, and I can't think that awareness of it escapes all but a small number of self-identifying atheists. If we were to total up the number of reasons for disbelief that float around out there, then, it seems to me that most self-identifying atheists should have at least one reason for disbelief known to them, and hence should be (by the prior definition) "strong" atheists.[1]

Distinctions between atheisms aside, one may wonder whether the word "atheist" should exist at all. As Sam Harris has argued, we don't have special words in our vocabulary for people who don't believe in fairies or unicorns. But if that is so, why do we have a special word for those who don't believe in god?[2] The underlying worry is that by having a special word to mark out those who don't believe in god over fairies and unicorns, illegitimate credibility is lent to the idea of god's existence. But in the minds of atheists like Harris, god's existence just isn't any more plausible than the existence of fairies and unicorns. To speak of "atheists" and "atheism," then, is to allegedly treat belief in god with more respect than it objectively deserves.

Whether or not having a word for atheism really does covertly slant people's judgments towards the plausibility of god's existence, I suspect that the reason why one exists is rather less exciting than linguistic subterfuge. The fact is that while most people in the world don't believe in unicorns or fairies, most of them do believe in the existence of something that can be placed under the category of "god." If in another possible world there was a large and established community of unicorn believers, I can easily imagine them having a word in their language to

---

[1] I readily accept that some ways of formulating the god hypothesis manage to avoid the problem of evil entirely (such as if we say that god is both non-moral and wholly non-interacting). In such cases, and in the absence of any other reasons to disbelieve, we are all weak atheists in respect to *those* kinds of gods. Such gods are not the usual targets of human interest, however.

[2] Harris (2004).

mark out the minority of people who did not believe as most others do. Such a term might be very useful if efforts were made by unicorn believers to convert nonbelievers, or more sinisterly, if they wished to treat nonbelievers differently from the rest. At any rate, it doesn't seem all bad for the cause of atheism that lack of belief in god has an identifiable label. One might just as easily argue that those who can't efficiently identify themselves in their position of nonbelief when arguing with believers in god (because a word for nonbelief in god doesn't exist) will have a harder time arguing for the superiority of their own position than otherwise.

As for atheism itself, it is sometimes accused by believers of being just another religion. This too is unfortunate. If the reason is to be that positive disbelief in something counts as participation in a religious viewpoint, note that this would leave us all belonging to an enormous number of different religions, for nearly everyone positively disbelieves in a vast number of things (from the existence of leprechauns to dragons and vampires). Surely it is absurd to think of ourselves as so widely religious as this, however. Moreover, it has to be at least somewhat unfair to religions like Christianity and Islam to say that monotheistic religious belief and disbelief in the Loch Ness Monster are just different manifestations of religiosity. I don't think that most Christians or Muslims would view their belief in god anywhere near as trivially as I view my disbelief in Nessy.

If the reason is to be instead that many atheists are just as passionate and vocal about their atheism as many religious people are about their religious beliefs, it is worth noting that there are a practically unending number of things that people are very passionate about that aren't religions, including music, sports, paintball, and politics. Moreover, many people hold religious beliefs and aren't particularly passionate or vocal about them. Enthusiastic passion for something can be neither a necessary nor a sufficient condition for that thing to count as a religion, then.

A third reason that might be given for why atheism is a religion is that it constitutes a worldview (or at least a pretty major element of one). While I don't disagree, it is clearly not the case that all worldviews are religious. Consider the belief that the world we experience is actually a simulation run on a very advanced alien computer somewhere. This might well be accepted as a worldview (or, again, a pretty significant part of one), for it tells us that our world is not "real" as such, but emerges from the technology and programming of an alien species. Are people who believe something like this necessarily committing themselves to a *religious* viewpoint? Well, why must they be? For philosophical reasons that we won't go into here, the possibility that the world is just a computer simulation is taken very seriously in the relevant philosophical literature, and it would be strange if that talk was *religious* rather than simply *metaphysical.*[3] And just in case it is thought that being metaphysical is enough to qualify something as a religion, note that the view that the world is *not* a hallucination or computer simulation is also a metaphysical viewpoint, but that does not appear to make it a religious viewpoint.

It is undoubtedly very difficult to give precise criteria for exactly when something should qualify as a religion. This is far from unusual when it comes to the meanings of words, though. As the philosopher Ludwig Wittgenstein pointed out more than half a century ago, the word "game" is extraordinarily difficult to define too—there is no way of defining the meaning of the word such that *all* and *only* games satisfy the definition. (If you're feeling ambitious, see if you can prove him wrong.) We may struggle no less to say what it is about something that makes it a religion, but the difficulty should not be thought to make extra room for atheism to stand as a religion. My suspicion is that calling atheism a religion has far more to do with trying to legitimize religious belief than it does with identifying some feature about atheism that meaningfully connects it with the world's religions. As Bill Maher memorably put it, calling atheism a religion is like calling abstinence a sex position.

The Problem of Meaningfulness

Another issue with atheism that is more difficult to do away with concerns the sense we have of our lives as meaningful. It has long been said by thinkers ranging from Dostoyevsky to Kant and Voltaire that belief in god's existence is fundamentally important for the meaningfulness of our lives. As the problem can be put, what is the value of living if god does not exist? How could anything truly matter if we are all going to end up annihilated by death?

No matter what conclusion we come to here, it will have nothing to say about the objective truth or falsity of atheism. God either will or won't exist, and the truth of it cares nothing at all for us. The question is still worth asking for the following reason, though: if it *is* the case that

---

[3] See, for example, Bostrom (2003).

we are widely incapable of psychologically withstanding the adoption of atheism without experiencing a tremendous depreciation in the value of our lives, and *if* considerations of things other than truth can properly enter into the question of how we should believe about any particular matter, it will potentially be a valid criticism to make of atheism that it does lead to a sense of meaninglessness. On the other hand, if atheism doesn't or shouldn't lead people to feel that their lives are less meaningful when everything is properly considered, or if it is *only* questions of the truth that are relevant to how we should believe, there will be nothing in this matter to fault atheism about.

So what actually is the alleged problem? The great Russian novelist Leo Tolstoy was able to set it out in a particularly vivid and biographical way.[4] At a time in his life when he had more than most others in Russia could have dreamed of, Tolstoy began to have doubts. An atheist since his late teens, Tolstoy achieved great fame and fortune and had a wife and children to care for. Yet whenever he asked himself "What is it all for?" or "Where does it all lead?" he could think of no satisfying answer.

As his need to find an answer intensified, he found that he could no longer put the question aside by focusing his attention on other things. While distractions had worked in the past, he noticed that he was becoming increasingly needful to know *why* he persevered in living, helping others, or taking care of himself. What lasting good did any of that ultimately do, either for himself or for others? So far as he could tell, the only real answer was none. Indeed, whether he enjoyed his life immensely or suffered horribly from it, he could discern no true or lasting consequence of that from a most expanded point of view. In the blink of a cosmic eye he would soon be permanently dead, and so too would everyone else who knew him not long after. At the end of a long enough timeline everything would ultimately be as if nothing had ever been. All the fruits of his labors and of his life would ultimately come to nothing. He found this a deeply despairing thought. As he put it,

> I had come to a precipice and saw clearly that there was nothing ahead of me but destruction. It was impossible to stop, impossible to go back, and impossible to close my eyes or avoid seeing that there was nothing ahead but suffering and real death—complete annihilation.[5]

---

[4] See Tolstoy (1884).
[5] *Ibid.*

Unable to free himself from his growing nihilism, he slipped into a depression.

Though the warmth and light of his life had left him, his daily routine did not change. He still got up in the morning, ate, drank, and slept just as he had done before. Indeed, he could not help but do these things, for it was his habit to do them. Yet it was not *life* as it once had been. Something was now absent, and it had left him when he had started to think about why his life mattered.

Tolstoy reasoned that human life is hopeless, much like the situation of a traveler who leaps down a well in order to escape from a great beast that is chasing him. Unfortunately, at the bottom of the well the traveler finds the mouth of a great dragon waiting to devour him if he should fall. The traveler therefore reaches out quickly and grabs hold of a twig that is growing from the side of the well. At this point the situation deteriorates, for two mice appear and begin gnawing away on the twig that is keeping him alive. If in the midst of all of this he should notice a few droplets of honey just off to the side, and which he could (with some effort) reach out to and eat, could he still genuinely enjoy their taste? But *how*, when the dragon waits below, the beast waits above, and time is all the while running out?

Tolstoy imagined four ways out of the dilemma: by the blessings of ignorance, by committing to hedonism, by killing ourselves, or by resignation to the fact that life is meaningless. In his own case he found that ignorance was not an option, for he had already glimpsed too much of the problem to put it from his mind, and as an intellectual it was in his nature to think about such things anyway. Nor was hedonism a realistic option, for he had already found that nothing in his life tasted nearly as sweet as it once did. While he praised suicide, he claimed he lacked the strength to overcome his crushing fear of death to actually end his life. The only other option was resignation to the fact of life's meaninglessness, but Tolstoy noted that this was no true solution at all. Nevertheless, it was all he had available; unable to live and unable to die, all he could do was hang perilously on the wall and wait for his time to run out.

As you can see, this is all pretty heavy stuff! Hardly heartwarming or inspirational reading. Torturous though he rationally found it, in the end Tolstoy reluctantly accepted a fifth possibility—to raise oneself out of the depths of nihilism by embracing faith in god. In doing this Tolstoy developed a (rather horrid, in my opinion) conception of the meaning of life as concerned with the salvation of one's soul by humble labor, suffering, mercy, the renunciation of pleasure, and a deep sense of connection with others in faith. In bringing relief to his nihilistic misery, Tolstoy found that faith simply *worked*, and did so where nothing else seemed able to.

In a postscript to his work detailing his struggles with nihilism, Tolstoy wrote about a dream he had not long after finishing writing it. The dream began with him lying on his back neither comfortably nor uncomfortably. When he began to wonder what it was he was lying on, he realized that it was a bed with a number of plaited strings hanging across it. Aware that the strings beneath him could move, he attempted to move the ones that were closest to his feet when they began to become uncomfortable. Unfortunately, as he did this he inadvertently managed to push them too far away, and in an effort to retrieve them, the ones that were supporting his legs were caused to give way. With both of his legs now hanging unsupported, Tolstoy tried to move his whole body to correct the situation. This caused some the strings beneath his body to slip and entangle, thereby making his situation only worse. The whole of his lower body now dangled downward, and, alarmingly, his feet did not feel any ground.

Frightened and uncomfortable, he looked about to see where he was. In doing this he saw that he was actually at a very great height—a height much higher than he could ever have imagined, in fact, and from which no detail of the ground could be seen below. Panicking, he felt as though he could slip at any moment if only the last few strings supporting his body gave way. As he felt himself getting closer and closer to falling and in a desperate attempt to find a solution, he looked upward. Above him he saw only an infinite sky, and he soon found that when he focused on this he was able to forget about the great distance beneath him. This helped calm him down, and as he continued to focus he sensed that he was not really in any danger of falling at all. He came to realize that he was actually being held in place somehow by a single support beneath his body, and that this supported him the best whenever he was looking upward. Soon after he became aware that the support was on a very tall pillar and that the stability of the pillar was unquestionable. As the dream scene came to a close, it appeared to him as if a voice said, "See that you remember," and he awoke.

Value and the Continuity of the Self

The idea that god is somehow essential for our lives to be meaningful is widespread. Like Tolstoy, many who ponder the meaning of life find that the thought of god's existence eliminates any nihilistic worries they may have surrounding it. It is easy to conclude from this that the issue of meaningfulness must be tightly bound up with belief or lack of belief in god. This inference is mistaken, however, for what most directly matters is not the existence of god but the continuation of our conscious identities beyond death. Belief in god only *appears* to solve the problem because belief in life after death and belief in god go hand in hand, such that in most cases to believe in the latter is to also believe in the former.[6]

But why might the shortness of life (and hence the finitude of our conscious identities) threaten life's meaningfulness? Unfortunately, the reason is not easy to discursively state, but I think it can be put in something like the following way: if this life is all there is for us, our lives do not possess any lasting significance. At some point in the future, all things will inevitably be as though they never were. We are forced by this to see that all the many different possibilities for our lives are, in their ultimate effects, exactly equivalent to one another. Whether we suffer terribly or live a life of opulent luxury, nothing about that will survive in its significance once time has marched itself on.

Why can't we find meaning in the significance of our lives as we live them, though? Why does it matter that our lives don't have unending significance—they still matter for us here and now, do they not? While it is possible to avert one's gaze and make every effort to see our lives only from within, Tolstoy found that once you have fully apprehended the problem from the outside it can be very difficult to put that view entirely aside from thought and avoid looking at it time and time again. Unfortunately, nihilism has a siren's call.

The fact is that however our lives might turn out for us, we will at some point not matter—not to others, and not to ourselves. This means that from within our own frame of reference we have only contingent importance to ourselves; we can matter to ourselves at the very most *only in passing*. The thought of this is not easy to ignore. By and large, most of us *want* to be of greater significance to ourselves than just in passing. The

---

[6] This isn't by any *necessity*, of course; it is perfectly possible to believe in god and yet have no belief in any associated afterlife. I take that situation of belief to be relatively uncommon, however.

idea that we must all die, and hence cannot matter to ourselves more than temporarily, calls into question the value of everything that is connected to us in value through the nexus of our own consciousness. The problem is that *everything* is connected to us through the nexus of our own consciousness, for without conscious existence everything is lost to us.

Our metaphysical continuation beyond death solves this issue by enabling us to matter more to ourselves more than just in passing. If we cannot escape our own existences any more than we can leap free from our own shadows, there would be no way of escaping the fundamental importance of ourselves to ourselves.[7] While the value of other things might come and go depending on how we value them, if we are inextricably tied to ourselves in consciousness, we stand as a permanent feature in our own scheme of values.

My suggestion is that the ability to project ourselves forward into an indefinite number of possible future states enables stable and rich valuing in our lives here and now. Our lives matter because the significance of what we experience with them will potentially always echo for us in some way, and *that* in turn matters because we, as conscious experiencers of ourselves, will always matter for us.

The Frustration of Death

An analysis of the problem of death by Keith Augustine does well to illuminate why it can cause a sense of meaninglessness. Augustine argues that the problem starts when we choose life goals for ourselves that death is likely to frustrate.[8] The psychology behind it is quite simple: if we feel we cannot succeed with what we centrally want to do or obtain in the course of living, we begin to feel as though there is no point to living.

Suppose someone is a bit of a romantic and wants nothing more than to experience unending love. The finitude of our lives obviously represents a rather great obstacle to that. While experiencing love is

---

[7] The only remaining sense in which we could "escape" ourselves, assuming our interminable metaphysical continuity, is by *changing* who we are. In other words, if it is not possible for us to not exist, given that we do, all that is left for us to do is to change who we are into something that satisfies us more and more. This is exactly what I have proposed life is spiritually all about, of course.

[8] Augustine (2000).

certainly possible in life, experiencing love with the security of it lasting forever is impossible if death will see us to a permanent end. Recognizing that, such a person may then come to feel as though their life has no point: what they most fundamentally want from it they cannot have. (You can see how this is consistent with what was suggested just a moment ago: if we want our lives to stand in a more permanent relation to ourselves than just in passing, and if death makes that impossible, a major desire we hold for everything that goes on within it is dashed. Because valuing anything requires consciousness, the importance of ourselves mattering more to ourselves than just in passing is really a kind of meta-value concerning how we want things of positive value to stand in relationships of value to us. Unfortunately, annihilation by death would mean that this meta-value can never be realized.)

Augustine suggests that the solution comes in being careful to choose our values so that the life goals we build upon them are not threatened by the inevitability of our deaths. His suggestion there is reminiscent of the fox in Aesop's parable who, having come across a bunch of grapes hanging down from a vine one day, finds that they are too high for him to reach. Rather than allow himself to be frustrated by this, the fox convinces himself that the grapes are actually sour, and hence that they would not be any good to eat even if he could get to them.

Augustine's proposal is similar but not identical to the fox's logic. We aren't to decide that a particular bunch of grapes is sour (and so engage in a kind of willful self-deception about the facts), but change ourselves so that grapes (and any other out-of-reach fruits in life) are just not objects of our desire in the first place. It is a matter of changing our values, not our beliefs about the facts, so that we can set ourselves in pursuit of only that which lies within human grasp. Anything else and we may begin to find that our lives start to seem meaningless.

As an explanation of where meaninglessness comes from, this account is intuitively plausible and, so far as I am aware, consistent with existing empirical research relating to motivation. Psychologists know that the strength of our motivation to try and achieve something is related to the value of that thing in our eyes and our expectations of success. Where something is highly valued and we think we can probably succeed with it, we will have a high level of motivation to try and achieve it. Where something is only lowly valued and we do not think we are likely to succeed with it, the motivation we will have to try and achieve it will be correspondingly low. If either the value or our expectation of success is high and the other is not, the level of our motivation to achieve it will suffer in some way.

Where I perceive a problem is in the idea that we can simply recast our values to accommodate a set of life goals that sits easily within the time frame that life affords. While the issue is complex, it seems unlikely that we hold enough power over how we value to simply abandon any problematic but important values and replace them with new ones simply because they (unlike the old ones) are achievable. At the very least we know that the power we hold over our own values is not unlimited. It would be great if things were otherwise, for that would mean we could value something trivially easy as the most richly meaningful thing we could ever do. In that case, our perfect happiness might be literally no more than a single eye-blink away.

Saying this is not to question the idea that people's values can and do change, and that they can and do change as a result of rational deliberation. Ironically enough, death happens to be excellent at bringing about these kinds of rationally-motivated changes in people. One can often find in the fallout from the death of someone close that people start to question their own lives and whether the things they are spending their time on are really the very best things they could be. Is earning more money, buying a bigger house, or seeking the recognition of other people for your work really *that* important? Or is spending more time with family, going on more adventures, and doing more each day to laugh and smile? A genre of art known as *vanitas* is explicitly aimed at inspiring these kinds of reflections. By presenting people with symbols of the swiftness of human life and the inevitability of death—skulls, clocks, watches, flowers, mirrors, half-burnt candles, decaying fruit, empty wine vessels, and so on—the idea is to remind people to spend their life in pursuit of what is truly important and worthwhile.

While the way in which we value is clearly open to change in response to philosophical reflection, this does not mean that the values we base our lives around are *so* available to adjustment that our interests in avoiding nihilism can freely determine them by an exertion of will. For my part, I don't think that mattering more to ourselves than just in passing is a desire that many people would find easy to abandon, and thus suspect that far more of a challenge is involved in implementing what Augustine suggests than appears to have been acknowledged.

Perhaps needless to say, the inherent difficulty of being unattached to the fact that we are conscious should hardly be surprising. After all, consciousness is perhaps the single most amazing, mysterious, and precious thing there is, and it is only through consciousness that anything comes to have value at all. If *anything* has value, then, it is surely consciousness itself, and the fact that we may not want to give it up does not strike me as a fault.

Not everyone feels the pull of that desire equally, or even at all, of course. While some atheists battle with feelings of nihilism, many others report seeing their lives as perfectly meaningful even though they are finite, and we have no reason to doubt them. The fact is that death *need not* be a problem so long as we either surrender or never acquire the importance of things that it stands to frustrate. So long as the goals we set for ourselves are well chosen, then, atheism can stand quite happily as a psychologically viable worldview. Whether everyone can actually manage their values well enough to avoid the problem of death in practice, however, is an open question.

Chapter 6
God, Ethics, and Moral Identity

With numbing regularity good people were seen to knuckle under the demands of authority and perform actions that were callous and severe. Men who are in everyday life responsible and decent were seduced by the trappings of authority, by the control of their perceptions, and by the uncritical acceptance of the experimenter's definition of the situation, into performing harsh acts... A substantial proportion of people do what they are told to do, irrespective of the content of the act and without limitations of conscience, so long as they perceive that the command comes from a legitimate authority.
—Stanley Milgram (1933–1984)

Divine Beings and the Character of Morality

It is often said that god's existence, or our belief in his existence, is necessary for morality. The reasons given typically come down to a set of three different claims about psychology, epistemology, and ontology. The psychological claim is that without god to administer punishments and rewards on the basis of our moral behavior, there would be insufficient motivation for people to live a moral life. The epistemic claim is that without god to instruct us about morality in a book of revelation, we would be unable to tell right apart from wrong and good apart from bad. The ontological claim is that if god did not exist, there would be no such thing as objective moral truth, and since objective moral truths are necessary for the viability of morality, morality needs god. My own view is that god's existence has very little to do with morality, and that the tendency of people to believe otherwise gives them bad reasons for belief. Since belief in god should not be rested upon bad reasons, I will argue against the truth of all three of these claims.

Let's look first at the psychological claim. Is it really true that belief in divine judgment, reward, and punishment is *necessary* for people to be motivated to live morally? Surely it isn't. Take the grizzly but imaginable example of an Orwellian society where cameras and microphones have been set up on street corners and in homes to record what people do and say. This information is stored and monitored by the Ministry of Ethical Standards for the slightest hint of ethical infraction. Anyone found guilty of doing something wrong, or failing to do something right, risks severe punishment. Theft and lying are punished by days or weeks of hard labor, while more serious crimes are punished by solitary confinement, physical discomfort, sleep deprivation, and even physical disfigurement. Sometimes, the perpetrators simply "disappear," never to be heard from again.

It seems fairly safe to say that anyone who found themselves living in such a society would have a compelling reason to live morally, at least as far as the government's ideas about that went. Terrible though such a society would be, it *would* be effective in achieving its moral purpose. This doesn't mean that instituting a regime of social terror for moral purposes would be *itself* morally justified, of course. Indeed, the fact that nobody would actually want to live in that kind of society makes you wonder how anyone could applaud religion for designing its metaphysical equivalent. As for heaven in the Orwellian society, it is superfluous. To get people to be moral, you don't need to create special rewards for anyone for being good—you only need to make the consequences of not being good so severe that nobody would sensibly fail to be.

Now, this doesn't mean that heaven and hell don't provide *more* of a reason for people to live a morally accordant life, but it does mean they aren't the only way for people to be so-motivated. Add to this consideration the fact that there are plenty of people who do not believe in heaven or hell, and who are fully committed to living in a moral way, and you have what looks like a pretty decisive refutation of the claim that divine judgment, punishment, and reward are psychologically necessary for moral motivation.

What about the epistemic claim—that without guidance from god we would be incapable of discerning right from wrong, good from bad? The example set by many atheists would once again appear to provide a straightforward refutation, for most atheists lead lives that are just as virtuous and morally upright as anyone else's.

There is a counterargument, though, and that is that atheists are only able to live morally because the ethical wisdom found in religion has become so infused in the fabric of society that avoiding its enlightening influence is impossible. Atheists are really the victims of a kind of false moral consciousness: they are able to tell right apart from wrong and good apart from bad, but only because religion has managed to get god's moral message across so effectively that it seems completely elementary and natural.

Putting aside the *ad hoc* nature of this account, are we to really think that without god to take us by the hand we would all look upon scenes of terrible pain, suffering, and despair with only pitiless stares of indifference as our response? This is a quite extraordinary claim to make, and certainly not a very flattering one. Beyond the evolutionary fact that we would not have survived this long as a social species without at least a rudimentary sense of morality to regulate our interactions with others, people's religious practices tell very strongly against the idea that they get their morality exclusively from god.

The fact is that most people tend to be quite selective about what they morally accept out of revelation, and will go to considerable lengths to avoid believing some of the worst of it (like that you should stone your wife to death if she isn't a virgin on your wedding night or kill your children for swearing at you). Doing this would be strictly impossible if everyone arrived at revelation as a moral blank slate, ready to absorb whatever it spills out of it without a single questioning thought. While the content of revelation certainly does influence the moral beliefs and values that people hold, we bring much to it before we even get to that point.

Finally, what about the ontological claim—that without god there would be no such thing as moral truth? According to divine command theory, what makes a particular thing right or wrong is that god decided that it should be so. If god had not existed to do this, there would be no morally true statements or claims, and hence no such thing as moral truth.

The most obvious criticism to make is that this implies there could have been a very different set of moral propositions selected by god as true, if only he had willed them to be. This in turn suggests a level of capriciousness about right and wrong that does not resonate very well with most people. We tend to think that torturing and killing children is morally wrong, and that it is morally wrong in a non-arbitrary way. That it *could have been right* if only god, having felt different on the day, had asserted that it was, and without changing any other relevant facts, is a rather difficult idea to accept. What if god had commanded that the rape and murder of anyone not of one's own religion is a supreme moral virtue—perhaps the very highest thing one might do in life? Would that make it so? The person who genuinely believes that all moral truth comes from god is in the unfortunate position of having to say that it would. Not only does this require adopting a highly deferential and accommodating mode of moral functioning, it is a very dangerous one, for it principally opens them up to committing horrors of all kinds if only they perceive them as having been declared right by god.

One attempted solution to this conundrum is to say that rather than having been decided by arbitrary decree on god's part, right and wrong emerge out of god's *character* or *nature*, and hence from the kind of being that god both is and isn't. Though it might sound like an improvement, this revised divine command theory doesn't help, for it is just as arbitrary for right and wrong to follow from god's being as it is for him to determine it by declaration. After all, why should we abide by a set of moral principles that are defined by god's being rather than by some other criteria? Whatever could it be about god that makes his nature the properly defining standard for morality?

One response might be that god's nature is essentially good, and because it is, it makes perfect sense that right and wrong should be defined in terms of it. What does this mean, though? If by calling god "good" we mean that god's nature conforms to some preexisting independent moral standard of goodness, it's not really god's nature but that independent moral standard that is defining moral truth. On the other hand, if we're simply saying, "Let's call "good" whatever it is that god is," this does nothing to justify why we should do that. We could just as easily write out moral statements on pieces of paper, throw darts at them, and call "good" whatever statements the darts happen to hit. What would justify us preferring god's "goodness" over the dart's "goodness"? The answer is hard to see.

Whether by decree or an outgrowth of being, then, the question of arbitrariness concerning morality when it is constructed around god appears to stubbornly remain. But if the alternative is true and morality is independent of god, what is moral truth, and where does it come from?

Free-Standing Morality

The objectivity of moral truth is often treated as a pivotal issue because of people's concerns about moral seriousness if moral truth is nothing more than subjective or cultural. Most of us would like to say that events like the Holocaust were profoundly morally wrong not simply because they were not to our individual or cultural *liking*, but because of what they were in themselves. This seems like a rather difficult thing to do if the truth of moral judgments is entirely relative to individuals or to cultures, though. If I say that bananas are unpleasant or that Vermeer's *Girl with the Pearl Earring* is beautiful, these are both aesthetic judgments that suggest nothing for how anyone else should think or feel—their truth belongs entirely to me in making them. Given this, if moral truths are subjective in the same way that aesthetic truths are subjective, it is hard to see how anyone could treat them with the level of seriousness we routinely do.

If moral truths are objective, though, the truth of a moral statement definitely *would* imply something for how others should think about it, for its truth would hold for all people regardless of their own beliefs about it. It is here that the usefulness of god comes in, for if we can say that it is *god* that determines moral truth, a moral statement's truth would be objective in at least the sense that a) it was not in any way dependent upon us, and b) is applicable to everyone.

Problem solved? Well, not quite, for as we just saw, the idea that god is responsible for the truth of moral statements has some serious philosophical problems. Even if that wasn't the case, though, I can't agree that moral seriousness requires treating moral truth as something that is purely objective.

What I will attempt to do in this section is show that while morality is neither dependent upon god nor purely objective in character, moral truth is still worth taking seriously. With that argument in place, the temptation that some people experience to try and link god with morality in order to secure moral seriousness can hopefully be lessened.

To begin, I think that any even half-plausible theory of morality needs to connect it with the fundamental aims of maximizing things like pleasure, happiness, and wellbeing, and minimizing things like pain and suffering. The concern for pleasure over pain and happiness over unhappiness would seem to be both universal and deeply rooted in human thinking. Nobody really needs to ask what the "good" of pleasure is or what the "evil" of pain is when they are experiencing them—we see it directly in the experiences themselves.

Given deep and universal interests of this kind, my suggestion is that what any system of ethical thought most fundamentally represents is a proposal for how we might best fit ourselves together with one another in a shared social space, insofar as there is some range of freedom over how that is done, and in respect to the realization of those centrally important human aims. Moral systems achieve this by devising ways for us to socially coexist and interact with one another via tremendously complicated sets of restrictions, obligations, and recommendations.

Let's flesh out this idea with some examples. Some actions cause harm to others and are prohibited as morally wrong as a result. Raping and killing someone else for your own pleasure would be an obvious example. Not all actions that cause harm to others are morally prohibited, however. A woman who turns down a man's invitation to go on a date with him might cause him to feel bad, but she could hardly be morally faulted for that. Whatever negative experiences her response might have caused, it was well within her entitlement to choose who she wants to date. That she chose to turn him down, then, is not a morally wrong thing for her to have done.[1]

Contrast that with cases where an action that causes good for others is regarded as morally obligated. If you happen to pass by a small child floundering in a pool, but do not act to save them because you don't want to get your clothes wet, most people would regard this as morally wrong. Indeed, if there was no personal risk involved in lending assistance to the drowning child then, depending upon where you are in the world, you may even have broken laws that require people to help.

Against this stand cases where an action brings about good for other people but is not regarded as morally obligated. I might do a great amount of good by telling someone a hilarious joke that sent them into a fit of belly-aching laughter for five minutes, but I am surely not morally *obligated* to tell them such a joke. I may or I may not tell it, but there is nothing requiring me to.

It is the assumption of morality that by defining what is morally permitted, prohibited, and required, a state of affairs can be entered into that best serves the aims recognized as fundamental within a given moral system (like happiness, wellbeing, avoiding suffering, and so on). In short, then, morality seeks to answer the very important human question, "How best can we all live together so as to get the most out of our lives according to what we mutually find most important about them from an experiential point of view?" What drives the evolution of systems of morality forward is the realization that not everything about a particular way of socially arranging ourselves in respect to each other contributes efficiently towards the realization of those moral aims.

---

[1] There are better and worse ways of saying no, of course, and particularly callous or belittling ways of doing that might be judged to be morally wrong. This is something quite separate from the choice to decline itself, however.

This is to give a very intellectualized gloss to ethical judgments, of course, and for the most part that is not how we actually experience them. We tend to *feel* the rightness or wrongness of situations and ideas much more than we explicitly reason that out about them. More often than not it just *seems to us* as if something is wrong or right, and there isn't any distinct pattern of thought that consciously leads up to that judgment. Despite that, if we're thinking about *why* something might count as right or wrong, it is natural to try and justify our judgments by appealing to the extent to which it either contributes to or detracts from positive human experiences and/or conditions of life.

If that is what morality is about, what are moral *truths*? Whatever they are, they don't appear to be truths in exactly the same way that the diameter of Earth being approximately 12,700 km at its equator is a truth. We can't measure the rightness or wrongness of a situation or event with scientific equipment, nor simply point to the truth of a moral statement in the way that we can with many empirical statements. None of this stops us from experiencing the appearance of moral truth as an integral part of many situations or actions, however.

There is a rather useful analogy that can be made here with language and meaning. Objectively speaking, words on a page are nothing more than highly ordered squiggles and lines and do not possess any intrinsic meaning. Our actual experience with written language is obviously rather different. As you are reading this sentence right now, for example, it will appear almost as if the words *themselves* somehow hold their meaning. How could that be, though, when words and sentences are nothing more than arrangements of symbols?

It is an illusion, albeit a very convenient one. It arises because our brains are so good at ascertaining the meaning of words and sentences according to the rules we have learned for them that we don't have to stop and consciously think about any of it. They work it all out for us, transposing the appearance of meaning into the words and sentences themselves so that, when we read them, we experience them *as though* they were intrinsically meaningful.

I suggest that something similar occurs in the case of morality: our brains place moral qualities (like rightness or goodness) so closely and efficiently with our comprehension of certain states of affairs and actions that it seems almost as if *those things themselves* objectively possess the moral qualities experientially associated with them. They don't, though. As a phenomenon, moral truths emerge only when minds meet worlds, and they exist only abstractly along the seam of the two.

You might think that this must mean that moral truth is nothing more than purely subjective, for what has effectively been said is that moral qualities like right and wrong are not found in the world but are imposed upon it by our brains, and all so efficiently and automatically that we mistake the world as the true source of them. What hope can there be in this for moral seriousness? Doesn't that mean that moral truth is subjective?

The key thing is that moral truths aren't *purely* subjective; more specifically, while morality does have a genuine subjective dimension to it, it also has an objective dimension as well. To see how that can be, consider an analogy with chess. The rules and conditions of the game of chess are decided entirely by convention. How many squares there are on a chess board, how many pieces there are per player, how many pieces there are of each type, the rules governing how those pieces move, what the winning and losing conditions of the game are, and so on, were all settled upon at some point so that the game of chess could exist. It could have easily been that there were 81 squares on a chess board instead of 64, or that the rook piece did not exist. Nevertheless, *given* the way the structure of the game has come to be conventionalized, there really are objectively better and worse ways of playing it. In other words, it's no accident that chess grandmasters consistently beat players of a lesser skill level; they are simply *objectively better* at chess than the people they play. This is only possible because what works and what doesn't is not itself directly decided by people, even if the structure of the game historically was.

The same sort of thing is true when it comes to morality. From the framework supplied by worldly facts and fundamental human aims, moral truths emerge that were *not themselves* chosen or decided. We each have minds capable of having certain phenomenological experiences, for example, and we inhabit a world that was formed in a certain physical sort of way. When we ask, "How best can we live together with one another to best achieve our most basic experiential interests?" note that however the answer goes, its truth is not directly decided by us. Instead, the answer comes from the relationship between the objective world and what we subjectively seek for ourselves in terms of our own experiences.

The analogy with chess can only carry us so far, for whereas chess is played in a competitive spirit against one other person, morality is played out with many people and has both competitive and cooperative aspects. Moreover, whereas in chess the rules and the winning conditions of the game are stable and uniform for all players, in life there is variation in the conditions that people live in, and also in what they hold to be most important (and hence worth cooperatively seeking). Some are poor while others are rich, some are fully-abled while others are disabled, some are women and some are men, some are heterosexual and some are homosexual, some are psychologically built in one way and some are psychologically built in others. The diverse needs of people and the things that enable them to achieve happiness in life cannot be assumed to be the same for all. For reasons like this, one may well wonder whether it is even possible to find a comprehensive moral framework that suits the fundamental interests of all or nearly all people in a satisfactory way. Thankfully, we don't have to answer that question here, for our immediate concern is simply with the ontological status of truth.

To put a concrete answer to the question, then: moral truth does not fit comfortably into *either* a subjective or objective classification, for it is *both* of them at the same time. But how can that be? I will once again use an analogy to illustrate—this time, with the nature of mathematical truth.

Most of us would probably say that if any truths are objective, it is mathematical truths. We say, "2 + 3 is necessarily equal to 5," and that it could not have been any other way. Interestingly enough, it could, for 2 and 3 added together only sums to 5 because we solve the equation using an arithmetical logic that treats numbers as intervals of equal size on an open line. (You might think of a piece of string that extends forever and has segments of an equal but arbitrary length marked out all the way along with numbers.) This is not the only way of arranging the logic of arithmetic. For example, if we chose to define numbers as intervals of equal length on a closed line, and define the number of those intervals as being just 4, then 2 + 3 would be equal to 1, not 5.[2] It is still true that *given* the standard logic of arithmetic, 2 + 3 is necessarily equal to 5, but then the truth of that is clearly conditional to the underpinning logic.

Morality is like this, too. Just as how light displays *both* particle and wave-like characteristics depending on the experimental conditions in which it is observed, and so cannot be said to be *just* a particle or *just* a wave in itself, morality has both an objective and a subjective character, and cannot be placed into just one or the other of those categories without losing sight of something very important about it.

---

[2] This example is taken from Sachs (1988).

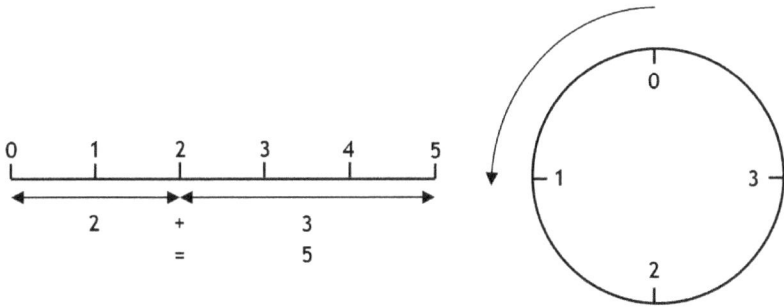

Figure 6.1: The logic of arithmetic. While 2 + 3 necessarily equals 5 using conventional arithmetical logic, we can get different results if we use a different underlying logic.

What I should stress is that since there are only so many ways of socially interrelating with one another in practice, *given* the facts of reality and our most basic experiential and situational aims in life, different ethical systems really can be *objectively* better or worse in respect to how well they facilitate or achieve those aims. If we all miraculously changed one day and adopted a different set of fundamental aims for ourselves, or if the world suddenly changed and became something altogether different for us, what is morally true could very likely also change. But this should not be any more alarming an idea than the fact that if you were to change the rules for how chess pieces move, or how many squares there are on a board, what strategies are likely to be effective in winning you the game are also likely to change. That doesn't mean that there are not objectively better or worse ways to play chess *given* the way it is now, though; it only means that what works and what doesn't is relative to the conventions of the game.

For this reason, I cannot agree that moral truth needs to be completely objective in order for there to be legitimate seriousness about morality. If we share a common mental architecture with one another, if we want essentially the same basic things as one another, and if the world really is basically the same for all of us, moral propositions can be sensibly regarded as normatively applicable inside of that common moral framework. Even though moral truth is not god-given in that case, it is still worth taking seriously—as seriously, at least, as we take experiences of pleasure and pain, happiness, and unhappiness. I.e., very seriously indeed.[3]

The Fragility of Good and the Stability of God

While god's existence may not be strictly necessary for the existence of moral truth, for the identification of moral truths, or for there to be motivation to live our lives morally, perhaps a purely secular approach to morality still fails to appreciate just how morally weak humans are in practice. Even if morality does not strictly *need* the idea of god, perhaps it still meaningfully benefits from it.

At a 2005 UN General Assembly meeting to commemorate the liberation of the concentration camps at the end of the Second World War, Nobel laureate and concentration camp survivor Elie Wiesel posed a deceptively simple question: how could otherwise intelligent, educated, and law-abiding people systematically murder men, women, and children by day, and then return home to their families in the evening to relax by listening to Bach and reading Schiller? The incongruity between the barbarity and civility of these images cries out for some sort of explanation. How could they have not been far too disturbed by what they had seen and done during the day to deal with such fine and delicate things towards its end?

The beginning of an answer can be found in the writings of the French political theorist Alexis de Tocqueville. Writing about 175 years

---

[3] There are many other deep issues with morality that this sketch of moral truth does not begin to address. For example, to say that pleasure, happiness, and wellbeing are fundamental ethical aims does not explain *why* those things should be regarded as such, or *why* other aims can't be positioned alongside them as fundamentally important. Furthermore, exactly *whose* wellbeing or happiness or pleasure should be regarded as the goal of any one person's moral thinking and commitment? If it somehow came down to a choice between my own happiness and that of three other people, for example, what would the morally correct choice be for me to make? The account given answers none of these questions. It is also tremendously complicated in practical terms by the fact that, if this claim about moral truth is right, how well a particular moral belief or value stands to promote pleasure or diminish pain can only really be decided in light of what *other* moral beliefs and values are held within the same ethical system of thought and which are relevantly connected to it. What this means is that the truth of individual moral claims (i.e., their adequacy in relation to the fulfillment of fundamental moral aims) is strictly holistic, and can be determined only by looking to the overall adequacy of the broader ethical whole in which they sit.

ago, de Tocqueville described a letter written roughly 175 years before him again by a pre-revolutionary French aristocrat to her daughter, who was away in the south of France. Writing from the city of Rennes, the letter proceeded very pleasantly up until she reported on recent local events. A new tax of one hundred thousand *écus* had just been imposed, and this was to be doubled and forcibly collected by soldiers if it was not paid within twenty-four hours. As part of this, a street of people had been evicted from their homes and the penalty for anyone else in taking them in was set at death.

What de Tocqueville found striking was the attitude the woman displayed towards the suffering of the evicted. She described how they had wandered around outside the city walls without any food or shelter, aimless and in tears, and she didn't appear to feel any bit the worse at the thought of it. In fact, she wrote approvingly of the execution of a violinist who had been arrested for stirring up a protest against the new tax, noting that after he had been broken upon the wheel (an excruciating method of execution where someone was tied to a wagon wheel and beaten with clubs to shatter their arms and legs), his body was dismembered and its parts sent to the different corners of the town to serve as a warning. Welcoming the fact that sixty more people were slated for execution the next day, she viewed it as an excellent lesson to the peasants to respect their governors and their wives, and to not "throw stones in their garden."[4]

What had gone so wrong for this woman? Why did she not *feel* for those who were suffering? As de Tocqueville noted, it couldn't have been because she simply felt nothing for anyone else, for she showed in the letter that she felt love for her daughter and concern for her friends who had fallen upon hard times. No, the problem, as de Tocqueville came to assess it, was that she had "no clear conception of what it was to suffer if one was not a noble."[5]

As a member of the aristocracy, she would have believed that she was innately superior to those in the lower classes. Indeed, so far as she and other aristocrats would have been concerned, she was a breed apart from them in substance, and a far better breed at that. This belief would have made it very difficult for her to truly imagine life from their point of view, and when you can't imagine yourself experiencing things as someone else does, it can be hard to feel for them when they suffer. The

---

[4] De Tocqueville (1863).
[5] *Ibid.*

problem wasn't that this woman wasn't capable of empathizing with other people, but that her beliefs stood in the way of her imagining herself in their shoes, and that in turn left her without empathy for them.

The importance of the imagination to our ability to feel compassion, and in particular about that, the way that our imagination can be obstructed by perceptions of difference, helps to explain quite a bit about our collective moral history. Consider that most paradigmatic example of a recent moral catastrophe, the Holocaust. Although many different groups of people, from gypsies to homosexuals, were sent to their deaths at the concentration camps, most of the Holocaust's victims were Jews, a people whom Nazi propaganda had depicted as dangerous and conspiratorial sub-human parasites whose existence was a continuing threat to higher civilization. While most Germans could be moved by the plight of those they recognized as fully human, many felt no equivalent emotional response to the suffering of Jews. Indeed, as an inherently evil abomination and enemy to all that was good and right, "the Jew" was something appropriately beyond the bounds of what should be afforded moral consideration. While the causal story behind the Holocaust certainly involves more than just the subversion of empathy by beliefs concerning racial superiority and perceived existential threats, that at least was one major part of it.

It is not just our beliefs that matter, though. Plato recounted the mythical story of the Greek shepherd Gyges who, while out walking one day, came across a great crevasse that had opened up in the ground. Climbing down into the gap, he found in there a metal horse inside with a hollow belly, and inside of that was a giant's skeleton with nothing on it but a golden ring. Taking the ring and putting it on, he soon discovered that it was no ordinary piece of jewelry, for if the collet on the ring was turned downward he would become invisible. Seeing its potential, Gyges used the ring to seduce the Queen, conspired with her to murder the King, and took the throne for himself.

The story of Gyges was intended to speak a wide truth about our unenlightened moral characters and the seduction of power. As Plato had one of the characters in *The Republic* explain, given power such as that which the ring affords,

> ...no man can be imagined to be of such an iron nature that he would stand fast in justice. No man would keep his hands off what was not his own when he could safely take what he liked out of the market, or go into houses and lie with any one at his pleasure, or kill

or release from prison whom he would, and in all respects be like a God among men.[6]

Plato went on to do his best to argue that those who *knew best* would know that no deep or lasting happiness can come from acting immorally, for the commission of immoral acts is in itself a source of unhappiness for those who know enough. Even if we accept that, most of us don't conduct our lives from a place of moral enlightenment. Imagine that you were able to bend the thoughts of those around you to your will, for as long as you liked and for as long as they remained within 50 meters. Using this ability you could make them think, feel and act in any way you wanted. Who among us would be so virtuous that they would never use this power to invade the minds of others and bend them to their own advantage? Who would not use it to help themselves procure sex, money, and power? The temptation would be colossal and I suspect that most would succumb, perhaps reasoning away their violations as somehow justified or legitimate, or at least as not too bad in the overall scheme of things.

It is rarely comfortable to confront the limits of our commitments to treating others well, of course, for so much of what we take to be valuable about ourselves comes from our moral ideals and their expression in our behavior. What the story of Gyges does is point to the uneasy possibility that we could find ourselves in situations where our moral treatment of other people would give way to our own selfish interests and desires. While that is unlikely to involve the discovery of magical rings in hollowed out horses, history shows that comparable situations both can and do arise. The result can be terrible.

At the end of the Second World War millions of women were raped by Russian soldiers as they took up positions across Eastern Europe. The situation was particularly bad in Berlin, the former stronghold of Nazi resistance, where girls as young as 12 and women as old as 80 were raped, including by gangs of drunken soldiers taking turns amongst themselves. Screams from the attacks rang out in the night air and were made all the more obvious to others by the fact that so many of the city's windows had been blown out by the Allied aerial bombing campaign. Many women wisely chose to hide in cellars or attics and to venture out in public only during the morning, a time at which they were less likely to be raped. Others chose to offer themselves to Russian officers in the

---

[6] Plato (n.d.).

hope that, by doing so, they might be protected from being raped by gangs. Fathers, husbands, and sons who attempted to intervene to stop the rapes were shot. Thousands of women ended up dying from their injuries—some were literally raped to death—and a great number of suicides and unwanted pregnancies resulted.[7] Like all moral tragedies that pass beyond a certain point in scale, we are left only to guess hazily at the enormity of the harm inflicted.

So how did it happen? It is far too much to believe that those who participated in the rapes (and it should be noted that far from every Russian soldier did, some being just as appalled by what their comrades were doing as we who read about it today are in retrospect) just happened to be all "natural born" rapists; that is, that the psychological profile of a significant portion of the soldiers enlisted in the Russian army at the time just happened to include so many men intrinsically disposed towards raping women and young girls. Vastly more probable, it seems to me, is that the rapes were committed by people who were in many ways quite morally *ordinary*—much closer to you or me than to some stereotypical moral villain. In fact their moral ordinariness was part of the problem, for they found themselves in a situation where they held great power over the people they abused, they could rape whoever they wanted with impunity, they had access to large quantities of alcohol to fuel their attacks, they were not discouraged from doing what they initially did by their military command, they had not seen their wives or girlfriends in a long time, and they burned for revenge after four savage and grueling years of bloody horror on the Eastern front.[8] Putting these different factors together, it is not hard to see how something as morally grotesque as what happened actually did.

The sensitivity of people's moral functioning to their external situation was illustrated very vividly in an experimental setting by Philip Zimbardo.[9] Zimbardo took 18 otherwise ordinary middle-class men and put them into a simulated prison environment. Randomly assigned into two groups by the flip of a coin, one group performed the role of the

---

[7] See Beevor (2002a) and (2002b).

[8] Beevor notes that as time went on the soldiers became more and more selective about who they raped, holding candles up to the faces of women in order to preferentially pick the most attractive among them. This suggests that the desire to inflict revenge upon the German population was only one of several motivational factors behind the rapes.

[9] See Haney, Banks, and Zimbardo (1973) for the original paper on the Stanford Prison Experiment, and http://www.prisonexp.org/ for an excellent overview.

"guards," who were responsible for the imprisonment of the other group, the "prisoners." While the guards wore uniforms and reflective sunglasses to anonymize their appearance and make them seem more authoritative, the prisoners were depersonalized by being forced to wear hospital-like gowns and being called by prisoner numbers rather than names.

As events unfolded, it was only a matter of days before conditions in the prison began to degenerate, with some of the guards developing what was later described as genuinely cruel and sadistic attitudes towards the prisoners. After a rebellion broke out on the second day, prisoners were punished by being stripped naked, forced to sleep on the ground rather than on mattresses, being placed in solitary confinement, and being taunted and intimidated. On a number of separate occasions, they were forced to do pushups as a form of punishment, prevented from washing themselves, and were required to clean toilets with their bare hands. As the experiment went on some of the inmates began to exhibit symptoms of severe psychological stress, including hysterical crying, rage, and disorganized thinking, and the study had to be abandoned less than halfway through the planned two-week duration. What the study showed was that, thanks to their social position and circumstances, ordinary people in the basement of a university building could experience a moral transformation of sorts and end up treating people they held power over in a truly appalling fashion in only a matter of days.

In light of these sorts of human moral frailties, it could be argued that there is a strong benefit to be found in retaining religious belief in god. After all, belief in god's existence, permanence, all-seeingness, and perhaps most importantly of all, his judgment and capacity for punishment, all help to ensure that people will be moved less by any morally undermining features of their present situations (like those of Gyges, the Russian soldiers, and Zimbardo's prison guards), and more by the timeless and universal principles of morality. Belief in god enables people to look past the temporary contexts of their lives and see themselves in an enduring metaphysical context of spiritual accountability.

That is one perspective. My own is that edifying the existence of a religiously-themed god is exactly what we should not be aiming to do, for not only does it require believing something that is both false and harmful, there is an incomparably more attractive alternative available: we can pour our efforts into trying to *understand* what it is about ourselves and the changing situations we might find ourselves in that either undermines or promotes our virtuous moral functioning. Though holding a better understanding of this aspect of our moral psychology would not *guarantee* morally consistent behavior, belief in a judging and punishing god clearly doesn't do that either. While it should go without saying that our moral frailty is a significant problem, the higher path forward surely rests in seeking greater knowledge for ourselves, not greater fear.

Chapter 7
Summary of an Idea

The only good is knowledge, and the only evil is ignorance.
—Socrates (469–399)

A Different Way of Seeing Life

The content of this book has been focused around three central claims. The first is that despite a long history of efforts indicating to the contrary, there is at least one plausible way of understanding the meaning of life from a spiritual point of view. Specifically, it is possible to plausibly understand life as something that was intended to help us move ourselves towards a deeper understanding of important truths of being. So understood, life is an opportunity to grow and develop in terms of who and what we metaphysically are by what we come to experience and the decisions we make in respect to ourselves in light of that.

An age-old philosophical problem was seen to confront acceptance of this view, however, and that was that there simply seems to be too much pain and suffering in the world to easily reconcile its existence with creation by a divinely good, capable, and knowing intelligence. If such a being really did create the universe, why did it choose to create one that can be so unpleasant for what lives within it?

It was argued that the answer lies in the importance of a range of values centered around things like autonomy, independence, and self-determination, and the need for those values to be respected by any system of life that god might come up with. So long as god is not *infinitely* capable, and hence capable of doing just anything whatsoever (including the logically impossible), the difficulty of balancing out moral concern for the experience of evils with other spiritually important values in a completely satisfying way reduces the pressure that the problem of evil builds up against the existence of a divine being. It was also argued that if our participation in life stems from a free and informed metaphysical choice on our part, as opposed to being something just blindly thrust upon us without our knowledge or consent, the significance of the problem of evil is reduced further still.

This was maintained to be at best only a partial answer to the problem, however. To the extent that we can still plausibly imagine god having been able to devise an experientially less-severe yet otherwise equally spiritually-effective universe, then even accepting the point that there are great difficulties involved in the balancing of the different values, the appearance of an excess in the level of pain and suffering found in the universe does constitute at least some disconfirmation of the existence of god.

Judgments concerning the actual extent of that disconfirmation will naturally vary between individuals, for the issue depends upon our appreciation of the relevant values involved, our understanding of the way in which those values are conflicted, our estimation of the capacities of god in virtue of his divinity, and the severity of the problem of evil as we see it from a moral point of view. It can be assumed that if god really does exist, he must have access to reasons that make up the moral distance we perceive between the world as it is and the world as we think it morally should have been, if it had actually been created by a divinely good, knowing, and capable being. Since we don't actually know of any such reasons ourselves, however, and can only postulate their existence in order to reconcile the universe's existence with its creation by a divine being, the problem still stands.

The second major argument of the book concerned the basic inadequacy of religion as a spiritual framework for understanding reality. While subjecting religion to critical analysis can be incredibly uncomfortable for believers to experience, it was argued that there are tremendous problems confronting the truth of both Christianity and Islam, including (but not limited to) the difficulty of believing that god would send down a revelation so heavily constrained in spatial and temporal distribution, that he would provide no independent reason to the vast majority of people to believe it, that the content of his revelation would contain such a collection of morally alarming, factually mistaken, internally inconsistent, and plainly absurd claims, and that he would give it over to humanity in such an inelegant and unappealing use of language.

While it brings me no joy to be the cause of anyone else's upset or distress, the grim fact is that the god imagined to exist by religion is a preposterously cruel and vicious being. The idea that he might be deeply interested in having his existence acknowledged by human beings, or in being worshiped and obeyed, or in keeping a metaphysical scorecard of our moral and spiritual failings, simply does not do any justice at all to the idea of god as divine. Indeed, I think that to call such a being divine is to make an unintentional mockery of that fundamentally guiding idea. Happily, religion holds no monopoly over the idea of god, for it is at bottom a *philosophical* rather than a religious concept, and the failure of religion to articulate a sensible way of spiritually thinking about existence should not be taken to indicate the hopelessness of doing so.

The third major component of the book consisted of an examination of whether there is any intersubjective justification for believing that life really does have a spiritual purpose to it. Because any such reasons cannot integrally depend on private personal experiences for the force of their strength, this naturally left aside any purely subjectively reasons individuals might have for belief (like private mystical or spiritual experiences).[1] The advantage of this approach, however, was that it allowed us to focus on reasons for belief that are principally open to all people as a rational foundation for human spirituality.

It was in this connection that the problem of cosmic fine-tuning was raised. Given the sensitivity of the existence of life to the details of the physics of the universe and the seemingly wide number of different possible ways the universe could have physically been, it appears to be nothing short of extraordinary that the universe has ended up with a physical character consistent with life. If god exists and was responsible for creating the universe, however, it makes perfect sense that it would allow for the existence of not just life, but conscious, intelligent, feeling, and morally apprehending life, for the value of that from a spiritual point of view is (by hypothesis) key to understanding why the universe exists in the first place.

Different ways of challenging the assumptions that this line of reasoning is built upon were looked at, as were common objections to the god hypothesis as an explanation of the universe and alternatives to it as a candidate for the best explanation of fine-tuning. It was noted how our judgment concerning the plausibility of different theories is affected by what features of those theories we take to be truth-indicating, and how there can be reasonable disagreement between people when it

---

[1] Since our analyses of evidence integrally depend upon our background beliefs, and since our background beliefs are shaped by our experiences in life, what I have just said is strictly misleading. Moreover, if a large number of people had remarkably similar mystical or spiritual experiences to one another, under varied conditions, and which all supplied specific and verifiable information which could not be easily explained in other ways, then even otherwise subjectively closed experiences might come to constitute a good reason for others to believe (in which case, they wouldn't be "closed" anymore). Nevertheless, I take there to be something sensible to the idea that fine-tuning is much more open to people as a reason for belief in god than subjectively private experiences.

comes to the details of that. It was also noted how practical interests (like avoiding harmfully-false beliefs) can affect the level of confidence we require in the truth of a theory before we will actually accept it as true.

While this complicates things a great deal, it was nevertheless suggested that the god hypothesis is a plausibly-true explanation of the universe, and to the point that it falls within the boundaries of reasonableness to tentatively believe that god exists and that our lives have a spiritual component of meaning to them. As it was argued, even if the god hypothesis does not exceed the multiverse or the deeper physics hypothesis as an explanation of fine-tuning, it can still be used as an explanation of the existence of the multiverse, or if not that, of the beautiful and simple physical laws that constrain the universe to a life-permitting condition (should many more than one of those underlying sets of physical laws have been possible). Indeed, there is at least some reason to think that that is where the god hypothesis more naturally belongs in explanation.

A number of other arguments were put forward throughout the book. One of these called for reconsideration of the antagonism that is often presented as existing between rationality and spirituality, and which is manifested perhaps most blatantly in the mystical and theological refusal to treat god as something capable of being rationally understood. It was argued that treating god as transcendently beyond the grasp of human knowledge does nothing more than make the idea of him meaningless, for no prediction, statement, belief or human thought could be true of him.

It was also argued that because the idea of god as a lawmaker, punisher, and redeemer has played such a prominent role in how we have thought about him, that it may now be quite difficult for many people to think in ways that lie completely outside of that conception. This is extremely unfortunate, for none of those ideas are natural to the idea of god in itself, and all of them do a tremendous amount of harm to it.

Lastly, the need for a "Copernican revolution" within human spirituality was urged. As it was said, it is not god but the nature of our thinking and its suitability-of-fit with the reality of being that should occupy the center of our spiritual attention. By treating god as the focus of what is spiritually important, religion has managed to get things almost entirely backwards.

The question of life's meaningfulness within an atheistic worldview also came up in the discussion. It was noted that while atheism does appear to present a genuine challenge to the meaningfulness of life, that as a philosophical issue this has far more to do with the termination of the self by death than the nonexistence of god. Quite naturally wanting to matter more to ourselves than just in passing, the inevitability of our impending deaths presents a rather great obstacle to that desire, and that can place a question mark over the significance of everything that stands in a relationship of value to us.

Even if the continuation of the self beyond death does matter, though, the problem of meaningfulness can only be a legitimate criticism to make of atheism if considerations *other* than that of truth appropriately enter into how we weigh decisions of belief. There is nothing about atheism being hard for many people to swallow that makes it false, and hence it is only if something other than the truth properly matters when it comes to making decisions about belief that this alleged fact itself will matter.

Finally, the connection between god and morality was examined. Against many people's views to the contrary, it was argued that god's existence is necessary neither for the existence of moral truths, for the successful identification of moral truths, or for there to be compelling motivation to want to live out our lives in a morally-accordant way. In an effort to alleviate concerns about moral seriousness if god has nothing to do with morality, a sketch of moral truth was presented whereby it is seen as something very much grounded in the world and human interests, as eschewing any easy classification as purely objective or purely subjective, and yet as something that is well worth treating seriously all the same.

If there is any core message to this book, it is that there is at least one way of looking at life spiritually that stands a meaningful chance of being true. On the view of life in question, each of us is a work in progress in a universe that functions as a crucible for our development. There is no debt that we owe for our lives, nor anything we might do in the course of living that could cause us to be divinely judged and condemned. Predicated upon a group of values that can be held up in the highest possible regard, the only thing left to say from a spiritual perspective is this: your life is beautiful, and it's for you.

Philosophical Glossary

Ad hoc – In Latin the phrase means "for this," though I prefer to think of it as meaning "for this case only." What a*d hoc* explanations represent are attempts to plug holes in explanations. The problem with them is that they do so in ways that are usually quite questionable and not independently testable for their truth. Someone might defend the idea that the events of 9/11 were perpetrated as part of conspiracy by the US government by alleging that the steel from the buildings was very quickly transported away from ground zero and melted down before any detailed inspections could be performed by experts. The reason for that, one presumes, was to destroy any evidence that explosives were used. When asked why those handling the removal of the steel deny that any such thing ever occurred, our protagonist might respond that those who handled the steel are quite obviously lying in order to cover up the truth. The latter explanation is *ad hoc* in the fact that it has no independent evidence supporting its truth, appears to be incapable of being tested, and is appealed to simply in order that the conspiracy theory does not have to be abandoned.

A posteriori – "From experience." If something is known *a posteriori*, it is known on the basis of experience. Examples of *a posteriori* truths are the propositions that "strawberries are red" and that "Ottawa is the capital of Canada." *A posteriori* contrasts with *a priori* (see below).

A priori – "Before experience." If something is known *a priori*, it is known independently of any experience of the way things are. Logical, geometric, and mathematical truths (like "1 + 1 = 2") are often put forward as examples of *a priori* truths, for their truth is known independently of any experience of the world.

Axiological – Related to the study of values, like the value of doing well by others, or experiencing beauty, or pursuing the greatest good for the greatest number of people.

Being – In its philosophical sense, *being* refers to the metaphysical nature and framework of existence, with special emphasis on that in terms of how it relates to us as conscious entities.

Empirical – Meaning by or from observation or experiment. An empirical fact about the world is an observable or experimentally-derived fact.

Epistemology – An area of philosophy dealing with questions related to knowledge, truth, and ways of knowing. What is it to know something? What justifies us in believing that something is true? What is it for a statement to be true? What is truth? These are all epistemological questions.

Deduction – A pattern of inference whereby conclusions are drawn that are intended to be conclusively shown as true on the basis of the premises they are drawn from. An example of a deductive argument is, "Socrates is a man. All men are mortal. Therefore, Socrates is mortal." As you can see, if both of the premises in the argument are true—i.e., if Socrates *really is* a man, and if all men *really are* mortal—we can know with perfect certainty that Socrates is mortal too. Deduction contrasts with induction.

Disutility – Negative utility (see utility).

Induction – A pattern of inference whereby conclusions are drawn that are intended to be established as likely or probably true on the basis of the truth of the premises they are inferred from. An example of induction would be, "Socrates was an Ancient Greek. Most Ancient Greek's loved the arts. Therefore, Socrates most probably loved the arts too." You can see that even if both of the premises are true, it is not necessarily the case that Socrates loved the arts, just more probable.

Metaphysics – By its Greek roots, the word means "beyond physics." As an area of philosophical inquiry metaphysics is concerned with the reality of things as they are at the most fundamental level, both inside and beyond the physical universe (if there is actually anything beyond it).

Nomological – Concerning the physical and logical laws of nature.

Ontology – The study or categorization of existing things and their properties. What kinds of things exist in the world? What properties do those things have? What is the difference between existing and not existing? Do numbers "exist"? If so, in what sense? Do unicorns "exist"? If so, in what sense? These are all ontological questions.

Phenomenological – Concerning the structure and quality of the conscious experiences. The phenomenology of the experience of seeing red, for example, will involve questions to do with the nature of redness as it comes to be subjectively experienced.

Proposition – A sentence that can be either true or false. "Mt. Everest is the highest mountain in the world" would be an example of a true proposition, for example, while "water weighs less than gold" would be an example of a false proposition. Examples of non-propositions include "what time is it?" and "yuck!" as neither of them is (or can be) true or false.

Utility – Most usually or ordinarily in ethics, the "good" of something. For example, hugs increase utility because they make people feel better, thereby promoting moral goods like happiness and wellbeing. Yay hugs!

Selected Bibliography

Achinstein, Peter. (1984). "The Pragmatic Character of Explanation." *PSA: Proceedings of the Biennial Meeting of the Philosophy of Science Association*, vol. 1984, pp. 275-292.

Alston, William P. (1991). *Perceiving God: The Epistemology of Religious Experience.* New York: Cornell University Press.

Armstrong, Karen. (1994). *A History of God: The 4000-Year Quest of Judaism, Christianity and Islam.* New York: Ballantine Books.

Aslan, Reza. (2005). *No God But God: The Origins, Evolution, and Future of Islam.* London: Arrow Books.

———. (2010). *Beyond Fundamentalism: Confronting Religious Extremism in the Age of Globalization.* New York: Random House.

Augustine, Keith. (2000). "Death and the Meaning of Life." *The Secular Web.* Retrieved from http://www.infidels.org/kiosk/article55.html

Bartholomew, David J. (1996). *Uncertain Belief: Is It Rational To Be a Christian?* Oxford: Oxford University Press.

BBC. (2012). "Pakistan acid attack parents 'feared dishonour'." *BBCNews*, 5 November, 2012. Retrieved from http://www.bbc.co.uk/news/world-asia-20202686

Barrow, John D. (2003). *The Constants of Nature: From Alpha to Omega.* London: Random House.

Beevor, Antony. (2002a). "'They Raped Every German Female from eight to 80'." *The Guardian*, 1 May 2002. Retrieved from http://www.guardian.co.uk/books/2002/may/01/news.features11

———. (2002b). *Berlin: The Downfall 1945.* London: Penguin Books.

Bloom, Paul. (2012). "Religion, Morality, Evolution." Annual Review of Psychology, vol. 63, pp. 179–199.

Bostrom, Nick. (2003). "Are You Living in a Computer Simulation?." *Philosophical Quarterly*, vol. 53, no. 211, pp. 243-255.

Bourget, David, and David J. Chalmers. (2013). "What do philosophers believe?." *Philosophical Studies*, forthcoming. Retrieved from http://philpapers.org/rec/BOUWDP

Boyer, Pascal. (2001). *Religion Explained: The Evolutionary Origins of Religious Thought.* New York: BasicBooks.

Bradley, Raymond. (2007). "The Meaning of Life: Reflections on God, Immortality, and Free Will." *The Secular Web.* Retrieved from http://www.infidels.org/kiosk/article745.html

Brawer, Roberta. (1996). *Inflationary Cosmology and the Horizon and Flatness Problems: The Mutual Constitution of Explanation and Questions.* Master's thesis, Massachusetts Institute of Technology. Retrieved from http://dspace.mit.edu/bitstream/handle/1721.1/38370/34591655. pdf

Chakravartty, Anjan. (1998). "Semirealism." *Studies in History and Philosophy of Science,* vol. 29, no. 3, pp. 391-408.

———. (2007). "Six Degrees of Speculation: Metaphysics in Empirical Contexts." In B. Monton (ed.), *Images of Empiricism* (2007), Oxford University Press. Retrieved from http://individual.utoronto.ca/anjan/downloads/monton_book.pdf

Carrier, Richard. (2001). "Our Meaning in Life." *The Secular Web.* Retrieved from http://www.infidels.org/kiosk/article113.html

CBC. (2012). "Pakistan parents killed daughter with acid for eyeing boy." *CBCNews,* 5 November, 2012. Retrieved from http://www.cbc.ca/news/world/story/2012/11/05/parents-kill-pakistan-girl-acid.html

Close, Frank. (2004). *Particle Physics: A Very Short Introduction.* New York: Oxford University Press.

Collins, Robin. (2002). "God, Design, and Fine-Tuning." In R. Martin and C. Bernard (eds.), *God Matters: Readings in the Philosophy of Religion.* New York: Longman Press, 2002. Retrieved from http://home.messiah.edu/~rcollins/Fine-tuning/Revised%20Version%20of%20Fine-tuning%20for%20anthology.doc

———. (2003a). "Evidence for Fine Tuning." In N. Manson (ed.), *God and Design: The Teleological Argument and Modern Science* (2003). New York: Routledge.

———. (2003b). "How to Rigorously Define Fine Tuning." Retrieved from http://www.lastseminary.com/cosmological-fine-tuning/How%20to%20Rigorously%20Define%20Fine-Tuning.pdf

———. (2007). "Universe or Multiverse: a Theistic Perspective." In B. Carr (ed.), *Universe or Multiverse?.* New York: Cambridge University Press. Retrieved from http://home.messiah.edu/~rcollins/Fine-tuning/stanford%20multiverse%20talk.htm

———. (2008a). "Modern Physics and the Energy-Conservation Objection to Mind-Body Dualism." *American Philosophical Quarterly,* vol. 45, no. 1, pp. 31-42.

———. (2008b). "The Teleological Argument: An Exploration of the Fine-Tuning of the Cosmos." In William Lane Craig and J. P.

Moreland (eds.), *The Blackwell Companion to Natural Theology*. Retrieved from http://home.messiah.edu/~rcollins/Fine-tuning/Abridged%20Version%20of%20Fine-tuning%20book.doc

Colyvan, Mark, Jay Garfield, and Graham Priest. (2005). "Problems with the Argument from Fine Tuning." *Synthese*, vol. 145, no. 3, pp. 325-38.

Craig, William Lane. (2003). "Design and the Anthropic Fine-Tuning of the Universe." In N. Manson (ed.), *God and Design: The Teleological Argument and Modern Science*. New York: Routledge.

Curd, Martin, and J. A. Cover. (1998). *Philosophy of Science: The Central Issues*. New York: W. W. Norton and Company.

DailyMail. (2012). "'It was her destiny to die this way': Confession of the mother who killed her daughter, 15, by dousing her in acid for just looking at a boy." 6 November, 2012. Retrieved from http://www.dailymail.co.uk/news/article-2228586/Killed-eyeing-boy-It-destiny-says-Pakistani-parents-killed-daughter.html

Davies, Paul. (2006). *The Goldilocks Enigma: Why is the Universe Just Right for Life?*. London: Penguin Books.

Dawes, Gregory. (2009). *Theism and Explanation*. New York: Routledge.

Dawkins, Richard. (1982). *The Extended Phenotype: The Gene as the Unit of Selection*. New York: Oxford University Press.

———. (1995). *River Out of Eden: A Darwinian View of Life*. New York: BasicBooks.

———. (2006). *The God Delusion*. Sydney: Bantam Press.

De Tocqueville, Alexis. (1863). *Democracy in America*. Trans. Henry Reeve, Francis Bowen ed. Third Edition, vol. 2. Cambridge: Sever and Francis. Retrieved from http://books.google.co.nz/books/about/DEMOCRACY_IN_A MERICA.html?id=gTX-uSzS2fAC

Drange, Theodore M. (1998a). "Incompatible-Properties Arguments: A Survey." *Philo*, vol. 1, no. 2, pp. 49-60.

———. (1998b). "The Fine-Tuning Argument." *The Secular Web*. Retrieved from http://www.infidels.org/library/modern/theodore_drange/tuning.html

D'Souza, Dinesh. (2008). *What's So Great About Christianity*. Tyndale House Publishers, Inc.

Earman, John, and Jesus Mosterin. (1999). "A Critical Look at Inflationary Cosmology." *Philosophy of Science*, vol. 66, no. 1, pp. 1-49.

Edwards, K, and E. E. Smith. (1996). "A Disconfirmation Bias in the Evaluation of Arguments." *Journal of Personality and Social Psychology*, vol. 71, no. 1, pp. 5-24.

Ehrman, Bart. (2009). *Jesus, Interrupted: Revealing the Hidden Contradictions in the Bible (and Why We Don't Know About Them)*. New York: HarperCollins.

Esposito, John L., and Dalia Mogahed. (2007). *Who Speaks for Islam? What a Billion Muslims Really Think*. New York: Gallup Press.

Gellman, Jerome J. (2005). "Mysticism and Religious Experience." In W. Wainwright (ed.), *The Oxford Handbook of Philosophy of Religion* (2005). New York: Oxford University Press.

Gillies, Donald. (1993). "The Duhem Thesis and the Quine Thesis." In M. Curd and J. A. Cover (eds.), *Philosophy of Science: The Central Issues* (1998). New York: W. W. Norton and Company.

Glover, Jonathan. (2001). *Humanity: A Moral History of Twentieth Century*. New Haven: Yale University Press.

Goldman, Alvin. (1999). *Knowledge in a Social World*. New York: Oxford University Press.

Goodin, Robert E. (2006). "The Epistemic Benefits of Many Biased Observers." *Episteme*, vol. 3, no. 3, pp. 166-174.

Graham, Dee, Edna Rawlings, Kim Ihms, et al. (1995). "A Scale for Identifying "Stockholm Syndrome" Reactions in Young Dating Women: Factor Structure, Reliability, and Validity." *Violence and Victims*, vol. 10, no. 1, pp. 3–22.

Greene, Brian. (2011). *The Hidden Reality: Parallel Universes and the Deep Laws of the Cosmos*. New York: Vintage Books.

Guth, Alan H. (1981). "Inflationary Universe: A Possible Solution to the Horizon and Flatness Problems." *Physical Review D*, vol. 23, no. 2, pp. 347-356. Retrieved from http://www.astro.rug.nl/~weygaert/tim1publication/cosmo2007/1 iterature/inflationary.universe.guth.physrevd-1981.pdf

Haney, Craig, Curtis Banks, and Philip Zimbardo. (1973). "Interpersonal Dynamics in a Simulated Prison." *International Journal of Criminology and Penology*, vol. 1, pp. 69-97.

Harris, Sam. (2004). *The End of Faith: Religion, Terror, and the Future of Reason*. Reading: The Free Press.

Hawking, Stephen. (1988). *A Brief History of Time: From the Big Bang to Black Holes*. New York: Bantom Books.

Hempel, Carl G. (1983). "Valuation and Objectivity in Science." In R. S. Cohen (ed.), *Physics, Philosophy and Psychoanalysis* (1983). Dordrecht: D. Reidel Publishing Company.

Henry, John. (2002). *The Scientific Revolution and the Origins of Modern Science.* Second Edition. New York: Palgrave.

Herant, Marc, Stirling A. Colgate, Willy Benz, and Chris Fryer. (1997). "Neutrinos and Supernovae." *Los Alamos Science*, no. 25, pp. 64-78.

Hitchens, Christopher. (2007). *God is Not Great: How Religion Poisons Everything.* New York: Hachette Book Group.

Hume, David. (1748). *An Enquiry Concerning Human Understanding.* L. A. Selby-Bigge (ed.). Retrieved from http://www.gutenberg.org/ebooks/9662

Ikeda, Michael, and Bill Jeffreys. (2006). "The Anthropic Principle Does Not Support Supernaturalism." Retrieved from http://quasar.as.utexas.edu/anthropic.html

James, William. (1996 [1902]). *The Varieties of Religious Experience: A Study in Human Nature.* Retrieved from http://www.gutenberg.org/ebooks/621

Jones, Jeffrey M. (2011). "In U.S., 3 in 10 Say They Take the Bible Literally." Gallup. Retrieved from http://www.gallup.com/poll/148427/say-bible-literally.aspx

Kant, Immanuel. (1996 [1781, 1787]). *The Critique of Pure Reason.* Trans. Werner S. Pluhar. Indianapolis: Hackett.

Kitcher, Philip. (2001). *Science, Truth, and Democracy.* New York: Oxford University Press.

Kross, Brian. (n.d.). "How Many Atoms are in the Human Body." *Jefferson Laboratory.* http://education.jlab.org/qa/mathatom_04.html

Kuhn, Thomas. (1957). *The Copernican Revolution: Planetary Astronomy in the Development of Western Thought.* Cambridge: Harvard University Press.

———. (1977). "Objectivity, Value Judgment, Theory Choice." In M. Curd and J. A. Cover (eds.), *Philosophy of Science: The Central Issues* (1998). New York: W. W. Norton and Company.

———. (1996). *The Structure of Scientific Revolutions*, Third Edition. Chicago: Chicago University Press.

Kukla, Andre, and Joel Walmsley. (2004). "Mysticism and Social Epistemology." *Episteme*, vol. 1, no. 2, pp. 139-158.

Lakatos, Imre. (1970). "Falsification and the Methodology of Scientific Research Programmes." In Lakatos and Musgrave (eds.), *Criticism and the Growth of Knowledge* (1970). Wiltshire: Cambridge University Press.

Laudan, Larry. (1983). "The Demise of the Demarcation Problem." In R. S. Cohen (ed.), *Physics, Philosophy, and Psychoanalysis: Essays in Honour of A. Grunbaum* (1983). Dordrecht: D. Reidel Publishing Company.

———. (1984). *Science and Values.* Berkeley: University of California Press.

———. (1990). "Demystifying Underdetermination." In M. Curd and J. A. Cover (eds.), *Philosophy of Science: The Central Issues* (1998). New York: W. W. Norton and Company.

Law, Stephen. (2010). "The Evil-God Challenge." *Religious Studies*, vol. 43, no. 3, pp. 353-373.

Lipton, Peter. (2004). *Inference to the Best Explanation.* Second Edition. New York: Routledge.

Livio, Mario, and Martin Rees. (2005). "Anthropic Reasoning." *Science*, vol. 309, no. 5737, pp. 1022-1023.

Lugo, Luls, Alan Cooperman, James Bell, et al. (2013). "The World's Muslims: Religion, Politics and Society." Pew Research Center, The Pew Forum on Religion and Public Life. Retrieved from http://www.pewforum.org/Muslim/the-worlds-muslims-religion-politics-society.aspx

Martin, Michael. (1990). *Atheism: A Philosophical Justification.* Philadelphia: Temple University Press.

———. (2001). "Wittgenstein's Lectures on Religious Belief." *The Secular Web.* Retrieved from http://www.infidels.org/library/modern/michael_martin/wittgens tein.html

———. (2002). "Justifying Methodological Naturalism." Retrieved from http://www.infidels.org/library/modern/michael_martin/naturalis m.html

McGrew, Timothy, Lydia McGrew, and Eric Vestrup. (2001). "Probabilities and the Fine-Tuning Argument: A Skeptical View." *Mind*, vol. 110, no. 440, pp. 1027-1038.

McMullin, Ernan. (1982). "Values in Science." *PSA: Proceedings of the Biennial Meeting of the Philosophy of Science Association*, 1982, pp. 3-28.

———. (1984). "The Goals of Natural Science." *Proceedings and Addresses of the American Philosophical Association*, vol. 58, no. 1, pp. 37-64.

————. (1990). "Rationality and Paradigm Change in Science." In M. Curd and J. A. Cover (eds.), *Philosophy of Science: The Central Issues* (1998). New York: W. W. Norton and Company.

————. (1993). "Indifference Principle and Anthropic Principle in Cosmology." *Studies in History and Philosophy of Science*, vol. 24, no. 3, pp. 359-389.

Monton, Bradley. (2006). "God, Fine-Tuning, and the Problem of Old Evidence." *British Journal for the Philosophy of Science*, vol. 57, no. 2, pp. 405-424.

Namnyak, M, Tufton N, Szekely R, et al. (2008). "'Stockholm syndrome': psychiatric diagnosis or urban myth?" *Acta Psychiatrica Scandinavica*, vol. 117, no. 1, pp. 4–11.

Paine, Thomas. (1794). *The Age of Reason*. eBooks@Adelaide. Retrieved from http://ebooks.adelaide.edu.au/p/paine/thomas/p147a/

Parsons, Keith. (2006). *Copernican Questions: A Concise Invitation to the Philosophy of Science*. New York: McGraw-Hill.

Pennock, Robert, and Michael Ruse. (2009). *But Is It Science? The Philosophical Question in the Creation/Evolution Controversy*. Updated Edition. New York: Prometheus Books.

Plantinga, Alvin. (2002). "Theism, Atheism, and Rationality." *Truth Journal*. Retrieved from http://www.leaderu.com/truth/3truth02.html

Plato. (n.d.). *The Republic*. Project Gutenberg. Trans. Benjamin Jowett. Retrieved from http://www.gutenberg.org/ebooks/1497

Quine, W. V. O. (1951). "Two Dogmas of Empiricism." In M. Curd and J. A. Cover (eds.), *Philosophy of Science: The Central Issues* (1998). New York: W. W. Norton and Company.

Red Jacket. (1805). "Address to White Missionaries and Iroquois Six Nations." *American Rhetoric: Online Speech Bank*. http://www.americanrhetoric.com/speeches/nativeamericans/chiefredjacket.htm

Rees, Martin. (1999). *Just Six Numbers: The Deep Forces that Shape the Universe*. London: Orion Books.

————. (2003). "Other Universes: A Scientific Perspective." In N. Manson (ed.), *God and Design: The Teleological Argument and Modern Science* (2003). New York: Routledge.

Ritcher, Burton. (2006). "Theory in Particle Physics: Theological Speculation versus Practical Knowledge." *Physics Today*, vol. 59, no. 10, pp. 8-9. Retrieved from http://www.physicstoday.org/resource/1/phtoad/v59/i10/p8_s1

Ross, Kelley. (2010). "Hume Shifts the Burden of Proof." *The Proceedings of the Friesian School, Fourth Series.* http://www.friesian.com/hume.htm

Ryan, Sean G., and Andrew J. Norton. (2010). *Stellar Evolution and Nucleosynthesis.* New York: Cambridge University Press.

Sachs, Mendel. (1988). *Einstein versus Bohr: The Continuing Controversies in Physics.* La Salle: Open Court Publishing Company.

Salmon, Wesley. (1978). "Religion and Science: A New Look at Hume's Dialogues." In M. Martin and R. Monnier (eds.), *The Improbability of God* (2006). Amherst: Prometheus Books.

———. (1990). "Rationality and Objectivity in Science or Tom Kuhn Meets Tom Bayes." In M. Curd and J. A. Cover (eds.), *Philosophy of Science: The Central Issues* (1998). New York: W. W. Norton and Company.

Shaw, George Bernard. (1923). *Saint Joan: A Chronicle Play in Six Scenes and an Epilogue.* Retrieved from http://gutenberg.net.au/ebooks02/0200811h.html

Singer, Peter. (1980). *Marx: A Very Short Introduction.* New York: Oxford University Press.

Sober, Elliot. (2003). "The Design Argument." In N. Manson (ed.), *God and Design: The Teleological Argument and Modern Science* (2003). New York: Routledge.

Solzhenitsyn, Aleksandr I. (1975). *The Gulag Archipelago, 1918-1956: An Experiment in Literary Investigations, books I-II.* Trans. Thomas P. Whitney. Harper & Row Publishers. Retrieved from http://ia600304.us.archive.org/29/items/Gulag_Archipelago_I/Gulag_Archipelago.pdf

Steinhardt, Paul. (2011). "The Inflation Debate: Is the Theory at the Heart of Modern Cosmology Deeply Flawed?" *Scientific American,* April 2011, pp. 36-43.

Steinhardt, Paul, and Neil Turok. (2008). *The Endless Universe: Beyond the Big bang.* London: Phoenix.

Stenger, Victor. (2007) *God: The Failed Hypothesis: How Science Shows that God Does Not Exist.* New York: Prometheus Books.

Strobel, Lee. (2007). *The Case for the Real Jesus: A Journalist Investigates Current Attacks on the Identity of Christ.* Michigan: Zondervan.

Swinburne, Richard. (1964). "Falsifiability of Scientific Theories." *Mind,* vol. 73, no. 291, pp. 434-436.

———. (1991) "The Justification of Theism." *Truth Journal.* Retrieved from http://www.leaderu.com/truth/3truth09.html

Thagard, Paul. (1978). "The Best Explanation: Criteria for Theory Choice." *The Journal of Philosophy*, vol. 75, no. 2, pp. 76-92.

Tolstoy, Leo. (1884). *A Confession*. Retrieved from http://flag.blackened.net/daver/anarchism/tolstoy/confession.html

Toulmin, Stephen. (1961). *Foresight and Understanding: An Enquiry into the Aims of Science*. New York: Harper and Row.

Vilenkin, Alex. (2006). *Many Worlds in One: The Search for Other Universes*. New York: Hill and Wang.

Warraq, Ibn. (2003). *Why I am Not a Muslim*. New York: Prometheus Books.

Weinberg, Steven. (1993). *Dreams of a Final Theory: The Scientist's Search for the Ultimate Laws of Nature*. New York: Vintage Books.

———. (1999). "A Designer Universe?." *New York Review of Books*, October 21, 1999. Retrieved from http://www.stephenjaygould.org/ctrl/archive/design/weinberg_designer.html

Wright, Robert. (2009). *The Evolution of God*. New York: Little, Brown and Company.

Index

www.ingramcontent.com/pod-product-compliance
Lightning Source LLC
LaVergne TN
LVHW051358080426
835508LV00022B/2881